GOD AND SKEPTICISM

PHILOSOPHICAL STUDIES SERIES
IN PHILOSOPHY

VOLUME 28

TERENCE PENELHUM

University of Calgary

GOD
AND SKEPTICISM

A Study in Skepticism and Fideism

D. REIDEL PUBLISHING COMPANY

A MEMBER OF THE KLUWER ACADEMIC PUBLISHERS GROUP

DORDRECHT / BOSTON / LANCASTER

Library of Congress Cataloging in Publication Data

Penelhum, Terence, 1929–
   God and skepticism.

   (Philosophical studies series in philosophy ; v. 28)
   Includes index.
   1. Skepticism. 2. Faith. 3. Faith and reason.
I. Title. II. Series.
B837.P45   1983   149'.73   83–6791
ISBN 90–277–1550–5

Published by D. Reidel Publishing Company,
P.O. Box 17, 3300 AA Dordrecht, Holland.

Sold and distributed in the U.S.A. and Canada
by Kluwer Academic Publishers,
190 Old Derby Street, Hingham, MA 02043, U.S.A.

In all other countries, sold and distributed
by Kluwer Academic Publishers Group,
P.O. Box 322, 3300 AH Dordrecht, Holland.

For Edith, for Claire,
and in gratitude for Andrew

CONTENTS

PREFACE

This book is an exercise in philosophical criticism. What I criticize are some variations on a recurrent theme in religious thought: the theme that faith and reason are so disparate that faith is not undermined, but strengthened, if we judge that reason can give it no support. The common name for this view is Fideism. Those representatives of it that I have chosen to discuss do more, however, than insist on keeping faith free of the alleged contaminations of philosophical argument. They consider the case for Fideism to be made even stronger if one judges that reason cannot give us truth or assurance outside the sphere of faith any more than within it. In other words, they sustain their Fideism by an appeal to Skepticism. I call them, therefore, Skeptical Fideists.

Skeptical Fideism is not a mere historical curiosity. Richard Popkin has shown us how wide its impact in the formative period of modern philosophy has been; and its impact on modern theological and apologetic reasoning has been immense. In my view, anyone who wishes to assess many of the assumptions current in the theologies of our time has to take account of it. I think, therefore, that there is a topical value in examining the figures whose views I discuss here – Erasmus, Montaigne, Bayle, and more importantly, Pascal and Kierkegaard. So while I have taken some pains to present their arguments in their own contexts, I have tried to evaluate them in a fashion that has application to philosophy of religion now, and I have also tried, in the last two chapters, to look at positions of contemporary philosophers that are similar to theirs, and to suggest how the lessons we can learn from their successes and failures can assist a better philosophical understanding of what faith is.

The structure of the book is as follows. In the first chapter I attempt to set the stage by a short historical discussion of Skepticism, which was seen by the Skeptical Fideists not as a creature of Descartes' imagination, but as an ongoing philosophical movement with its roots in antiquity. I then distinguish two kinds of Skeptical Fideism, which I call Conformist and Evangelical. Chapters 2 and 3 discuss the Conformist kind, found in Erasmus, Montaigne, and, I think, Bayle, and try to argue that its appeal to thinkers of considerable acumen can be explained, though not justified, in a way that deepens our

understanding both of Skepticism and of faith. In Chapters 4 and 5 I examine
the Evangelical Fideism of Pascal and Kierkegaard (as we find him in the
Philosophical Fragments), and try to show that, for all their insights, they are
deeply mistaken to suppose that the Skeptical critique of reason does faith
a service, even an unwitting one. The only argument we find in their writings
which has sufficient merits to support their case is one which I call the Parity
Argument — the popular argument which says, roughly, that the Skeptic
shows us that our common-sense beliefs lack intellectual foundations, and in
showing us this makes it clear that the assent that faith requires is analogous
to the assent we give, without resistance, to the tenets of common-sense. In
Chapter 6 I examine Hume's philosophy of religion, which can be viewed as
a sustained attempt by someone who takes this bleak view of common-sense
to fend off the Parity Argument and reject faith. I claim that Hume fails, but
in Chapter 7 I look at some recent versions of the Parity Argument in order
to show that its value for the Fideist is very limited. In the final chapter I
indicate some of the implications of what has gone before for our understanding of what sort of state faith is.

This study is limited in two important ways. I have, first, made no attempt
to argue the wider philosophical question of how far the Skeptics' assessment
of the powers of human reason is correct, although it has been necessary to
discuss the question of the coherence of classical Pyrrhonism. The issue that
concerns me is the narrower one: should a skeptical assessment of reason be
welcomed, rather than resisted, by the religious apologist? The second limita-
tion on the study is that I have confined myself to the Christian religious
tradition, which is of course the one which the writers I am examining were
defending or attacking. As scholarly knowledge of other traditions grows,
such a restriction may look parochial. I think, however, that questions about
the rationality of a religious tradition, and about the value of philosophical
enquiry or speculation to a religious tradition, have to be considered in relation to each such tradition, before issues of higher generality about religion-
in-general can be considered profitably. My competences, strained already
(as will be obvious) in what follows, do not extend to non-Christian traditions
sufficiently for me to go beyond the topics of this book at the present time.
In a work that discusses the limits of reason so often, this is, I hope, an
acceptable excuse.

Calgary, October 1982   T.M.P.

ACKNOWLEDGMENTS

No philosopher can hope to identify all the sources of his reflections, but there are two people without whose work I could never have made any progress on the topics I deal with here. The first is Richard Popkin, whose writings on the Skeptical tradition in modern times have been indispensable. The second is Myles Burnyeat, whose scholarship and philosophical insight, encountered in print, in lectures, and in conversation, must take all the credit for any understanding of classical Skepticism that this work may show.

A good deal of the work for this book was done during two recent half-sabbatical leaves, spent in Cambridge University. I am grateful to the University of Calgary for those leave periods, and to the Social Sciences and Humanities Research Council of Canada for Leave Fellowship support. I would also like to express thanks, from my wife and myself, to the Master and Fellows of Corpus Christi College, and particularly to Dr and Mrs Barry Cross, for the warm welcome we received into their Leckhampton community on the first of these visits; and to the President and Fellows of Clare Hall, who did so much to make us a congenial academic environment on the second. I am much indebted also to the members of the Divinity Faculty at Cambridge for their many kindnesses and the stimulus of association with their work. And our special thanks to Dr Joan Cooper and Jean Smith for the home-away-from-home we had at Wytherton while these things were happening.

Some passages in the chapters have appeared previously in print, and I am happy to acknowledge the permissions given for me to use them again here: 'Human Freedom and the "Will to Believe" ', in 1979 Transactions, Fourth Series, Vol. XVII, and 'David Hume 1711–76; A Bicentennial Appreciation', in 1976 Transactions, Fourth Series, Vol. XIV, © The Royal Society of Canada; "Hume's Skepticism and the Dialogues" in McGill Hume Studies, edited by D. Norton, N. Capaldi and W. Robison, © 1979, Austin Hill Press.

I should add that some earlier reflections on the historical themes considered here are to be found in my essay "Skepticism and Fideism" in the volume The Skeptical Tradition, edited by Myles Burnyeat, to be published in 1983 by the University of California Press.

Thanks are due, in addition, to the following for the approval of quotations: Selections from Pierre Bayle's Historical and Critical Dictionary, translated and edited by Richard H. Popkin © 1965; *Thought and Knowledge*, by N. Malcolm, © 1977 Cornell University Press; *Sextus Empiricus*, in the Loeb Classical Library, © 1967 by Harvard University Press: William Heinemann Ltd.; *The Essays of Michel de Montaigne, Vol. II*, by Michel de Montaigne, translated by Jacob Zeitlin, © 1935 Alfred A. Knopf, Inc.; *He Who Is*, by E. L. Mascall, © 1954, Longman Group Ltd.; *Death and Immortality*, by D. Z. Phillips, © 1970, Macmillan, London and Basingstoke; *Descartes: Philosophical Writings*, translated by E. Anscombe and P. T. Geach, © 1966, Van Nostrand Reinhold (UK) Company Ltd.; *Faith and Reason*, by Richard Swinburne, 1980, Oxford University Press; *Metaphysical Beliefs*, edited by Alasdair MacIntyre, 1957, *Christianity at the Centre*, by John Hick, 1968, and *Taking Leave of God*, by Don Cupitt, 1980, © SCM Press; *Luther and Erasmus: Free Will and Salvation*, The Library of Christian Classics, Vol. XVIII, translated and edited by E. G. Rupp and P. S. Watson, © 1969, the Westminster Press; *Philosophical Fragments*, Søren Kierkegaard, translated by David Swenson, © 1936, 1962 and *Concluding Unscientific Postscript*, translated by David S. Swenson and Walter Lowrie, © 1941, 1969 by Princeton University Press; *Pascal: Pensées*, translated by A. J. Krailsheimer (Penguin Classics), © 1966 by A. J. Krailsheimer.

I am grateful to Keith Lehrer for his patience and encouragement. And last, but by no means least, I want to thank Marion Harrison and Saidah Din for typing all this.

My wife has shared the task of checking the proofs. But without her love and support there could have been no book at all.

Ah, what a dusty answer gets the soul
When hot for certainties in this our life!

Meredith, *Modern Love*

All we have gained then by our unbelief
Is a life of doubt diversified by faith,
For one of faith diversified by doubt:
We called the chess-board white — we call it black.

Browning, 'Bishop Blougram's Apology'

Due sense of the general ignorance of man
would also beget in us a disposition to
take up and rest satisfied with any evidence
whatever, which is real. . . . If a man were
to walk by twilight, must he not follow his
eyes as much as if it were broad day and
clear sunshine? . . . how ridiculous would it
be to reject with scorn and disdain the
guidance and direction which that lesser
light might afford him, because it was not
the sun itself!

Butler, 'Upon the Ignorance of Man'

CHAPTER 1

TWO KINDS OF FIDEISM

INTRODUCTION

When philosophers have discussed the relation between faith and reason, they have usually done so by asking whether or not faith met certain standards of rationality set, or assumed, by themselves. Those philosophers who have tried to defend faith, have, therefore, usually been concerned to show that faith conforms to those standards: that it is, in other words, a rational state of mind or attitude toward life. Such a defence seems to concede in advance that if faith cannot be shown to conform to such standards, the rational man must reject it. The most well-known version of such attempts to defend faith is that associated with St. Thomas Aquinas, who seeks to show that although faith involves the person who has it in assenting to propositions which human reason cannot itself show to be true, the authority which proclaims these propositions, namely the Church, has intellectually acceptable credentials, since some of what it teaches *can* be shown by reason to be true, and that which cannot be established in this way does have reasonable evidence to support it.[1]

But not all defenders of faith have accepted the implications of this pro-cedure. Many, especially those under the influence of classical Protestant thought, have held that such a procedure subordinates faith to human rea-son in an unacceptable way. They have believed, for example, that human thought-processes are corrupted by sin as deeply as other human activities are, and that faith is man's one and only way of salvation from the effects of this corruption. To insist that the claims of faith have to be judged by the standards of philosophical systems of human origin is to corrupt one's response to these claims from the outset.

The insistence that faith needs no justification from reason, but is the judge of reason and its pretensions, is usually called Fideism. As I have de-scribed it, it is a theological doctrine, since the concept of sin is a theological concept. But Fideism can be supported by many different arguments, and some of them, even though theologians have put them to use, have philoso-phical origins.

I want in this book to examine a number of such arguments that originate in the literature of philosophical Skepticism. I shall say that any attempt to show that faith is immune to the demands of reason by using arguments from this source is a form of Skeptical Fideism. I shall apply this title to the views of philosophers who explicitly recognize that their arguments have this ancestry, and to the views of those who do not recognize this even though it is so. (In the latter cases, of course, I shall have to give some justification for likening their views to those of the former group of philosophers.)

Superficially, it is not so hard to see why arguments of the kind I shall examine might appeal to some apologists. One ground for rejecting intellectual criticisms of faith is the supposed inability of human reason to make competent judgments on the subject-matter on which faith pronounces: reason's finitude, as distinct from its corruption. Once an apologist appeals to reason's finitude, he might well be tempted to espouse arguments which suggest that reason is not only incompetent in those things on which faith pronounces, but is far less competent than most of us suppose in more pedestrian matters; so that its powerlessness to pronounce on things transcendent is merely a manifestation of its universal impotence.

This temptation may be understandable, but it is hard for anyone familiar with the major developments in epistemology in modern times to see the resulting alliance as natural. Philosophers are used enough to the fact that the word 'Skeptic' connotes someone with doubts that extend more widely than religious doctrines (even though this restriction is still common enough among laymen). But how can someone who casts doubt on all our common-sense and scientific judgments about ourselves and our world be thought of as a potential ally of faith? For faith surely consists in, or at least involves, beliefs about transcendent realities, whereas Skepticism casts doubts on our beliefs in everyday facts. Faith surely is prized as a source of commitment and assurance, whereas Skepticism offers nothing but suspension and doubt. So the natural philosophical allies of faith have always been thought to be the more rationalistic and speculative thinkers who have not considered wider metaphysical truths about man's place in the universe to be unobtainable, but have attempted to discover them, and to show that they coincided with what faith also tells us about man and his relationship to God. How can someone who thinks it is doubtful whether tables and chairs even exist be a source of support for those who proclaim the doctrines of the Fall and the Resurrection and the Last Judgment?

To compound this, most philosophers no doubt suppose that even if their numbers are decreasing, people of faith are fairly easy to find; yet real Skeptics are not. Examples among philosophers, perhaps, are the Descartes of the First *Meditation* and the Hume of Book I of the *Treatise of Human Nature*. But since Descartes himself says that he is taking up a position he plans to reject, and since Hume confuses us by saying in several places that human beings cannot really take Skepticism seriously, even these instances are questionable. On the whole, Skepticism has been discussed in recent years as a position which no one holds, but which it is one of the basic duties of serious philosophers to refute. (It is a duty which some consider has finally been discharged by Wittgenstein.)

Although this is not a primarily historical study, some historical comments are therefore necessary for the phenomenon of Skeptical Fideism to be intelligible. The most important of these relate to changes in the perception of Skepticism itself.

SKEPTICISM, CLASSICAL AND MODERN

The tradition of Skeptical Fideism in modern times was the result of the rediscovery in the Sixteenth Century of the writings of Sextus Empiricus, and of the impact which that rediscovery had upon philosophers and theologians. Our own awareness of the importance of this phenomenon in the early history of modern philosophy is the result of the splendid scholarly labours of Richard Popkin. Among his many services to the self-understanding of philosophers has been his perception of the influence of Skepticism in its classic, Pyrrhonian form, on the work of such diverse figures as Descartes, Pascal, Hume, and even Kierkegaard. My own reflections in this book would have been quite impossible without these.[2]

But although Popkin has woken us from our dogmatic slumbers, the awakening is still incomplete. Many still think of Skepticism as something that Descartes not only tried to refute, but somehow invented. This mistake inevitably has the effect of making students of philosophy think of Skepticism as consisting in that special version of it which Descartes developed in order, as he saw the matter, to refute finally the Pyrrhonian tradition which had revived in his time. To see the changes which Descartes made in the Skeptic position in order to develop his own system, it is first necessary to rehearse what preceded him.

The classical Skeptic tradition lasted over five hundred years. It is usually said to have begun with Pyrrho of Elis (about 360 to 275 B.C.), and to have developed subsequently in two main phases: the Academic phase, represented most famously by Arciselaus (about 315 to 241 B.C.) and Carneades (about 213 to 129 B.C.), and the later Pyrrhonist phase, developed by Aenesidemus

(about 100 to 40 B.C.) and systematically expounded and illustrated by
Sextus Empiricus (about 160 to 210 A.D.). The writings of Sextus are our
major source of knowledge of the whole Skeptic tradition (and often of
the philosophers who were the targets of Skeptic criticism), although in
the case of the Skeptics of the Academy, we can also draw on the writings
of Cicero.[3]

A brief acquaintance with the writings of Sextus gives the impression
that the Skeptic way consisted in the endless use of destructive arguments,
especially if one assumes before one looks at them that the Skeptic is one
who, after the fashion of Descartes in the First *Meditation*, doubts everything. But although the Skeptics did indeed build up a battery of arguments
that undermined the constructive positions of their opponents, and although
the dialectical employment of these arguments undoubtedly came to be
pursued largely for its own intrinsic fascination, it is essential to bear in mind
that the Skeptic movement was, in its origins, and always at least in its profession, a practically-oriented movement, designed as an alternative to the
other practical philosophical schools of the Hellenistic age, namely Epicureanism and Stoicism. When the Skeptic refers to Dogmatists, it is usually to
these schools, especially the Stoic, that he refers. *Their* practicality is always
recognized by historians,[4] but since the time of Descartes the practical
orientation of Skepticism has commonly been overlooked. It can most
clearly be seen in Pyrrho, whose travels to India with Alexander are often
said to have been among the sources of his particular form of asceticism;[5]
but it can be detected throughout, and is quite explicit in Sextus' *Outlines
of Pyrrhonism*.

Skeptic questioning was supposed to yield a spiritual benefit. Like Epicureanism and Stoicism, it offered a way of life that based itself on the cultivation, not of worldly goods, but of an appropriate inner state that would
prevent the vicissitudes of life from penetrating the soul of the practitioner
and disturbing his peace. The purpose, then, is the banishing of anxiety.
Skepticism differed from Epicureanism and Stoicism in the procedures it
offered for the cultivation of this inner state. The Epicurean recommended
the pursuit of simple and undemanding pleasures. The Stoic recommended
the passionless pursuit of ends set by the divine order. Both such recommendations, especially that of the Stoics, required the possibility of a dependable
knowledge of reality to ensure the wisdom of one's choices. The Skeptic, by
contrast, sought inner peace through non-commitment, or suspense of judgment. The way to inner peace is through withholding assent to any dogma
about what the realities are, and recognizing the incapacity of human reason to

determine them, both in the realms of fact and of value. The very multiplicity of the competing knowledge-claims of current philosophical systems showed, to the Skeptic, that the certainties from which the consolations of these systems were supposed to follow were unreal, and that the competition between contending dogmas is itself a major source of confusion and anxiety. To avoid it one must decline to dogmatize on either side of controversies.

The complex, and often tedious, batteries of Skeptic arguments, which range from accounts of the odd ways of exotic tribes, to remarks about how sticks seen in water look bent and how things look yellow to men with jaundice, are designed to induce the suspense of judgment which was thought to follow upon the recognition of the intellect's limitations. A particularly important feature of these batteries of arguments is the collection of dogmatic reasonings on both sides of some disputed issue: the assemblage of both good and bad reasoning on each side is thought to induce suspense of judgment by leaving the reader in a state of equipoise between both sides, from which the step to suspense of judgment is either short or non-existent. (It is not, of course, necessary for such a procedure that the Skeptic who marshals these arguments should consider them all to have merit.) The Skeptic claim was that the consequence of such suspense would be an inner calm or unperturbedness — *ataraxia*.

Obviously a movement of this sort would require those identified with it to proceed, for the most part, by *ad hoc* criticisms of those forms of Dogmatism that confronted it. So the individual Skeptics, particularly Carneades, are traditionally represented as fierce destructive dialecticians. But in spite of this, Skepticism does seem to involve some minimal positive commitments, at least on the surface; and these apparent commitments are obvious sources of difficulty for it. There are natural criticisms to the effect that Skepticism is internally incoherent: that it teaches suspense of judgment, yet does so on the apparently dogmatic ground that knowledge of reality cannot be obtained; and that in recommending suspense of judgment it espouses a principle that such a procedure will have good results in leading to *ataraxia*; so that its own practice requires both a claim to knowledge about human nature and a claim about what state of mind is good. There are also practical criticisms: the most obvious one of these is the claim that no one can consistently suspend judgment, since daily life requires us to make decisions, and no one can take decisions without abandoning suspense. Skepticism, then, is said by its critics to be incoherent in principle and impossible to execute in practice.

Not surprisingly, it is in their varying responses to these criticisms that the major Skeptics seem to have differed from one another. Since Sextus is our major source, and has his own preferred resolution of these difficulties, his portrayal of these differences might be inaccurate. But, as he represents the matter, the Academic Skeptics and the Pyrrhonists divide in the following way.[6] He says the Academics compromised the tradition begun by Pyrrho in two respects. First, they lapsed into negative dogmatism by denying outright the possibility of real knowledge. Second, they claimed that the Skeptic can live in the world by recognizing that there are probabilities or likelihoods even though there are no certainties, and allowing himself to be guided judiciously by these. The Pyrrhonians regarded this concession, if indeed they are correct in ascribing it to the Academics, as compromising, indeed abandoning, suspense.

Sextus tells us that the Pyrrhonian evades the alleged difficulties in the Skeptic way in a different manner. First, he is not recommending his way on the basis of any theoretical generalizations or value-judgments for which he is proselytizing. The way is rather a stance or attitude or habit of mind which he is evincing and illustrating in his writings and arguments. This stance or attitude is one in which the enquirer is driven, by the sheer multitude of arguments on each side of the question which the Dogmatists dispute, to a point where their felt equivalence induces suspense in him. Quietude (*ataraxia*) is not, then, a condition which is sought after as a perceived good, but one which follows 'as if by chance' upon a suspense which in its turn has come upon the enquirer and was not actively chosen by him. Second, neither the suspense nor the quietude is understood in a manner which is inconsistent with the continuance of daily activities. The latter-day Pyrrhonian does not engage in ascetic withdrawal from the affairs of the day as Pyrrho himself appears to have done. He rather yields to appearances and to local opinion in the least stressful manner. His difference from those around him consists in his yielding to their opinions without subscribing to them. He yields in an undogmatic, or uncommitted, or belief-less way. Sextus describes this accommodation as follows:

Adhering, then, to appearances, we live in accordance with the normal rules of life, undogmatically, seeing that we cannot remain wholly inactive. And it would seem that this regulation of life is fourfold, and that one part of it lies in the guidance of Nature, another in the constraint of the passions, another in the tradition of laws and customs, another in the instruction of the arts. Nature's guidance is that by which we are naturally capable of sensation and thought; constraint of the passions is that whereby hunger drives us to food and thirst to drink; traditions of customs and laws, that whereby we regard piety in the conduct of life as good, but impiety as evil; instruction of the arts, that whereby we are not inactive in such arts as we adopt. But we make all these statements undogmatically.[7]

Such a statement certainly requires interpretation in its details, but it is clear that the Skeptic suspense does allow involvement in day-to-day activities. The involvement, however, takes place with a good deal of *arrière-pensée*: the Skeptic may share with his fellows an experience of the appearance of goodness and of conformity to reality in what they say and do, but does not follow them in judging that the appearances are veridical. He is, therefore, in, but not of, their world. Sextus makes no pretence that such uninvolved participation eliminates all stress. So the practical accommodation extends to the understanding of *ataraxia* itself:

We do not suppose, however, that the Skeptic is wholly untroubled; but we say that he is troubled by things unavoidable; for we grant that he is cold at times and thirsty, and suffers various affections of that kind. But even in these cases, where ordinary people are afflicted by two circumstances — namely, by the affections themselves and, in no less a degree, by the belief that these conditions are evil by nature — the Skeptic, by his rejection of the added belief in the natural badness of all these conditions, escapes here too with less discomfort. Hence we say that, while in regard to matters of opinion the Skeptic's End is quietude, in regard to things unavoidable it is 'moderate affection'.[8]

In summary, then, the Pyrrhonian Skeptic is presented by Sextus as an enquirer who does not deny, as his Academic counterpart is alleged to have done, that knowledge is possible at all, and does not meet the practical exigencies of daily life by accepting that although there is no knowledge we can be guided by probabilities. Instead, he yields to the same appearances that influence his fellows, but does so without either asserting or denying that these appearances correspond to realities. Sextus puts this by saying that the Skeptic's 'criterion' is the appearance (*phainomenon*). It is most important to avoid interpreting this anachronistically, yet very difficult for post-Cartesian readers to do so. The most tempting way to understand what Sextus says is to read him, as many have, as a phenomenalist like Berkeley or even Russell. But in spite of the obvious verbal derivation, this does justice neither to him nor to them. It is integral to modern phenomenalism that it seeks to rid us of the need for the appearance-reality distinction by telling us in some manner, metaphysical or metalinguistic, that appearances are in some sense all that there are, so that we can cast off all our lingering doubts about the nature of the reality that lies beyond them, or is supposed by non-phenomenalists to do so. Sextus, however, suspends judgment about whether or not appearances match 'non-evident' realities: a state of mind that essentially requires the use of the very distinction that the modern phenomenalist is proposing we abandon.

Recognizing this difference, however, is only a beginning. A claim to knowledge for Sextus (the sort of claim which, in common with his Academic counterparts, though not in their manner, he is trying to persuade us to abandon) is a claim that this or that appearance does, or does not, conform to reality — that the honey, for example, does not merely seem sweet, but is. It is judgments of this kind, about non-evident realities, that have generated those Dogmatic disputes from which the Skeptic way is to free us. From this it follows that the Pyrrhonist, though he does not dispute how the appearances are, does not regard the recognition that they are thus and so as itself a claim to knowledge. In the context of Skeptic reasoning such a suggestion would be paradoxical, even though since Descartes it is a philosophical commonplace to make it. The questions that concern Sextus are always questions about alleged non-evident realities beyond appearances, and it is these that he is speaking of when he asks whether knowledge is possible, or as he expresses it, whether Anything True Exists. Even if it is true that the distinction between appearances and realities is one that can only be invented by Dogmatists, it is also true that Skeptics have nothing they can say without using it. It is an important truth of history that it is only post-Cartesian philosophers who have said that appearances *are* realities. When considering the nature of the practical accommodations that Sextus recommends, this has to be kept constantly in mind.

In addition to this, the Skeptic's suspense, while extending to all judgments about the consonance or disparity between appearances and realities, does not embrace the proposition that there are external realities that are non-evident to us. For what the Skeptic is helping us to do is to live in a world in which knowledge of them is not available. More than this, however: the Skepticism of Sextus does not extend to the existence, or even, in any significant way, to the similarity, of other minds than the Skeptic's own. The Skeptic is thought always to live in a community whose customs and assumptions differ from those in other communities. The relativity of opinions about reality to the communities in which they are found is one of the more common Skeptic reasons for not assenting to the correctness, either of the opinions of the local community or contrary ones found elsewhere; but the yielding to appearances that Sextus commends is an uncommitted conformity to those one finds around one and toward which one naturally leans. Such arguments and accommodations require the assumption of a world full of thinkers and observers who live in societies that have different opinions, as much as they require the use of the distinction between appearances and realities. The menace of Solipsism cannot be stated coherently in such a context, even if it can be in some other.

These remarks are enough to show that the questioning of the Pyrrhonist are in certain key respects less extensive and omnivorous than the doubts of the post-Cartesian Skeptic. They also imply that in another respect they are wider in their scope. Epistemological Skepticism since Descartes has tended to focus almost exclusively upon the problem of the 'External World': roughly, the question of whether or not our sensory experiences can give us knowledge of the physical world from which we assume we derive them. It is natural, therefore, to assume that when Sextus talks of appearances he is speaking of sensory experiences, sense-data, visual and auditory images, and the like. This is reinforced by the fact that he often does do this, and by the fact that a very great many of the Skeptical arguments, especially those derived from the Academis Skeptics, were directed against the Stoic claim that some of our sensory experiences (some of the 'phantasms', or imprints on our souls from without) carry with them undeniable marks of their authenticity, and are therefore infallible guides to the reality which the Wise Man must know in order to guide his conduct. These arguments are often the very ones that reappear, usually unacknowledged, in the writings of early modern epistemologists — including the bent sticks and the jaundice. But there is little doubt that Sextus intends the notion of yielding to be understood much more widely than this. To conform beliefless to local moral customs is to yield to appearances, for example. To treat a patient's medical symptoms without speculating on hidden physical conditions is another way of yielding to appearances. So, finally, is the philosophical statement of the Skeptic way itself. For in each of these cases one is saying how it appears to one, and not claiming how it really is, or is not, for this is the essence of Dogmatism. It is this last which makes Skepticism, as Sextus sees the matter, both coherently statable, and practically liveable.

So, very roughly, the Skeptic will assemble all those arguments that Dogmatists have used to show that it not only appears that p, but really is, and then will assemble all the arguments that contrary-minded Dogmatists have used to show that even if it appears that p, it is not; this assemblage will bring upon him an incapacity to judge either that p, or that not-p. This will not make it cease to appear to him that p (or, perhaps, in his situation and society, that not-p), but it will enable him to live with his fellows who insist that p by conforming in his actions to their beliefs without sharing them. This will free him from all the mental disturbance which attends the assent to

p, and that which attends its denial, and will confine his vulnerability to those affects which attend the mere appearance that p, which he does not, and indeed cannot, dispute. In the process of attaining this state, he will of course have freed himself from the disturbances attending the disputations about whether or not p is really so; and by reviewing and transcending all the philosophical arguments for p and against it, he will have reached the point where he is free of all inclination to interpret the appearances in his life. The Socratic dialectic has, in an ironic way, come full circle: it is the examined life that is rejected.

This needs qualification, however. While there is nothing in principle, one may suppose, to prevent the Skeptic from discovering that what the appearances indicate for him is a practice that is in his society a minority one, or even a revolutionary one, it is obvious that the overwhelmingly likely result of the Skeptic attitude will be conservative patterns of action, and the continued practice of traditional crafts and recreations undisturbed by questions of ultimate value or meaning. Such questions will have been withered away by the very processes of reasoning they generate in other philosophers. But this shows that the Skeptic is not someone whose stance is indistinguishable from that of unreflective common sense, or that he considers ordinary folk to live in a condition of pre-philosophical innocence. If this were true, the Skeptic's questionings would only be directed against competing philosophical schools, and would pass the layman by. It is true that the standard targets are philosophical Dogmatists, the Stoics in particular, but there is also no question that the unlettered are also considered to be the victims of Dogmatism, and to be subject to perturbation and unhappiness because of the unfounded judgments that they make. So although the Skeptic's outward practice may not differ from that of his unphilosophical fellows, he is someone who *returns* to common practice after extinguishing his wish to justify or undermine it, and returns to a common practice that is disinfected, for him, of those specious underpinnings of belief and valuation that have given it meaning, and have helped to establish it, for those with whose behaviour he allows himself to conform. One cannot throw away the Skeptic's ladder without first climbing it. In this Skepticism resembles other anti-philosophical philosophies, like those of Hume and Wittgenstein, and differs fundamentally from those of Reid and Moore, who extol the philosophical wisdom they find among non-philosophers.

Whether or not the key notion of yielding to appearances is clear enough for the attempt to be successful, it is clear that the Pyrrhonism of Sextus rests upon a careful and sophisticated attempt to respond to the charge of impracticality directed against earlier forms of Skepticism. This charge is, strangely, repeated in modern times by the two thinkers who show, in many ways, the greatest understanding of Skepticism and the deep influence of it — Pascal and Hume. Perhaps this, too, can be laid at the door of Descartes. Certainly Descartes, in attempting to refute a revived and vigorous Pyrrhonism, changes the character of the Skeptic way in the process of presenting it; and it is this changed version of it that has become most familiar to modern students of philosophy.[9]

The first change Descartes makes is in presenting Skepticism as a wholly theoretical exercise; not only in the sense usually understood, that his own adoption of it in the First *Meditation* is purely methodological, and in that sense not sincere, but also in the sense that he does not even suppose it to be a position which *anyone* can sincerely espouse. The doubts of the Skeptic, as he presents them, are unnatural and even insane. This enables him to make them more radical. He first of all does this by saying that it will be part of his method to suppose that everything he does not find it wholly impossible to doubt is false. He then proceeds to make the supposition that all his sensory judgments are, therefore, false, since there is no unquestionable criterion for distinguishing false ones from true ones; he follows this by making a parallel suggestion about the conclusions of rational demonstration on the ground that his intellectual processes may be corrupted by a deceptive deity. His purpose, of course, is to insist that in the very supposition of this universal deception there is one truth which one is inevitably committed to accepting as true and beyond all question, namely the *cogito*. From this he proceeds to argue that the mind's knowledge of its own contents is also indubitable, and that among these contents there is, it turns out, one idea that can serve as an undeniable representation of reality beyond — the idea of God. Henceforward philosophers have been more and more inclined to suppose that the Skeptic is someone who is caught in a predicament — the predicament in which he knows his own existence, and the nature of his own ideas, but is haunted by the anxiety that there may be no reality beyond those ideas, so that he has no body to inhabit and there are no minds other than himself. This is a completely different situation from the one in which the classical Pyrrhonist saw himself, which was one in which quietude could come from recognizing that the world which he and others like him inhabited was one in which we could live satisfactorily by assenting to appearances but not disputing about the realities which lay behind them.

A further important difference between the Cartesian Skeptic and Sextus is to be found in the implications of their respective views of suspense. In the

Fourth *Meditation*, Descartes propounds a general theory of the voluntariness of belief, in order to show that human error cannot be blamed on the mere finitude of the intellect with which the creator has endowed us. In this theory, judgment is always a voluntary act in which the will assents to what the intellect presents to us. The moral of the story is that one should assent only when the grounds for doing so are complete — so that the Cartesian skeptic has rightly withheld his agreement until such time as the grounds have been shown to be conclusive. This picture of suspense of judgment as a voluntary choice is one it is natural to read into Sextus also. But to do this leads quickly to a paradoxical result. Since suspense is the normative Skeptic state of mind, and is supposed to lead in its turn to quietude, then if it is a state that can be achieved by sheer choice, the Skeptic, it would seem, might as well elect to adopt it on all occasions without first of all labouring so mightily to produce all those batteries of countervailing arguments to induce it. It would seem, rather, that suspense is a state that follows upon the psychologically equivalent effects of the countervailing arguments that the Skeptic examines, and cannot be construed as an action on the Cartesian model any more readily than the way things appear to him or the quietude that suspense itself gives rise to. The importance of this lies in the implied consequence that the Skeptic way as we find it in Sextus cannot be undermined by arguments that show belief to be involuntary. Of course, it does not follow from this that the Skeptic's characterization of the effects of Dogmatic arguments or philosophical perplexities is accurate in other ways.

Reminders of the differences between classical Pyrrhonism and Cartesian Skepticism are important when one turns to the work of other modern thinkers who respond to the revival of interest in Skepticism in the Renaissance and after. In recognizing that Descartes' own concern with Skepticism is itself one such response, we can see that thinkers who wrote after him, such as Pascal and Hume, may well not understand Skepticism in his terms, however radically he may have influenced them, and can certainly be taken to have independent access to versions of the Pyrrhonian tradition other than the recast version he presents.

For an account of such versions one must refer to Popkin.[10] What emerges immediately from even a brief acquaintance with his classic study is the intricate involvement of the revival of Skepticism in early modern times with theological disputes. One of the fruits of this involvement has been the Skeptical Fideist tradition, in which Skeptic argumentation is used in the interest of faith. Before attempting to make this tradition intelligible, and before examining some of its examplars, it is worth while looking to see what Sextus himself says about religion.

Naturally, it is of a piece with what he says about the Skeptic attitude toward all affairs of life. In the *Outlines of Pyrrhonism* he prefaces his summary of Dogmatic positions on the gods with this comment:

Although, following the ordinary view, we affirm undogmatically that Gods exist and reverence Gods and ascribe to them foreknowledge, yet as against the rashness of the Dogmatists we argue as follows.[11]

This is a natural application of following

a line of reasoning which, in accordance with appearances, points us to a life conformable to the customs of our country and its laws and institutions, and to our own instinctive feelings.[12]

The much lengthier theological discussions of M IX conclude, as always, with the introduction of Skeptic suspense, and with the additional comment that such suspense is not only a response to the balanced arguments of theistic and atheistic philosophers, but also a response to the divergency of views to be found among ordinary people.[13]

Precise interpretation of this stance may not be easy, because the fundamental concept of beliefless yielding to appearances is not a pellucid one, and we have here a particular application of it. But this application produces something very different from the conscious abstinence from religious practice that is entailed by those attitudes toward faith that are now called 'skeptical' in non-technical speech. For Sextus, assuming of course the existence of widespread local religious observance, says the Skeptic will participate in those observances, and will assent to the formulae of worship verbally. He will, however, abstain from inner commitment, it would seem, even on the very existence of the deities whose being and wisdom he will outwardly subscribe to in worship. One might call this stance one of beliefless piety. The piety subscribed to is seen as traditional, customary, and as embodying how things will seem to the member of the practising group.

It is interesting to see how this compares with the position adopted by the Skeptic (i.e. Academic) participant in Cicero's *On the Nature of the Gods* — the work on which Hume openly modelled his *Dialogues Concerning Natural Religion*. Cotta's main function is to attack the arguments for theism as these have come from the Stoic protagonist, Balbus. But Cotta does this, not as an atheist, but as a practitioner, indeed a functionary, of traditional religion. To Cotta religion is a matter of tradition and should remain so.[14] This comparison should not, however, make us think that the Skeptic stance can in any way be equated with a simple religious faith uncontaminated by theological argument. The Skeptic stance is a post-theoretical, not a pre-theoretical, one. The Skeptic continues with the ritual and the formulae of his tradition, self-consciously seeing it as a tradition and *not believing* it, yet not denying it. Contemporary analogies may well come to the reader's mind; but at this point my purpose is merely historical — that of identifying the particular form of undogmatic religiosity which Sextus accepts.

It is surprising, in the light of this, to see the extent of the attraction which Pyrrhonism exerted on thinkers deeply engaged in the theological wrangles of the Reformation period. For it is here that the revival of Pyrrhonism seems first to have entered the mainstream of Western thought in modern times.

SKEPTICISM AND FIDEISM

Initially, the use of Skeptic notions in theological controversy seems to have been a mere matter of the adaptation of particular arguments from one sphere to another. The Protestant insistence that the traditional claims of the Roman Church to interpret the Christian revelation were unfounded, and that Scripture alone was the vehicle of the Word of God, gave rise to questionings reminiscent of those the Pyrrhonists had engaged in.[15] If the Church and its traditions were to be put aside as sources of authoritative interpretation, what was then to happen when readers of Scripture did not agree on its meaning? To leave the matter to individual decision or inspiration appeared to leave no way of distinguishing between theological appearance and divine reality; yet to introduce some criterion distinct from Scripture itself or the reader's inclination to interpret it in a particular way reintroduces difficulties similar to those brought against the Catholic teachings by Protestants in the first place. Such disputes were to lead, in purely epistemological contexts, to the Cartesian doctrines of natural light and clear and distinct ideas — neo-Protestant conceptions which make it readily intelligible that the writings of Descartes, for all his Catholicism, should have found their way onto the Index. The Skeptic disputations that are echoed here, of course, are those surrounding the refutations of attempts to define 'the criterion' — in Dogmatic contexts, that which would serve to tell us which appearances conformed to reality and which not. Although neither side had a monopoly on the use of Skeptical or anti-Skeptical argument, it is easy to see that the Catholic would have more temptation to use Skeptical manoeuvres, since he would be inclined to recommend the return to tradition in a time of anxious disputation: a return which bears some resemblance, if we do not look too hard, to the Skeptic's acceptance of local religious consensus.

This temptation is one to which two famous figures appear to have yielded in a more self-conscious way. The first of these is Erasmus, in his famous debate with Luther about the freedom of the human will. The second, and for our purposes more important, is Montaigne. What each of them appears to do is to recommend the wholesale importation of Skeptical attitudes into Christian thought: to present Christian faith as a manifestation of Skeptical accommodation. To many this might seem a grotesquely implausible understanding of what faith is, but I shall attempt shortly to make it more readily intelligible, and to show much later that it has seductive contemporary counterparts. The only thinker of real philosophical sophistication who espoused it in early modern times after Erasmus and Montaigne is Pierre Bayle. At least, it is the position which it seems to me most natural to read into the best-known of his multitude of comments on the relation between faith and reason. The attempt to represent Christian faith as analogous to the Pyrrhonian conformity to appearances I shall call Conformist Skeptical Fideism. To avoid clumsiness I shall speak, for short, of Conformist Fideism, though this briefer title is intended only to refer, of course, to a form of Fideism which makes use of Skeptic argumentation. In the next chaper I shall deal, quite briefly, with the versions of it we find in the three thinkers I have named. I do not think it is hard to show that the arguments which support it are weak, or that the consequences which follow from it are unacceptable, particularly for anyone who wishes to preserve or defend Christian faith. This, however, creates an obligation, which I shall try to discharge in a speculative way, of showing the sources of the attraction which Skepticism could have in this context for thinkers of such obvious gifts and reputations. I shall defer until much later some latter-day analogues of Conformist Fideism which now attract attention.

Skeptical Fideism, however, has taken another, and in general much more influential, form. Its proponents have recognized that Skeptic belieflessness and Christian faith are indeed the polar opposites they seem. But they have nevertheless seen Skepticism as a tradition which has, unintentionally, served the cause of faith by exposing the inability of human reason to provide grounds for the commitment faith embodies. In doing this, Skepticism has, in their view, prepared the way for divine grace to generate faith without philosophical obstacles. For on this view, the attempts of natural theology to ground faith in reason are, as it has been put in our own day 'a sustained attempt to replace conversion by argument'.[16] On this view, whose proponents are not, of course, themselves Skeptics, the appropriate outcome of an immersion in Skeptic argument is not belieflessness, with or without observance, but *belief* — belief, nevertheless, without the pretence of metaphysical credentials. I shall call .this position Evangelical Skeptical Fideism, or Evangelical Fideism for short. Here the shortened title does have the disadvantage of suggesting that there can be no form of Fideism with an evangelical thrust which does not draw on Skeptic arguments, and this is clearly not so; but it has the advantage of making it a little clearer that the works I shall discuss, though drawing substantially on the works of the Skeptics, do not embody any form of Skepticism themselves. They merely share some of the Skeptic's reasons for despair about the claims and credentials of human reason. The two thinkers who most famously represent Evangelical Fideism are Pascal and Kierkegaard, and I shall seek to assess this stance by comments on appropriate aspects of their work.

These two forms of Fideism are clearly incompatible, even though individuals may oscillate between them. What they share are the two premises that the Skeptic has exposed the claims of the Dogmatist, and that the Dogmatist is not, therefore, the defender of the faith that he may think himself to be, but its competitor. To assess either position, one has to take an independent look at what faith is. I shall also attempt this task at a later stage, when the questions that such an enquiry needs to answer have become clearer.

NOTES

[1] His position on this theme is expounded in the *Summa Theologiae* 1a.1, and the *Summa Contra Gentiles*, Book One, Chapters 1–8. His account of faith is to be found in the *Summa Theologiae* 2a2ae, 1–7.
[2] See particularly the two books, *The History of Scepticism from Erasmus to Spinoza*, University of California Press, Berkeley, 1979, and *The High Road to Pyrrhonism*, Austin Hill Press, San Diego, 1980. An important additional source is his Selections from Pierre Bayle's *Historical and Critical Dictionary*, Bobbs-Merrill, Indianapolis, 1965.
[3] The writings of Sextus are available in four volumes, edited and translated by J. B. Bury, in the Loeb Classical Library, Heinemann, London, 1967–8. *The Outlines of Pyrrhonism* (PH) is in Volume 1, and the treatises commonly referred to as *Against the Mathematicians* (M) are in the remaining three. The most important of Cicero's writings for our purposes are the *Academica* and the *De natura deorum*; these are also available in one volume of the Loeb Classical Library, with translation by H. Rackham. There is a good English version of the latter by H. C. P. McGregor, *The Nature of the Gods*, published by Penguin (Harmondsworth), 1972.

A philosophically sophisticated account of the epistemological development of classical Skepticism is Charlotte Stough, *Greek Skepticism*, University of California Press, Berkeley, 1969. *Doubt and Dogmatism*, edited by M. Schofield, M. Burnyeat, and J. Barnes, (Clarendon, Oxford, 1980) is a most valuable collection of papers on Hellenistic thought, with much emphasis on Skepticism. A useful though less subtle presentation of Sextus is Philip P. Hallie's *Scepticism, Man, and God*, Wesleyan University Press, Middletown, 1964. I am most particularly indebted to the writings and lectures of Myles Burnyeat. Many of his arguments are presupposed in what follows here; they can be found particularly in two essays: 'Can the Sceptic Live his Scepticism?' (in *Doubt and Dogmatism*) and 'Idealism and Greek Philosophy: What Descartes Saw and Berkeley Missed' in *The Philosophical Review*, XCI No. 1, 1982.

[4] The practical, indeed religious, dimension of Epicureanism and Stoicism is not only commonplace among historians of philosophy; it is brought out in more general studies like A. D. Nock, *Conversion*, Oxford University Press, 1933 and E. R. Dodds, *Pagan and Christian in an Age of Anxiety*, Cambridge University Press, 1968. Stoicism gets much attention as a religious alternative in Paul Tillich's *The Courage to Be*, Nisbet, London, 1952.

[5] On Pyrrho's Indian Connection see Everard Flintoff, 'Pyrrho and India', *Phronesis* XXV, 1980.

[6] See Sextus, PH I, 226–231.

[7] PH I, 23–24.

[8] PH I, 29–30.

[9] On Descartes' method of doubt and its relation to Skepticism see Chapter 2 of Bernard Williams *Descartes: The Project of Pure Enquiry*, Penguin, Harmondsworth, 1978, Chapters 2–4 of E. M. Curley, *Descartes Against the Skeptics*, Blackwell, Oxford, 1978, and Burnyeat's essay 'Idealism and Greek Philosophy' referred to in Note 3 above.

[10] For Descartes' relation to the Skepticisms of his own time, see the first nine chapters of Popkin's *History of Scepticism*.

[11] PH III, 2.

[12] PH I, 17.

[13] M IX, 191–192.

[14] See *De natura deorum* I, 60–62.

[15] See Popkin, *History of Scepticism*, Chapter I.

[16] Alasdair MacIntyre, 'The Logical Status of Religious Belief', in *Metaphysical Beliefs*, SCM Press, London, 1957, p. 210.

CHAPTER 2

CONFORMIST FIDEISM – I

ERASMUS, MONTAIGNE, AND BAYLE

It is not surprising that attempts to recommend a particular version of Christian faith as the outcome of Skeptical disillusionment with reason and an example of Skeptical calm and detachment, should seem to many to be so obviously implausible that their authors were accused of insincerity or concealed apostasy. Both Montaigne and Bayle are most commonly read, in fact, as anti-religious figures who veiled their agnosticism under thin disguises in order to avoid persecution or inconvenience. I do not think that these judgments are correct, though I do agree that the attempted assimilation of faith to Skeptical detachment and conformity cannot work.

The first famous example of such apparent assimilation is to be found in Erasmus. At least, this is how he was read by Luther, whose understanding of his target has usually prevailed. Erasmus is not clear on this issue, and gives Luther some excuse for reading him in the way he does. No doubt Erasmus' main reason for publishing an argument on the Catholic side of the Reformation controversies was his conviction that the doctrinal divisions on which Luther was insisting, and for which Erasmus himself felt such distaste, were destroying the unity of Christendom and making simple, unfactional piety impossible. The particular dispute on which he chooses to intervene, namely that of the efficacy of the human will in the progress toward salvation, is one where he believes that Luther's doctrinal claims were undercutting the moral effort on which simple piety depended. This concern for simple faith, understood in largely moral terms, was compounded by a scholar's weariness with the interminable doctrinal disputes of the Fathers and Schoolmen. In venturing to censure Luther, however, he ran headlong into the classic representative of an altogether different understanding of what faith is; and in using language that echoed the Skeptics he gave his opponent a devastating weapon with which to demolish his case.

Probably Erasmus' view of his own argument was that he was importing into theology a Skeptic indifference that would permit simple piety to continue unsullied by sectarian differences. It is very doubtful if any more clearly-thought scheme existed in his mind for fusing Skeptic and Christian attitudes. The work in which he tried to introduce this apparently healthy uncontentiousness was the *Diatribe Concerning Free Choice*, dated 1524.[1] It is formally a response to an earlier work of Luther's whose title begins with the term 'assertio'.[2] In this work Luther had stated that free choice is a 'fiction', and that the human will makes no contribution of its own to salvation, which is due wholly to the activity of divine grace. Erasmus says at the outset that

> So far am I from delighting in 'assertions' that I would readily take refuge in the opinion of the Skeptics, wherever this is allowed by the inviolable authority of the Holy Scriptures and the decrees of the Church, to which I everywhere willingly submit my personal feelings, whether I grasp what it prescribes or not.[3]

This is not an unambiguous endorsement of Skepticism, and the arguments Erasmus goes on to use reflect this ambiguity.

We can find echoes of Skeptical themes when Erasmus insists that 'Christian godliness' does not require us to engage in theological disputation about divine foreknowledge or the efficacy of the will, and that there are matters which God does not wish us to penetrate but only to "contemplate, as we venerate himself, in mystic silence". To insist on exploring them is divisive, morally harmful, and generative of paradoxes. The total argument is plausibly read as a recommendation to do our Christian duty by striving to turn from evil to good, yet ascribing any good we achieve not to our own powers but to God – all the while declining to worry about any inconsistencies that over-eager dialecticians can generate from this. This is very close to the Skeptic's recommendation to fall in with tradition while avoiding interpretation. But most of the detailed argument is in favour of one of the competing dogmatic solutions, in this case a middle-road theology which holds the will to be free, but in need of grace to stir it to decision and to make its decisions effective. While he marshalls texts on both sides of the controversy in an apparent imitation of Skeptic practice, he does so only to re-interpret those texts which would otherwise favour Lutheran doctrine.

Luther's reply[4] is wholly single-minded by contrast, and is made much easier by Erasmus' inconsistencies. He represents these as the inevitable outcome of an attempt to mix two incompatible traditions. Two points in particular are worthy of note for our present purposes. First, Luther accuses Erasmus of contradiction in saying on the one hand that the freewill question is not one which the simple believer has to settle, but saying on the other that godliness requires both moral effort and divine mercy. Such theological advice embodies an attempted doctrinal solution to the very controversy that

Erasmus says one had best avoid. The theological problem, then, cannot be evaded by the participant in the Christian life. The attack here is not primarily on the muddles in Erasmus' logic, but on the suggestion that anti-dogmatism is a real possibility for the believer. Such attempted disengagement can only destroy faith, and not preserve it.

The second, and more fundamental, charge that Luther brings is that the Skeptic and Christian attitudes are fundamentally at odds:

> For it is not the mark of the Christian to take no delight in assertions; on the contrary, a man must delight in assertions or he will be no Christian. And by assertion . . . I mean a constant adhering, affirming, confessing, maintaining, and an invincible persevering; nor, I think, does the word mean anything else either as used by the Latins or by us in our time.[5]

It is all summed up in the famous sentence:

> The Holy Spirit is no Skeptic, and it is not doubts or mere opinions that he has written on our hearts, but assertions more sure and certain than life itself and all experience.[6]

This famous confrontation brings several important issues into sharp focus. It is usually thought that Luther's obvious tactical victory is due to his having a more accurate understanding of what faith is than Erasmus has, or implies. I think that this is correct, but the situation is more complex than it seems on the surface. Let us look first at the extent to which Erasmus duplicates the classical Skeptic's stance; for if he duplicates it at all closely, this would detract from Luther's insistence that Skepticism and 'the Christian mind' are incompatible. For there can be no question of the sincerity of Erasmus' intent to defend, not to undermine, Christian piety as he understood it. His understanding of it is one which, as he states it here, includes 'piety' (which can be taken to include both religious observance and moral conduct), a reticence to engage in doctrinal dispute, and a submission to authority. It is easy to see that analogies with classical Skepticism are strained in key respects. The submission to authority is offered as a source of potential exceptions to Skeptical suspense of judgment: this can only mean that Erasmus considers it possible that there are some doctrinal disputes on which the Church may well insist that a decision between interpretations be made in one way. It is also true that the moral requirements of Christian piety, as he understands them, also involve a degree of assent to moral authority which is not consonant with Skeptical distance. But however strained the analogies may be, they are present. The detachment that Erasmus recommends is offered as a way of evading one of the major issues which had separated Luther from the Church.

The acceptance of authority is an obvious analogue of the Skeptic conformity to tradition, and the adherence to tradition is a (probably deliberate) echo of Cotta's understanding of piety as a matter of custom. We need a further clue to explain Erasmus' failure to perceive how strained his analogy is; but Luther's ire is in part due to 'his recognition that it does have a superficial appeal.

What Luther's criticisms force us to see is the gulf that separates the two thinkers' understanding of what faith is. There are three key differences that appear in this exchange. First, Luther insists that the Christian mind is not detached, but intensely committed. Second, he insists that this commitment involves not an 'invincible persevering', which might seem to correspond to the moral requirements of Erasmian piety, but repeated *assertion*; this of course refers to the Christian need to confess the faith openly, but it has the additional purpose of stressing that what the Christian confesses is the acceptance of certain essential doctrines about ultimate realities and his own relationship to them — doctrines of the very sort on which it is the essence of Skepticism to suspend judgment. Finally, the commitment he has insisted upon is characterized not only by resolution but by *certainty*. There is no place in his view of the Christian mind for the doubts and hesitations and alternatives which have driven Skeptics, and Erasmus following them, to talk of detachment.

There have always been, and always will be, many Christians who consider that the path of Christian conduct is more central to the faith than that of doctrinal assertion. In so far as his views of the Christian way are an expression of this form of Christianity, Erasmus can be seen as recognizing the importance of commitment as much as Luther does. But to that very extent, he is departing from the enervating conformity which Sextus admits. Such conformity yields, as Sextus himself says, a moderation in attitude that would, in the Christian tradition, bring down the judgment levelled by the author of the *Apocalypse* on the Loadiceans.[7] On the second of the differences I have just outlined, two issues must be distinguished. There is the issue of how far, in the case of any particular Christian assertion, one is involved in theological controversy. One can at least say here that it is implausible to suggest that such controversy can be avoided in all cases, even if Erasmus is right that it can be in the matter of the freedom of the will. There is also the more fundamental issue of how far it is correct, or even coherent, to suggest that one can have faith without thereby holding beliefs about what the Skeptic calls nonevident realities. The onus certainly seems to be on the one who thinks this is possible or desirable to offer some analysis of faith that is consistent with this, and Erasmus does not offer us one. It does not follow from this, however, that Luther is right when he insists that such beliefs have to be 'more sure and certain than life itself'. If such certainty is required by faith, then Skeptical attitudes are wholly opposite to it. The fact that most of those who have faith, and most of those who do not, take it for granted that Luther is right in this, is what makes the attempt to graft Skeptical ideas onto Christianity seem odd to the point of paradox when first considered, and has ensured that those who followed Erasmus in this attempt have been suspected of disguised apostasy.

The most famous of these figures is Montaigne, whose essay *Apology for Raimond Sebond*, published in 1580, became the most famous of all modern Pyrrhonist texts, and the source of much of the concern with Skepticism in early modern philosophy. The essay served to introduce dozens of Skeptical arguments, and many of the standard Skeptical examples, to a wide literary audience. Montaigne's motives have been much debated. He was widely taken as undermining religious faith − it is his influence when so interpreted, for example, that Pascal is trying to combat in the *Pensées*. But if this reading of his intentions is the right one, it is contrary to the surface sense of many things that he says. I shall assume that the surface sense is the correct one, though such a reading undoubtedly fits only if we assume that Montaigne's acceptance of Christianity is, as Popkin says, an 'unexcited' one.[8] I think his motives in writing this enormous and shapeless essay were in part similar to those of Erasmus: to offer an intellectual antidote to violent sectarianism, both that of the Protestants and that of their over-zealous persecutors among the French Catholics. His method is much more radical and much more philosophical than that of Erasmus: though not an original philosopher, Montaigne follows Sextus in undermining confidence in the power of human reason to arrive at truth in any sphere, by the use of reason itself. His explicit statements to this effect take him perilously close to negative dogmatism, but the avoidance of inconsistency is not his primary concern. Indeed, the stance Montaigne adopts is a twofold one that is deeply at odds with itself.

The nominal structure of the essay centres round two objections made by critics to the natural theology of the Fifteenth Century Spanish thinker Raimond Sebond. Montaigne had translated Sebond into French at the request of his father. The defence Montaigne offers is an odd one. Sebond had tried to give a rational demonstration of the major articles of Christian faith. Montaigne considers two objections to this that had been made by critics. The first is that faith should not be based on reason at all (something Montaigne himself says at the end of the essay). His answer is that *within* faith reason can be of great service: a manifestly irrelevant response. The second objection is that Sebond's actual arguments are weak. Montaigne answers this by arguing at length, with assistance from Sextus, that the greatest human minds have been unable to find the truth about any subject-matter, so there is no particular reason to be dismayed if the arguments of Sebond are not compelling, since they are as successful as any others are! Sebond disappears from sight as Montaigne assembles argument after argument, in Pyrrhonian fashion, to undermine our confidence in the sciences, our senses, philosophy, and all manifestations of human intellect. The impact of his assemblage of arguments has, in spite of his unoriginality, been very great. Both Descartes and Pascal, in their very different ways, absorb much of what Montaigne says, the former in his rejection of the senses as a possible source of true knowledge, the latter in his depiction of reason as unable to pass beyond chronic ambiguities in its search for truth on ultimate human concerns.

Montaigne himself, however, draws two morals. The first is explicitly Catholic, traditional, and conformist. Man, placed individually in history, and unable to rise above the relativities that derive from this, must recognise his inability to do so, and should submit to the religious forms and teachings that surround him, rather than try arrogantly to assert or deny them from an objective standpoint that is impossible for him. Such arrogance is equivalent to that of the dogmatist who supposes himself capable of telling us what things are really like in themselves without regard to the fact that he only has access to the appearances of things that depend on the physical placing and condition of his sense-organs. This position is almost purely Pyrrhonist. It is found, for example, in the following passage:

Now, from a knowledge of this volatility of mine, I have accidentally begotten in myself a certain steadfastness of opinion and I have not much altered those that were original and native with me. For whatever semblance of truth there may be in a novel idea, I do not easily change, for fear of losing by the bargain. And since I am not capable of choosing, I take the choice of other men and keep myself in the station in which God has placed me. Otherwise I could not save myself from rolling perpetually. In this way I have, by the grace of God, with no perturbation and disturbance of conscience, preserved my faith intact in the ancient beliefs of our religion, amid so many sects and divisions that our age has produced.[9]

The second moral is more general, is in principle acceptable equally to Protestants and Catholics, and is the more familiar and influential form of Skeptical Fideism. Since neither the senses nor reason can guide us to reality, we have to accept that our own resources are inadequate to grasp it. To

someone humble enough to recognize his inability to rise above his limitations, access to truth comes through divine grace, as a gift.

> Nor can a man rise above himself and humanity; for he cannot see but with his eyes,
> nor take hold but with his own grasp. He will rise if God will extraordinarily lend him
> his hand; he will rise by abandoning and renouncing his own means and by suffering
> himself to be uplifted and upraised by means purely celestial.
>   It belongs to our Christian faith, and not to his Stoical virtue, to aspire to that divine
> and miraculous metamorphosis.[10]

This form of Fideism seems to mean that when the disillusioned seeker
abandons the dogmatist's quest for ultimate truths, he can nevertheless attain
to them because divine grace will step in to fill the place he has emptied for
it. The words Montaigne uses suggest that such a miraculous transition will
be characterized by conscious surrender to God, and by the very assertion of
ultimate truths which the subject has previously given up. The outcome will
be not belieflessness but belief. The two morals are patently inconsistent with
each other, and it is tempting to read Montaigne as though he were hinting at
a non-religious meaning by leaving their inconsistency on the very surface of
his work. If we wish to produce a more coherent statement from what he
says, however, I think we can do so in the following way, which depends
upon assuming that faith, for Montaigne, though real enough, was indeed the
'tepid' thing that Popkin suggests it was.

   We can take Montaigne to be suggesting that when the enquirer abandons
the pretensions of reason and relaxes into incurious conformism, this process,
viewed theologically, is a Providential passage from anxious seeking into
tranquil faith: a passage from the stormy sea into the safe haven of the
Church. The credal pronouncements which the subject will then make, and
the observances he will then follow, are in fact the ones that God has
ordained for man's salvation. Man's own rational enquiries cannot show this
to him, but the very abandonment of the search for truth will lead him into
the right way by Providential provision. If we read him this way, the huge
fissure that seems to separate the two morals that he draws can perhaps be
plastered over.

   Two obvious comments must be made, however. The first is that such an
identification of conformist conservatism and faith cannot give us faith as
Luther understands it. (It could only do so if the conformity were entered
into deliberately as a device to replace hesitation by something psychologically quite different, as Pascal later suggested.) The second is that such acqui-
escence assumes a readily-identifiable local consensus from which the seeker

has been temporaily disturbed, and to which he can easily return. This may indeed have been the situation of Montaigne's Catholic readers faced by disputes with Protestants, and this no doubt accounts for the way in which Montaigne's lead was followed by other Catholic Pyrrhonists, such as Charron.[11] Such consensus is virtually unknown in our day, and such a relationship to a religious tradition is rare also.

There has been at least as much suspicion of Bayle's intentions as of those of Montaigne. The *philosophes* of the Enlightenment used his *Historical and Critical Dictionary* as a treasure-house of Skeptical argument with which to attack Christian dogma, and it has been the most common view of him that his frequent professions of faith in the Reformed Chruch are deliberate obfuscations, designed to keep him out of trouble. But there is a body of scholarly opinion which inclines to the view that his professions are sincere, though the faith they express must certainly have been devoid of enthusiasm. In favour of the negative reading, there is, first and foremost, the obvious obsessive relish with which Bayle repeatedly demonstrates the lack of rational support for Christian doctrines, and the way he undermines the moral and historical authority of the Scriptures (at least the Old Testament). In favour of the sincerity of his statements of faith, we have the elaborate arguments of the famous Clarifications added to the second edition in response to the censures of Church authorities, and the repeated fideistic assertions in the main body of the work: plus the fact that the disapproval of Church authorities would not have represented serious calamity for him in the Holland of his day. He retained his Church membership until his death; and for him it represented the tradition to which he had returned after his brief acceptance of Catholicism as a young man. To Bayle the acceptance of tradition would mean the acceptance of Protestant tradition: and Bayle is in fact the only major Protestant Skeptic.[12]

The historical question of Bayle's private intentions need not concern us unduly; but it is my purpose here to see how far Bayle's professed position is sufficiently coherent to have convinced him, or to have seemed to him to be convincing enough to state to others. On the surface, his position is that of what I have called Evangelical Fideism. He speaks of the Pyrrhonists as a school of philosophers with opinions that would doom them to hell,[13] but claims that their arguments, plus the many of his own that resemble theirs, serve to reveal the impotence of reason when faced with divine mysteries. The realization of its impotence should make us turn, unquestioningly, to faith. Faith as he represents it appears to be much the same moralistic piety that Erasmus took it to be. So when he insists that one should leave rational disputation and take refuge from its uncertainties in faith, he does not appear to see this as the adoption of one side in a doctrinal dispute, but to be urging his readers to turn away from such disputes altogether. Faith, then, supplies the calm that Pyrrhonian argument can not alone supply, but for which it is still, in spite of this, a precondition. It is a precondition of it because in such Skeptic argument reason shows its possessor its own incapacity to lead him to assurance. We find these sentiments expressed in this paragraph from the Third Clarification:

Theologians should not be ashamed to admit that they cannot enter a contest with such antagonists (i.e. the Pyrrhonists), and that they do not want to expose the Gospel truths to such an attack. The bark of Jesus Christ is not made for sailing on this stormy sea, but for taking shelter from this tempest in the haven of faith. It has pleased the Father, the Son, and the Holy Ghost, Christians ought to say, to lead us by the path of faith, and not by the path of knowledge or disputation. They are our teachers and our directors. We cannot lose our way with such guides. And reason itself commands us to prefer them to its direction.[14]

In spite of the use of some anti-Skeptical language, therefore, I would suggest that Bayle belongs more in the camp of the Conformist Fideists than their Evangelical counterparts. For him, faith serves as the unreflective conclusion of a quest which ends only in the abandonment of argument. If what one comes to rest in is (as it no doubt is) one of the dogmatic positions about which the argument has raged, one does not come to rest in it as the winner in the argument. Nor, it would seem, does one properly come to rest in it if one has not been through enough of the argument to see the latter's futility. We are not here confronting a thinker who recommends us not to reason, but someone who recommends us to reason in order to recognize reason's incapacity. Hence it is desirable for those in the faith to be fully acquainted with all the disputes about its doctrines, not merely to recite these unheedingly. This also from the Third Clarification:

There are so many people who so little examine the nature of divine faith and who so rarely reflect on this act of their minds that they have need to be removed from their indolence by long lists of the difficulties that surround the doctrines of the Christian religion. It is through a lively awareness of these difficulties that one learns of the excellence of faith and of this blessing of heaven. In the same way one also learns of the necessity of mistrusting reason and of having recourse to grace.[15]

This brings us to an aspect of Bayle's Skepticism that distinguishes it from that of Montaigne. Bayle shows relatively little interest in those arguments of Sextus that undermine the claims of the senses as guides to the nature of the real world. His main concern is with the anti-metaphysical arguments Sextus offers, and in particular with the attacks upon theological and scientific doctrine. Naturally Bayle's actual targets are the theologians, mathematicians and physicists of his own day. Again and again he seeks to undermine their rational pretensions by uncovering inconsistency and paradox in their theories. The assumption that Sextus appears to have made, that such theories lie, somehow, behind the everyday beliefs of the common man, is not obviously present in Bayle. What we find is the repeated demolition of attempts to defend scientific and theological doctrines against charges of absurdity. The most famous of these are the arguments in the remarks to the articles 'Manicheans' and 'Paulicians' showing that no coherent Christian response to the problem of evil is possible, and the assertion of the paradoxical character of Christian doctrines in Remark B to the article 'Pyrrho'. In the latter he has an imaginary philosophical *abbé* point out that the doctrine of the Trinity contradicts the self-evident maxim that things which are not different from a third thing are not different from each other; that the Incarnation contradicts the principle that the union of a human body and a human soul is sufficient to constitute a person; and that the Catholic doctrine of the Eucharist contradicts the self-evident principles that a body cannot be in more than one place at a time and that a substance cannot be taken away without its accidents being taken away also. In each of these cases, there is a clear incompatibility between accepting the Cartesian standard of clarity and distinctness and accepting the Christian doctrine. The inclusion of the Catholic teaching of transubstantiation must show that Bayle (a Protestant) is not arguing that each of these doctrines is known to be true in spite of the principle it violates; rather he is insisting that faith involves the abandonment of this most central and prestigious intellectual standard.

In the Clarifications, Bayle defends the orthodoxy of his position by reference to Scripture. His texts are Pauline; in the Third Clarification he chooses I Corinthians 1:17 – 2:14, where Paul contrasts the truth of the Spirit and the wisdom of men; in the Second Clarification he quotes II Corinthians 5:7, where Paul contrasts faith and sight. Faith, says Bayle, "produces a perfect certitude, but its object will never be evident. Knowledge, on the other hand, produces together both complete evidence of the object and full certainty of conviction. If a Christian then undertakes to maintain the mystery of the Trinity against a philosopher, he would oppose a non-evident object to evident objections".[16] This mixture of Pyrrhonian and Cartesian notions offers two grounds for Bayle's fideism: first, the Christian faith proclaims mysteries, which are necessarily non-evident realities, and therefore beyond the reach of reason in the way Skepticism has always understood reality to be beyond it; second, there is a necessary connection, as we would now express it, between mysteriousness and non-evidence, so that faith and knowledge are incompatible. Bayle here draws on traditional understandings of faith, and in particular of Paul's contrast between faith and sight; and he is enabled to do so by assuming the Cartesian equation of knowledge and self-evidence.

Is it, however, possible to assert doctrines while simultaneously holding that they contradict self-evident principles? To many such a question seems straightforwardly psychological. Some, reading it this way, would say the answer was obviously "Yes"; others, that the answer is obviously "No". Bayle is in the former camp, though he offers some argument, in remark M to the Article on 'Spinoza':

One may cry out that he is not sincere; and that our mind is not made in such a way, that it can accept as true that which a geometrical demonstration shows is completely false. But is this not setting yourself up as a judge in a case in which it can be objected that you are not competent? Have we any right to decide what goes on in another's heart? Do we know the human soul sufficiently to declare that such and such a combination of views cannot be found in it? ... For it must be observed that there is no contradiction between these two things: (1) The light of reason teaches me that this is false; (2) I believe it nonetheless because I am convinced that this light is not infallible and because I prefer to submit to the proofs of feeling and to the impressions of conscience, in short, to the Word of God, than to a metaphysical demonstration. This is not at all the same as believing and not believing the same thing at the same time. That combination is impossible, and nobody ought to be allowed to offer it as his justification. ... The Abbé de Dangeau speaks of certain people who have religion in their minds but not in their hearts ... I believe that one can also say that there are people who have religion in their hearts, but not in their minds. They lost sight of it as soon as they seek it by the methods of human reasoning. ... But as soon as they no longer dispute, and as soon as they listen only to the proofs of feeling, the instincts of conscience, the weight of education, and the like, they are convinced of a religion; and they conform their lives to it as much as human weakness permits.[17]

In spite of Bayle's protestations, most philosophical readers of this passage will no doubt feel inclined to question the logical possibility of the state of mind that he describes — either by denying the sincerity of the profession of the negative proposition or denying the sincerity of the profession of the positive one. On the other hand, Bayle is not alone in his insistence upon its reality, which is also proclaimed or implied by Evangelical Fideists, particularly Kierkegaard.

This likeness underlines the difficulty of fitting Bayle, or the professed position of Bayle, into the Conformist-Evangelical division I have adopted.

I have chosen to present him as a Conformist because of the obvious lack of fervour in his religious professions, and because of the obvious fact that faith appears in his writings always as the end-product of a process of skeptical questioning and counter-questioning, as a latter-day substitute for suspension as a source of quietude – not, as in Pascal and Kierkegaard, as a dominant stance from which skeptical argument functions as a heaven-sent barrier to false philosophical constructions. Even though Bayle's professions of faith are sincere, it it his skepticism that dominates his work: he genuinely is a Skeptic and a Christian together, whether this is consistent or not.

I have two brief footnotes to this. First, Bayle's insistence that Christian doctrines are false by Cartesian principles of clarity and distinctness emerges as a more powerfully *Skeptical* move if his faith in those very doctrines is accepted as genuine. For it then amounts, as Popkin has pointed out,[18] to an attempted refutation of Descartes' claim to have established clarity and distinctness, in the goodness of God, as the criterion of truth: for it can be no such thing, if it can yield false results! God has given us an intellectual instrument he requires us in the last resort to abandon. Second, Bayle suggests in Remark H to the article 'Zeno', that since there is no refutation of Zeno's arguments against the reality of motion, or of other arguments like Zeno's which he has himself offered against the reality of extended bodies, our only way of evading Zeno's negative results is by faith. This again offers faith, here in a wholly secular context, as the equivalent of Pyrrhonist accommodation.[19] It is also a source of a common fideist argument, or cluster of arguments. These say, in their negative version, that religious faith is no worse off by rational standards than many common sense commitments which daily life requires of us. They say, in their positive versions, that Christian faith is merely an extension in another sphere of a natural trust we give unhesitatingly in non-religious matters. The implication of this sort of argument is that the unbeliever who does not adopt rationalist defences of his common sense commitments is inconsistent in withholding assent from the claims of faith. This challenge was taken particularly seriously by Hume, whom Bayle influenced considerably.

Let us now review some of the major questions which have been raised in this brief review of the most important classical exponents of Conformist Fideism.

(1) Each of the figures we have considered has tried to commend not only the arguments, but also the attitudes, of classical Skepticism to Christians. The wrathful response of Luther reflects a puzzlement that arises even more for any reader at a distance from the original debate: a puzzlement that

attitudes so clearly incompatible as those of Skepticism and faith can be grafted together. My first comments will be an attempt to make this more nearly intelligible. In so doing I shall try to illuminate some important but neglected features of each.

(2) I hope that my comments on this first question will make it possible to examine a second. There have been at least two places where philosophers have questioned the logical possibility of a professed state of mind. One of these is the state of mind of the classical Pyrrhonist as Sextus presents it. Can one in fact yield to appearances and thus function among one's fellows while simultaneously suspending judgment about everything which they believe? The second is the state of mind professed by Bayle when he tells us that we can embrace Christian doctrines in faith while acknowledging that they are contrary to reason, not merely unproven. He tells us that this is not a matter of holding two contradictory beliefs at once. Both these professed states of mind have seemed to incredulous hearers to be psychologically impossible states which are yet being recommended to them as the results of heroic feats of will! To examine the difficulties that both have caused it will be necessary to digress a little, in the next chapter, to discuss the old and knotty question of the voluntariness of belief, and then to apply some results of that digression to the understanding of these paradoxical professions.

There are other questions that have arisen which I hope to comment upon after examining Evangelican Fideism.

(3) One of these is found in Bayle's suggestion that faith is requisite in secular as well as religious contexts. It has appeared to many that the traditional contrast between faith and reason is at least exaggerated. The rationalist theologian has attempted to reduce the contrast by giving rational support to Christian doctrines, but Bayle's suggestion points to another way — that of arguing that many of the secular beliefs of common sense or science with which faith is contrasted are themselves beliefs which we cannot justify by reason either, so that the contrast is a bogus one for that reason. This argument has many shades of emphasis, and what may serve to refute one version of it will not necessarily serve to refute another. But since a general name for all of them is convenient, I shall say they are all versions of the Parity Argument. To assess them effectively, the results of all the discussions in this book will be necessary. At this stage we can at least see that the Conformist Fideist will incline to infer from the Parity Argument that an uninvolved or moderated conformity is an appropriate response both to the claims of faith and to those of secular appearances and conventions.

(4) There is a curious agreement between our three Skeptics and Luther – and indeed their other opponents. All seem to agree that faith is characterized by certitude. Erasmus merely argues that those theological issues which generate uncertainty for the scholar are not central to faith. Montaigne and Bayle speak of faith as a refuge from doubts and dissensions, and make no suggestion that one could combine it with hesitation or ambivalence. Indeed this is what makes our first question such a puzzling one. The assimilation of the traditions of Skepticism and faith might naturally be expected to raise questions about the assumption that faith involves certainty, but it is not so presented. I shall try to argue as the book proceeds that the assumption is a mistaken one, unless expressed with the most careful qualifications.

(5) The Conformism I have claimed to find in all three writers is linked with the assumption, made by Cicero and Sextus, that religious piety is a matter of participation in the traditional forms of ritual in a particular community. This contrasts sharply with Luther's insistence on the centrality of *assertion*. The natural thrust of Conformist Fideism is toward the reduction, or even elimination, of the role of doctrine in faith. In recent years the non-credal understanding of faith has been growing in influence. Ironically, in spite of the Skeptic sources of its main stance, it is sometimes associated today with the claim that Skepticism has been exposed as incoherent by the investigation of common thought-forms and linguistic practices. The question to be considered, therefore, is whether an Erasmian piety, with little or no doctrine, is faith at all, and whether faith can be defended in the face of doctrinal uncertainties by non-dogmatic interpretation.

SKEPTICISM AND FAITH

Some of the preceding may have made the attraction of Skepticism for certain apologists intelligible, but the sharp contrast between the Skeptic and the Christian ways remains obvious. We must go a little deeper into the nature of each in order to offer suggestions on the reason why Erasmus, Montaigne, and Bayle, to say nothing of lesser figures such as Charron[20] or Huet[21] felt it possible to fuse them.

In spite of the fact that modern readers can only see Skepticism through the eyes of Descartes, it is essential to recognize that even those fideists like Bayle or Pascal who came after him saw him as a thinker who sought to refute the classical Skeptic tradition; hence his more radical version of it, and his refutations, could not eradicate the aspect of that tradition which he chose to ignore: its practicality. Skepticism was a competitor of Epicureanism and Stoicism, offering, as they claimed to offer, a way to inner peace and freedom from anxiety; it was not, as Descartes made it in order to reveal its supposed impossibility, an unnatural theoretical indulgence to be humoured in the study. When this is kept before us, its appeal to a certain type of religious believer becomes easier to understand. For all its dialectical rigmaroles, it offers what would be called in religious parlance a saving way of life. It offers a way of escape from those immoderate affections that, in its view, derive from ascribing non-evident (in present-day religious jargon, transcendent) value to human activities in which we all, perforce, engage, and from ascribing ultimate truth to judgments that we all, in order to conduct our daily business, must make. The ultimate enemy, therefore, is anxiety. The Epicurean tried to contend with it by reducing the occasions for its occurrence to the minimum, which was to be done by confining one's aspirations to simple, low-budget satisfactions. The Stoic sought to contend with it by identifying the dictates of his own will with those of a cosmic reason, and thereby extinguishing the passions from whose demands and frustrations our anxieties arise. Both of these ways, in the Skeptic view, presuppose a power to gain knowledge of cosmic realities and ultimate values that there is no reason to suppose we have. The way to root out anxiety is to eliminate the urge toward knowledge of the non-evident that is a condition of the unhappy involvements the Epicurean and the Stoic seek to avoid. Their only remedy is to offer competing commitments, which can have no better basis in knowledge than the ones they are designed to supplant, and which must be, in their turn, deflated at their source.

This view of the sources of human ills bears striking resemblances to actual religious traditions, particularly to the anti-metaphysical forms of early Buddhism. The fact that Pyrrho is said to have journeyed to India with Alexander can generate interesting speculation about influences, which I am not competent to judge.[22] But it is easy to find examples in both Hindu and Buddhist traditions of the claim that dissatisfaction is due to ignorance (*avidyā*), the latter being understood as a compulsion to make false judgments about the permanence, substantiality, and value of the human soul and the objects to which it relates itself, and that this compulsion manifests itself in the speculative attempt to seek for truth in thought-forms, or categories, that cannot express it. The way to enlightenment and peace is to be found by the elimination of such compulsions. The one who has eliminated them will not cease to live and work among the rest of us, but will do so in an uninvolved and tranquil manner, neither ascetic nor indulgent, but moderate.

My purpose in drawing attention here to this analogy is not to claim (whatever this would mean) that Skepticism is a religious movement, nor to fuel historical theses about sources, but to indicate that the likeness between Skepticism and key elements in two major religious traditions may serve as a clue to the attraction which certain Christian apologists felt for it. It would be the sort of attraction which religious contemporaries feel for religious traditions other than their own, but do not feel for competing secular systems or even for some groups within their own faith. It comes from seeing that the target of their procedures and the reward of their procedures are understood in like ways. Unfortunately, just as the likenesses between Christian and Hindu or Buddhist traditions are, though real, readily exaggerated by those who see them, so the likenesses between Christian faith and classical Pyrrhonism, though real, could only seem as great as they did to the Conformist Fideists if they were not examined too closely. The likenesses between some strands of Hinduism or Buddhism and Pyrrhonism are far greater than the likeness of either to Christianity.

How far can the real likenesses between Pyrrhonism and Christian faith be thought to extend? Both involve a dissatisfaction with the disturbance and anxiety associated with the commitments of the world of secular common sense. Both hold that the products of human speculation and dogmatism are unable to advance us to a stage where we are free from them. Both recommend, as a cure for these anxieties, not physical disengagement from the common sense world, but a kind of participation in it, and acceptance of the demands of its customs and authorities, that is less than the participation we find in others, but enables us to live and work among them free of their unhappy entanglements. We can live in their world without being of it. The detailed articulation of this state of living is a matter of the greatest difficulty in both cases, but the fundamental notion of a combined detachment and involvement is clearly the same.

This can help us begin to understand the motives of the Conformist Fideists. They see the faith they commend as the ultimate outcome of the reasonings they copy from Sextus. They identify this faith with a predominantly practical conformity to a tradition which they say we should not try to justify. Each of them sees the quiet faith they commend as a tranquil contrast to the hot-blooded and destructive enthusiasms of his day. Each sees these enthusiasms as the product of dogmatic disputes which can be brought to an end only by a recognition of our incapacity to reach truth by means of them. And each is able, from his personal position, to equate this quiet faith with a scholar's minimal participation in the knockabout world from which he can maintain a protective inner distance.

The purpose of our enquiry, however, is not primarily that of entering in imagination into the attitudes of historical figures, It is that of understanding faith and Skepticism better. To do this, I shall first state the obvious contrasts that the Conformist Fideists glossed over. I shall then try to examine the similarities a little further.

The contrasts are vital, but easy to state. A religion modelled on classical Skepticism could only be a very unreligious religion. In the first place, its emotional tone could only be an enervating and tepid one. This is the most obvious source of Luther's protests. Even though faith does indeed distance the one who has it from many everyday involvements, so that it matters less to the man of faith whether the particular objectives he shares with his secular fellows are actually attained (for fanaticism is a perversion of faith), his serenity is nevertheless combined with a commitment that in the normative cases of faith must be described not as moderate but as passionate and total. In the second place, this commitment is characterized as a trust in God, and said to lead to, and be due to, a love of God: language which, on all normal interpretations, implies a dogmatic view of non-evident realities which, even if beyond the powers of reason, is totally at odds with the openness and agnosticism which defines the Skeptic's stance. Such commitment indicates, further, that the man of faith does not reach his detachment from ordinary involvements by refraining from judging them, but by judging them from a supposedly transcendent viewpoint which makes the secular man's evaluation seem myopic. This shows, thirdly, that there is no way of reconciling the whole Skeptic way with the faith of the Christian, since it will always be a matter of legitimate controversy within the faith whether its commitment and its detachment are properly attained by abandoning the hope of reaching truth through reason, or, as the tradition of natural theology in the West has always held, by the prior exercise of reason in the demonstration of religious truths. The only coherent way in which an apologist for faith can draw upon the armory of the Skeptic is by rejecting the Skeptic way as a whole, but maintaining, within his own tradition, that reason is not the best path to faith; so that the Skeptics have conveniently shown the pretensions of reason, as we find them in the work of natural theologians, to be empty ones. This is the way of the Evangelical Fideists, to whom I shall turn shortly.

First, however, I wish to look deeper at the likenesses on which Conformist Fideism traded, and to pick out two important features of Skepticism that can help us understand faith better. For in respect of these two features, Skepticism and faith are duplicates of each other. The first of these is what I shall call their need for reminders. The second is the way that each involves a special kind of self-distance. The likenesses only exist if we bear in mind, again, that it is Skepticism as a practical way of life, allegedly productive of tranquillity, that we are examining.

One reason why Montaigne and Bayle were suspected of insincerity in their protestations of faith was their obvious delight in the production of Skeptic arguments and the destruction of the intellectual props of theology. Surely, a reader must ask himself, no one who has really abandoned the pursuit of truth through reason, and has taken refuge in the haven of faith, would be as eager as this to keep returning to the disputes he says we should evade? If he meant it, surely he would give them up, not spend his life lovingly polishing them? Bayle says reviewing them is good for the Christian; whether or not he really meant it, I suggest that for someone who thinks abandoning the pretensions of natural theology is the way to faith, what he says is sound, and that the mere fact of a recurrent return to Skeptic argument is not a sign of insincerity. For it reflects an inevitable concern common to Skepticism and faith alike: the concern to *sustain* the stance that the subject has taken up. The language of psychological passivity that Sextus uses obscures this somewhat in the Skeptical case, but it is true in both cases. We can see this most easily if we consider the oldest and most plausible criticism of Skepticism: that it is not humanly viable.

This criticism receives its best-known expression in Hume.[23] He can quite properly be called a Skeptic himself, since he accepts many of the Pyrrhonian arguments, and adds to them. But he insists that they are *vain* arguments. They do show that our natural beliefs are without rational foundation; but since these beliefs are entrenched in our natures by forces that are quite distinct from the reasoning to which philosophers appeal in their arguments, philosophical arguments like those of the Skeptics cannot dislodge them. The Pyrrhonian's 'cavils' only produce a 'momentary amazement and confusion', which we cannot sustain when we leave our studies. This is, in his view, all to the good, for if we could sustain it, the effect would not be liberating, but paralyzing and distressing. So Hume claims Pyrrhonism to be doomed to failure, and happily denies any power to his own negative arguments.

Hume's criticism here shows less acquaintance than one might expect to find with the details of Sextus' position, since the concept of moderate and beliefless participation is surely designed to deal with just this sort of attack. Let us take Hume as conceding, however, that Skeptic questioning does make us draw back for a moment from our ordinary commitments; what he then says, it seems, is that even this amount of suspense cannot be kept up, since our natures force us to lapse from it. Hume, indeed, recommends that we should make sure that we are rooted in society in such a way that the temptations to go into the study and risk the renewal of this suspense, are not too strong or too frequent. But in this concession and recommendation we have the elements of a perfectly good Skeptic answer — one which, somewhat disguised, Montaigne and Bayle have actually given. If one can counter inclinations to doubt and to suspend judgment by placing oneself in those market-place situations where the inclination to believe is at its strongest, it is presumably also possible to counter the inclination to *believe* by placing oneself, as frequently as necessary, in situations where Skeptical arguments can weaken it. Doubt can be sustained and protracted as well as belief. And what from one viewpoint is a lapse from humanity into unreal detachment, is from another an escape from over-attachment into a more natural spiritual independence. The Skeptic stance is something that can, and should be, sustained, by the use of frequent reminders of the inadequacy of all dogmatic efforts — reminders which Bayle says it is good for the soul of the Christian to have on record for review. We can even go further, and say that someone who follows a way of thought in which he regularly extinguishes his inclinations to commitment by the examination of arguments for and against each dogmatic position, can be said to live his Skepticism in spite of his occasional lapses into commitment in the marketplace. Here he might feel he is succumbing to outside pressures to believe, but that his overall performance can entitle him to say he does not believe really. For most of the time the suspense he engenders in the study stays with him in the marketplace, so that he conforms with his fellows undogmatically. What counts in judging any lapses is the fact that he is following a way of life which enables him to *contend* with them.

I do not suggest that the answer I have just given can be found in the text of Sextus. On the contrary, there are important elements in his text which would make it impossible for him to respond to Hume in quite this way, and I shall return to these shortly. I claim merely that the obvious plausibility of Hume's insistence that we cannot keep up philosophical doubts all the time, does not show that no one can live the Skeptic way. For no one can be accused of not living according to a preconceived way merely because he lapses from time to time under the influences of forces in his nature or his environment. But I return for the moment to the analogy between Skepticism and faith.

For the analogy here is a close one. Faith, also, is a stance toward daily experience which has to be sustained by reminders, and which those who have it claim to yield spiritual benefits of the deepest importance. The strengths claimed for faith are that it enables us to reduce anxiety and over-attachment to the goods of the world, and that it thereby opens our natures to love. The pressures of the world do not make these easy prizes, and con-stantly threaten them when they are achieved. The reminders that help to sustain faith are primarily prophetic and sacramental — though in the eyes of some, they also include philosophical reflection. These reminders serve to recall to the believer that which he holds to be true about his relation to God, and to renew his response to that supposed relationship. This relationship is said to be one that consists in part of divine promises that reassure the believer that God's purposes will eventually win out in history. The believer's relative freedom from the anxieties that would otherwise beset him is the fruit of that reassurance. It also involves the judgment that such anxieties are reasonable ones if the reassurance is not available. This of course involves an interpretation of experience which goes far beyond the appearances to which the Skeptic confines himself, and from which he would therefore withdraw. But the two offer competing ways of release from the strains of human anxiety.

I have suggested that Skeptic suspense can properly be ascribed to some-one, even in the face of temporary lapses into conviction. The converse is clearly true of the person of faith. For such a person, conviction can properly be ascribed in spite of periods of doubt. For doubt can, notoriously, occur within faith, and need not destroy it. It will not destroy it if the doubter *contends* with the doubts which he has, and sees them, and the marketplace pressures which produce them, as lapses which he has to reduce in power and force. Clearly reflection, *de facto* philosophical in character, will often be the way in which he contends with them.

In both lived Skepticism and lived faith, therefore, there is a crucial two-way relationship between reasoning and the emotional life. Reflection supports a mood which one may have only imperfectly, but has firmly enough to muster intellectual resources in its defence, to ward off judgments which might undermine it and generate anxiety and disturbance. So each appears from outside to be at odds with common sense, even though its practitioner's behaviour might conform with it. For one seems, at some level, to be obstinately doubting the indubitable, and the other seems, often because of his loud proclamations, to be obstinately believing the incredible.

It is this analogy which probably led Montaigne and Bayle, in both cases inexcusably, to stare past the obvious and fundamental opposition between Skepticism and faith, and suppose that the rehearsal of Skeptic argument and counter-argument could be the appropriate propaedeutic, and the appropriate sustainer, of *faith*. They should have known better; indeed those who do not read them as I have done here insist they did know better. But even when we allow that any religious establishment is prone to allow too much accommodation with common sense, and even when we allow that the evils of fanaticism and factionalism were the ones most obvious and urgent in the minds of Montaigne and Bayle, they cannot be acquitted of confusion. It is a confusion, however, from which we can learn. In detecting its sources, it is possible to understand both faith and Skepticism better.

The role of reasoning in sustaining the stance of the Skeptic, or the stance of faith, is connected with a second feature in which the two are analogous. It is one which we could not expect the Skeptic to explore, but which the literature of faith has often explored. Not only does each way involve the concerns of the world in which he moves and acts, however different the cause of this distancing may be; each, in so doing, involves him in distancing himself from those facets of his own being which can undermine the stance he takes up. He is required to think that those parts of his psyche, in particular his desires and reactive emotions, which lead to and manifest over-attachment, are, though indeed a part of him, yet not ideally so; that in some sense he is not identified with them in the way he is identified with those aspects of his being which he is detaching. This device of metaphorically externalizing some passion that one considers should be otherwise is characteristic of religious understandings of man and of salvific modes of thought.[24] It is found, for example, in the Stoic understanding of the relation of the wise man to the desires that beset him, and in St. Paul's distinction between the flesh and the spirit. In such understandings of human nature, the norm adopted is the total absence of the externalized force; the use of the externalizing device in one's thinking is the consolidation of a policy of combating it; and if the policy is successful, the outcome is a progressive reduction in the number of occasions when lapses due to the offending force take place. Pyrrho is on record, by tradition, as seeing his own lapses into conviction as a sign that he had not rid himself of his ordinary humanity.[25] No understanding of faith or Skepticism can be successful if this pattern of thinking and self-judgment is not recognized to operate deeply within each. When it is recognized, however, we can see better why they were mistakenly assimilated: this happened because they are, though opposite, mirror-images of one another.

NOTES

[1] The text of the Erasmus–Luther debate that I cite here is that contained in *Luther and Erasmus: Free Will and Salvation*, ed. by E. G. Rupp and P. S. Watson, Westminster Press, Philadelphia, 1969.

[2] Its full title was: Assertio omnium articulorum M. Lutheri per Bullam Leonis X novissiman damnatorum, 1520.

[3] Erasmus, *op. cit.*, p. 37.

[4] It is entitled *The Bondage of the Will*.

[5] Luther, *op. cit.*, p. 105.

[6] *Op. cit.*, p. 109.

[7] See Revelation 3:15.

[8] See Chapter III of Popkin's *History of Scepticism*.

[9] From *The Essays of Michel de Montaigne*, trans. Jacob Zeitlin, Alfred A. Knopf, New York, 1935, Vol. II, p. 233.

[10] Montaigne, *op. cit.*, p. 269.

[11] See Popkin, *op. cit.*, Chapter III.

[12] For the more standard view of Bayle see Howard Robinson, *Bayle the Sceptic*. Columbia University Press, New York, 1931; the positive interpretation, which I follow here, is argued in Karl C. Sandberg, *At the Crossroads of Faith and Reason: An Essay on Pierre Bayle*, University of Arizona Press, Tucson, 1966. For a comparison of Bayle with Montaigne, see Craig B. Brush, *Montaigne and Bayle: Variations on the Theme of Skepticism*, Martinus Nijhoff, The Hague, 1966. The more positive reading of Bayle is defended by Popkin in the introduction of his Selections from the *Historical and Critical Dictionary* (Bobbs-Merrill, Indianapolis, 1965) and in his article, 'Bayle' in the *Encyclopedia of Philosophy*, ed. by Paul Edwards, Macmillan, New York, 1967. Quotations from Bayle are from the translations in Popkin's selections; with author's permission.

[13] At least he quotes from La Mothe le Vayer to this effect in Remark C to the article 'Pyrrho' (Popkin, p. 208).

[14] Third Clarification II; Popkin, p. 423.

[15] Third Clarification VIII; Popkin, p. 435.

[16] Second Clarification; Popkin, p. 414.

[17] 'Spinoza', Remark M; Popkin, pp. 298–299.

[18] See Popkin, *op. cit.*, footnote pp. 199–200.

[19] The equivalence is not, of course, an exact one. See Sextus, PH III, 64–81, and M X, 168.

[20] See Popkin, *History of Scepticism*, Chapter III.

[21] See Popkin's article 'Huet, Pierre-Daniel' in *Encyclopedia of Philosophy*, and the references in *The High Road to Pyrrhonism*.

[22] See Note 5 to Chapter I.

[23] See below, Chapter 6.

[24] For a general discussion of the significance of this device, see my essay 'Human Nature and External Desires', *The Monist*, Vol. 62, 1979.

[25] See Diogenes Laertius, *Lives of the Philosophers*, Book IX. This aspect of Pyrrhonism is emphasized in Burnyeat, 'Can the Sceptic Live his Scepticism?', and is discussed further below.

CHAPTER 3

CONFORMIST FIDEISM – II

THE COHERENCE OF PYRRHONISM

I have argued that the appeal of Conformist Fideism was due to some deep similarities between classical Skepticism and Christian faith. I have also argued that Skepticism can be defended against the common criticism that it is unlivable if we are prepared to see it as a pattern of living which, like faith, makes use of the intellect to sustain an emotional attitude as consistently as possible.

This does not show, however, that the self-understanding of a particular Skeptic thinker is a coherent one. I have already indicated that the description of the Skeptic way that I have offered in defence of psychological criticism does not fit the text of Sextus. It does not fit his text for a clear reason: I have outlined a way of living and thinking which represents the assemblage of intellectual reminders of the limits of reason as a matter of conscious *policy*, designed to sustain suspense of judgment for the purpose of avoiding commitment and the mental disturbance thought to accompany commitment. Sextus, however, does not present the Skeptic way in this manner. This is because he is trying to avoid two traditional complaints about Skepticism, not one. He is trying to avoid the complaint that no one can live Skeptically; but he is also trying to evade the argument that the Skeptic must make some dogmatic assertion, albeit of a negative sort – such as the assertion that reason is impotent to arrive at truth, or that truth cannot be apprehended, or that nothing is certain. Since assertions like this are paradoxical, the critic of Skepticism seems to have an easy victory available to him.

To evade this, Sextus does four things. First, he makes a sharp distinction, at the very beginning of the *Outlines*, between his own school and the Academic school, saying that the Skeptic keeps on searching for truth, whereas the Academics say that it cannot be grasped. Second, he insists, as we have seen, that the statements the Skeptic makes as part of his engagement in the world are made undogmatically. Third, he interprets this to be a matter of the Skeptic expressing how things seem, passively, to him at the time of utterance. Fourth, he applies this understanding of Skeptic pronouncements to all statements, including those which express Skeptic methods or attitudes.

If we take these at their face value, the Skeptic is not involved in a commitment to general principles, positive or negative, about the nature of realities or the value of modes of life, but is merely announcing how he feels at the time of speaking or writing. On the surface the charge of incoherence, which depends on the Skeptic's holding at least one general negative belief, is evaded, since he cannot correctly be accused of holding any beliefs whatever, even if he uses forms of words that would encapsulate such beliefs when used by others.

For all its ingenuity, and for all the psychological reality that I have agreed to ascribe to the Skeptic's ongoing doubts and suspense of judgment, the stance Sextus presents to us is open to severe criticisms. The key element in the fourfold tactic just outlined is the third, which is undermined by a serious ambiguity.

There is a problem, when reading Sextus, of deciding on the scope of the Skeptic techniques and the Skeptic suspense. Do these apply to all opinions whatever, or only to metaphysical or religious or scientific opinions? I have interpreted him in the former way, and inferred that the Skeptic sees himself as differing not only from dogmatic philosophers but from the unlettered public, who are also judged to be infected by dogma; so when he relaxes back into local tradition, he does so by accepting that things seem to him much as they seem to others, but does not follow them in the supposed further step of imputing what appears to be so to reality. So when Sextus says that the Skeptic is merely expressing how he is affected, or how he feels, he is saying that he is, like his fellows, the involuntary product of the influences of environment and tradition, so that when some action, for example, seems morally appropriate to him, he realizes that this attitude of his is the result of his time and place, and does not judge it to be an instance of some universalizable principle which transcends particular times and places. In adopting local consensus in this undogmatic fashion, he is staying within the appearances, which are, in themselves, not under his control. The notion of staying with the appearances, however, has another and more restricted application, which to a modern reader can obscure the difficulty which lurks in the notion of undogmatic participation. Many of the best-known Skeptical arguments are about the reliability of sense-perception. Here it is easy for a modern reader to accept that one might passively receive certain appearances, and agree that they are thus and so, but refrain from committing oneself on whether they conform to realities beyond themselves. To inheritors of the Cartesian tradition, this is as familiar as can be. It is also easy for us to interpret this in a special way: as a concession that sensory appearances *really are* thus and so, whereas physical realities may or may not be. This tempts us to read Sextus as something he is not: a Twentieth-Century phenomenalist. For Sextus has to adopt a stance which does not only fit sense-perception, but other forms of judgment besides.

But this produces a difficulty. Such a general stance cannot treat confining oneself to the appearances as a matter of saying only how things look, or sound, or feel. Even if this model often dominated Sextus' mind, he has to have a stance which embraces opinions, or utterances, of a much wider class than this. Once this is admitted, however, it seems to allow only one inter-pretation of the concept of staying with how things appear — that of indi-cating merely *what seems to be true*. But to say what seems to be true to one is to say what one is *inclined to believe*, which in Sextus' universe of dis-course can only be to indicate what one is inclined to believe of reality.[1] Even if the language of passivity is correct to use here (and I think it is), to say how things appear to oneself is to say what one is inclined to believe about them. If this is combined with a Skeptic suspense of judgment as to how they really are, the total state of mind that the Skeptic expresses when conforming to appearances undogmatically is one in which he inclines to think that *p*, though he suspends definite commitment whether or not *p* is so, since he has found no reasons to believe that *p* is so that are stronger than those that can be given for thinking it is not so. This state of mind is one which Sextus describes to us in order to show that the Skeptic can act when he must, and will experience moderate, though not intense, affections. What are we to make of this state of mind?

In order to evaluate it, we must first decide whether or not Sextus is right to speak of believing as something that happens to us, rather than as some-thing that we do. Philosophers have divided sharply on this. Those who see belief as a matter of free choice include Descartes[2] and Aquinas.[3] Those who claim it is not a matter of choice include Spinoza[4] and Hume.[5] It is necessary to make a decision on this matter in order to be in a position to interpret the difficult notion of *inclining to believe*,[6] which I have used to construe the Skeptic concept of agreeing to appearances. If belief is a free action, then inclination to believe will be something like a desire or a temptation. If, on the other hand, belief is a passive condition, inclination toward it is a mild or early stage of that condition itself. In the former case, one can be inclined to believe but refuse to do it. In the latter case, the distinction between incli-nation to belief and belief is one of mild and substantial degrees of the same phenomenon. If Sextus is right that what the Skeptic does when he expresses his Skepticism is give voice to an affection which is a product of tradition, environment, exhaustion of rational capacity, and the like; and if I am right in holding that what he is doing is expressing an inclination to believe certain things about Skepticism or about those matters on which he is conforming to the habits of his fellows; then Sextus, contrary to his own self-understanding, is telling us that the Skeptic differs from his fellows in having mild beliefs where they have strong ones, not in not having beliefs when they do. This is, I think, exactly the case.

BELIEF AND WILL

The language in which we speak of our beliefs makes it appear that they are actions, things that we do; yet some of our idioms suggest they are passive states that happen to us. Both are easy to illustrate. Suppose, during an election, a candidate says, "According to my opponent, my tax reduction scheme will bankrupt the Government in five years, but I prefer to believe that the economy is strong enough to sustain the needs of government with lower taxes". On the surface, when he says he prefers to believe this, he implies that even though he could, if he chose, believe what his opponent does, he has elected to believe something more cheerful. On this interpretation of his idiom, his believing what he does is an action he has chosen to perform, when he could equally well have chosen to do something else. But the very same candidate might easily have said, in the same context, "My opponent said that my tax reduction scheme will bankrupt the Government in five years, but I cannot believe the economy is too weak to meet the needs of government without the present rate of taxation". This idiom suggests that his opponent's view is one that the speaker is *unable* to hold, which would seem to imply that his own view is not one he has chosen, but one he has had forced upon him. Most of us would feel that the two ways of speaking say much the same, yet their surface implications appear to be quite opposite. The candidate will no doubt be proud to believe what he does, yet on one reading he is proud of an achievement, and on the other he is proud of an incapacity. Take another example. We often say that something proposed to us is very difficult to believe, or that we are very reluctant to believe it. These forms of words suggest that to believe it is to do something which we can manage with an effort, although circumstances or desires may stand in the way of our managing it. It is striking, however, that we do not carry on from this and talk as though believing in the face of these obstacles is an accomplishment. On the contrary: the beliefs of which we are most vain, and which we are most apt to urge upon others, are those we think it impossible *not* to hold, which are forced upon us. In the realm of action, if something is forced upon us, this counts as an *excuse* for our having done it; in the realm of belief, it counts rather as a sign of our wisdom and good sense. So if belief is an action, it is an action of a strange sort. It must also be conceded, however, that if in believing we are passive, we are passive in an unusual way! So the division on this question among major thinkers is not surprising.

It is also too simple. It is associated to some degree with differences in the understanding of what freedom is in the realm of action. Philosophical theories here have tended to fall into two groups. One type of analysis argues that being free is a matter of being unimpeded in the exercise of one's preferences: that I am behaving freely if I am doing what I want to do without hindrance. If this is what freedom is, then my actions can be perfectly free even if there is never any real alternative for me to what I do, for my freedom will consist in the fact that what I do is what I want, and I am allowed to do it. Freedom understood this way Hume calls 'liberty of spontaneity',[7] and he points out, as many have since, that it is very common, and that its existence is fully compatible with the determinist's belief that all human actions have causes and can be predicted by science. Those who have opposed this analysis of freedom have been those who have wished to resist the determinist's thesis. The analysis of freedom that has appealed to them has represented it as consisting of openness of options. On this view, if I have acted freely, then I have had the power, at least until the action has begun, of doing something else. Even if what I did was something I very much wanted to do, and no one hindered me, my action was not a free action unless I had the power not to do it. (And if my action was done freely, it might well have been an action that I did not *want* to do, since I may have decided that the best of the alternatives was not, unfortunately, the one which I wanted.) Hume called this alleged power of alternative action 'liberty of indifference'; and like the true determinist that he was most of the time, he denied that it ever exists, or that we have any need of it.

When philosophers have debated whether believing is free, they have usually taken this to be the question of whether it manifests liberty of indifference. I cannot here debate the wider question of whether liberty of indifference actually exists in the realm of action. I confine myself to the question of whether our thought and language about our *beliefs* show that we consider them to manifest it. With an obvious (and orthodox) reservation, I shall argue that they do not.

It is a significant fact of intellectual history that Sextus and Hume, who take the negative view in this matter, do not argue for it, but appear to offer it as a consequence of their denial of the power of reason to justify our beliefs. This is significant because if the picture of belief as an open choice between alternatives is attractive, it is because it seems to fit those occasions when we *cogitate*: when we try to weigh the arguments for or against some opinion, in order to see, as we put it, what we ought to believe. These occasions look very like those other times when we try to decide what to do, and have two or more alternative actions to choose between.

How alike are they? Not alike enough, I suggest, to support the theory we are examining. Both in the theoretical circumstance, when we weigh beliefs, and in the practical cases where we consider actions, we may indeed not know which way to jump, because the reasons on each side balance too well. Suppose, however, that some information comes in that makes the answer obvious. In the theoretical case we will then say that we can no longer doubt what we must believe. This means that we *do* now believe that to which the new information points. But in the practical case, even though we may say that there can no longer be any doubt what we must do, it is a lamentable fact about our freedom of *action* that we are still able to hold back, or to do something else. The same disparity appears at an intermediate stage. If I think that the evidence I have makes one opinion more likely to be true than another, I may say that I am more inclined to believe the one than the other. But this is as well put by saying that I partly believe the favoured one. In a practical situation, even though I may be more inclined to do one thing than to do the other, I can still do the other. When I see what I should do, I still have to do it. But when I see what I should believe, I believe it already.

Sometimes circumstances force our hand in practical matters. Whatever the pros and cons of the new job offer, I must either accept it tomorrow or reject it tomorrow, on the information available to me at that time. Similarly, even though there are so many more things I want to know about the parties' policies, I have to vote tomorrow on the basis of what I know then, and there is no time left to form opinions. But of course there is – in this respect I have more leeway in my beliefs than I do in my actions. Once I make my practical choice, I am committed and cannot go back. But even though I may also have to act as though I believe one party to be clearly better than another, this necessity does not compel me to *believe* that it is. What life forces from me is action without belief. It does not force belief without information. The upshot of all these considerations seems to be this: that even when we are weighing alternative beliefs, if the process issues in a real choice the result is not a belief; and if it issues in a belief, it is not because of a real choice.

I would hold, then, that even though some forms of speech suggest that belief manifests liberty of indifference, this does not justify holding that it does manifest it. Some account of the existence of such forms of speech is, of course, in order here, and I shall have some unoriginal remarks on this below. For the moment, it is worth a brief digression to examine another, rarely considered, suggestion: that perhaps beliefs can manifest liberty of spontaneity — that sometimes we believe what we believe because of the un-impeded exercise of our wants, even though this does not represent any choice between real alternatives.

This suggestion looks very implausible, and the reason is easy to find. We all know that many people (or at least *other* people) believe things for which there are no good reasons. Very often they believe these things, we say, be-cause they *want* to believe them. Now when people believe something be-cause they want to, we think of them as victims of psychological or economic or social forces, not as free agents. We excuse them, at best; we do not praise them. Surely, an objector might say, these are the very people who exemplify liberty of spontaneity with regard to their beliefs, since they are believing what they believe because they want to? Surely our attitude to this sort of belief proves that this theory of freedom in belief must be mistaken?

This criticism would be confused. Suppose I were the son of a highly suc-cessful business tycoon. After his death, let us further suppose, I discover evidence that convinces everybody else that he made his money by embezzl-ing company funds at key points in his career. I continue to believe that he made every penny through vision and honest toil. My critics will no doubt say of me, either in pity or in censure, that I believe that because I want to believe it, and what they say will probably be true. But what is it that they are saying? Bernard Williams has made it clear[8] that in such cases there is no ground for holding that the subject wants to hold a particular belief. It is not true that I would believe my father made his money honestly *because I want to believe* that he did. For it is not that which I want. What I want is *that my father should have made his money honestly*. It is this that my friends are saying: namely, that my wish that my father should have behaved honestly is making me believe that he did so — not that my wish *to believe* that he did so is making me believe that he did so. If they are right, then my continued belief in my father's honesty is not an example of the unimpeded implementation of a want that I have. For in this case *I* cannot implement the want I have at all, for many reasons. I am not getting what I want, even though my critics are right in saying that the belief I hold is a result of *a* want which I have. To say I am getting what I want would be like saying that when

I put money in a machine to get coffee and get soup instead, I must be getting what I want because my want was the cause of my getting what I got. In general, believing something because we want to is not an example of liberty of spontaneity, because the wants that generate the beliefs in these cases are not wants of which the beliefs are the intended objects, or the intended satisfactions.

There is, however, a class of beliefs to which the concept of liberty of spontaneity does apply. Paradoxically, these are beliefs we often say we cannot help holding. I refer to beliefs for which the grounds seem conclusive, and over which we are unwilling to admit the possibility of error. There is a discussion of these in Descartes.[9] He holds, of course (and I have argued, mistakenly) that we have liberty of indifference when the grounds for the beliefs we consider are inconclusive grounds; but he also wishes to emphasize that there are other occasions when the grounds for conclusions are indubitable – indeed he bases his positive epistemology on these. The favored cases are the demonstrations of logic and mathematics, and the first principles of his own philosophical system. He does not, however, wish to say that we are not free when we accept these, for he regards them as the paradigms of the mind's free exercise of its faculties. So he adapts his understanding of freedom to accommodate them. No one would say, comfortably, that when an action is so obviously good that I cannot consider choosing another, I must be somehow less free than I would be if the alternatives were even, for it is on these occasions that our powers of action are most dynamically released; nor, surely, am I less free when the grounds for a conclusion are so strong that the possibility of its being false cannot be entertained. Descartes even goes so far as to say that "the indifference that I am aware of when there is no reason urging me one way rather than the other, is the lowest grade of liberty; it argues no perfection of free will, but only some defect or absence of knowledge; for if I always saw clearly what is good and true, I should never deliberate as to what I ought to judge or choose; and thus, though entirely free, I could never be indifferent". When a conclusion is obvious, the illumination of the understanding is followed, he says, by a great inclination of the will. So although Descartes has need to say that there is liberty of indifference with regard to belief, he also says that our most laudable conclusions do not exemplify it, but exemplify liberty of spontaneity; or, as he puts it, that "our impulse towards what the intellect presents to us as worthy of assertion or denial, as a thing to be sought or shunned, is such that we feel ourselves not to be determined by an external force". We are unhindered in grasping what we want to find – what is 'good and true'.

Perhaps this combination of two distinct theories is inconsistent, as Descartes states it. But it does seem to me that his use of the idea of liberty of spontaneity here is sound; that however unsatisfactory this may be as a source of analysis of freedom of action, it fits the cases to which Descartes tries to apply it here. The enquirer who is convinced by a sound demonstration, or an obvious good, will attain, in the very moment when he sees he has no real alternative, the very thing he may have been seeking for years: the final truth about a subject-matter that has hitherto puzzled him.

To summarize: I have argued it is wrong to say that believing something is a matter of choosing between two or more options, either one of which we would equally well adopt if we so elected. Although, on the surface, this understanding of what happens seems to fit those times when we try to make up our minds between alternatives, it misrepresents even these. I have also suggested that we can find more merit than we might expect in the view that the formation of belief could be an example of liberty of spontaneity, of the unimpeded exercise of a want — a suggestion which is present in Descartes, and seems best to fit those beliefs we proudly offer as inevitable. This suggestion seems to me to be correct as far as it goes, provided we are careful to identify the want which the belief satisfies as the desire to attain the truth about some subject-matter, and not as the desire for the supposed facts that we allow ourselves to believe in when we indulge in wishful thinking.

This is manifestly incomplete. For it remains obviously true, and very important, that we have control in some sense over what beliefs we form, that we can properly be praised or blamed for the manner in which we form them or change them, and that we can even develop policies about the formation and tenure of our opinions. Some have talked as though we ought to believe certain things out of moral obligation, or prudence. There is H. H. Price's example of the Victorian ladies who considered it a moral duty always to believe, whatever the evidence, that their betrothed were impeccably virtuous.[10] Whether or not we would praise them today, we would still think it a natural or a moral deficiency in a parent to be able to believe in the dishonesty of his or her children as easily as strangers or policemen are. As for believing out of prudence, it is something very commonly recommended to us by evangelists: many of them say, repeatedly, that it is a necessary condition of salvation to believe certain things about one's relation to God. Whether or not they misrepresent the character of their faith when they say these things, they do say them. And what they say is not obviously absurd. For one thing, it seems to work, as far as one can tell. That is to say, people do end up believing the things the evangelists tell them they need to believe, apparently as a result of hearing and accepting these prudential arguments. So there is plenty of evidence to suggest that each of us can exercise some degree of control over his beliefs.

But this can be accommodated without saying that believing can be done at will. It is quite common for philosophers to hold that belief can be controlled indirectly, though not directly. The distinction between direct and indirect control of one's states and actions is by no means a completely clear one, but it is an easy enough one to introduce informally by examples. If I decide to clench my left fist (as a political gesture, for example) I can do it, just like that — unless I am partially paralysed and unable to control the movements of my left hand. If I were so handicapped, I could still clench my left fist by using my right hand, over which I still had normal control, to bend the fingers of my left hand together. In such a case it seems appropriate to say that clenching my left fist would be something I could do, or perhaps that the clenching of my left fist is something I could bring about, indirectly, whereas clenching my right fist was something I could do directly, or perhaps, just do. Among actions, it has been argued that there are some which 'normal' persons will always do, if they do them, directly, and others which can only be done indirectly, because in order to do them one has to do something else directly — for example, tying a shoelace can only be done by moving one's fingers in a certain complex manner, so that tying a shoelace, though not a sophisticated performance, is nevertheless indirect. Actions which are done by a normal person directly have been called basic actions.[11] Although I find this concept helpful in reflection on action-theory, it is not really necessary to use it here. To claim that beliefs can be controlled, but only indirectly, is to claim that (i) believing is not an action at all, but that (ii) it can be made to happen, or be modified, or made to cease, by the performance of actions, that (iii) the actions which have these consequences can be freely chosen, and therefore commanded or recommended, so that (iv) it is proper to apply moral or prudential evaluations to the beliefs that we have, at least in those cases where such actions can be taken.

This seems to me a correct understanding of the alleged voluntariness of belief, which I will express by saying that some, at least, of our beliefs, are under our indirect control. One of the ways in which one can indirectly control one's beliefs is, of course, by considering evidence and reasoning about their subject-matter. Another is by choosing to change emotional and environmental factors which also affect what we believe — by choosing our associates, by restricting or widening our access to relevant information, and the like. On this view, a command or recommendation to believe (or disbelieve) something will have to be understood as a command or recommendation to choose those actions which will bring about the onset or the cessation of the belief in question; and someone who successfully obeys such a command, or carries out such a recommendation, has to be understood as having performed actions which have had the desired consequence. Someone who refuses to believe something for which the evidence is strong is, on this view, someone who persists in taking steps which fend off the impact of the evidence which would otherwise be likely to bring about the change in his beliefs which he would like to avoid — by declining to read the relevant documents, by listening only to those who believe what he does, and the like. Such indirect control over our beliefs is open to moral and prudential appraisal in its turn: not only is it possible to suggest that we ought to get ourselves to believe p, or that we would be prudent to get ourselves to believe p; it can also be argued that the only means by which such a result can be achieved are in themselves immoral, or imprudent, or irrational, and the like. There can, in other words, be a great deal of disagreement about policies of belief-formation: about what can be called doxastic ethics.

If the view I have adopted here is correct, it does not follow, of course, that those who command or recommend beliefs hold it themselves. They may or may not. Pascal, for example, does.[12] Aquinas and Descartes do not. Their claims about moral responsibility for our beliefs can probably be retained on the view we have adopted. But it may be a matter of importance in other ways that someone who commands or recommends a belief does not recognize that the instruction can only be carried out indirectly. If he does not recognize this, he is likely to have seriously mistaken views about what it is possible for his hearers to do. He is likely to think that because they can respond to what he says and achieve the end-result he wants, his command has been obeyed in a manner quite different from the only logically possible one.

There are two ways in which such a mistake can be made. I shall try to bring them out by using our evangelist as an example. If he commands his hearers to believe, and they do come to believe, he (and indeed they) may think, mistakenly, that their believing is an act which they have suddenly come to be able to perform because he (acting perhaps as a vehicle of divine grace) has broken down moral hindrances that have hitherto stood in the way of their performing it. They will join in construing what has occurred on the model of the will being freed to overcome temptations and moral weakness. This may have the effect of including within these moral obstacles the serious consideration of evidence and argument that weighs against what they have now come to believe to be true; and even of representing the weighing of *positive* evidence as a form of temporizing in the face of temptations. So even the most favorable philosophy will come to be judged as a form of spiritual corruption. This will, of course, locate very real spiritual obstacles, such as idleness, prejudice, self-seeking, fear, and the like, in the wrong place. They are in fact obstacles which will impair a hearer's willingness to consider those facts on which his beliefs should depend; but the mistaken picture of what converts have done will make it seem that they are obstacles to something which is not in our direct control at all – namely the acceptance of that to which these facts point. The ultimate form of this mistake is, of course, the confused and vicious assumption that faith and reason are somehow contradictory notions.

There is a second and deeper form of misinterpretation that can follow from a mistaken voluntarist view of belief. It is the fundamental assumption that a command to believe (a command, that is, to believe directly) is intelligible. I am inclined to say it is self-evidently unintelligible, because I am personally unable to imagine a response to it, other than to imagine the hearer saying "How?" and the speaker answering by suggesting actions which would bring the belief about. Because this sort of answer could be supplied, it is easy to overlook that in supplying it the original command is being interpreted as an indirect one. But since some have supposed that the command can be understood in a direct manner, I must proceed obliquely, by argument. I make the following suggestions.

(1) A command of the form 'Believe that *p*' is not shown to make sense as a direct command because some who utter it and some who respond to it credit the onset of belief to the power of divine grace sweeping aside human obstacles. The power of divine grace can readily be said to sweep aside obstacles to the performance of those actions (such as attending to evidence, listening to prophets, reading the scriptures) which, unimpeded, will lead to belief. It makes eminent sense to say, if divine grace is a fact, that it can dispose us to receive the truth; not, however, to say that when we have received it, it will enable us to elect to believe it. What it makes no sense to say we do, it does not make any more sense to say grace enables us to do.

(2) If belief could be commanded directly, it should be possible for us to be told to adopt it, or to withhold it, whether there are reasons favoring it, or reasons against it, or neither. I have already said that I do not think this is what evangelists do, even if some may think it is what they do. But it is interesting to look at the two sophisticated voluntarists that I have referred to. Aquinas, who holds that faith is at the command of the will, has difficulty

in accommodating this to his insistence on the rational strength of its pream-
bles, and of sustaining the blameworthiness of the devils when they believe
God exists because infallible signs of it force them to do so.[13] Descartes urges
us to suspend judgement when our ideas are not clear and distinct, but tries
to induce this suspense by using Skeptical arguments against the senses. In
neither case does their practice suggest a confidence in the real possibility
of a simple appeal to choice. Sextus is surely nearer to a correct perception of
our powers when he seeks to draw us toward suspense through the devious
paths of argument and counter-argument, without any suggestion that we can
arrive at it directly.

(3) It is sometimes suggested at the popular level that we can adopt a
belief on a trial basis; we will then find its rewards will confirm its truth and
will not turn back. This has, I think, to be interpreted in its turn as something
other than what its surface language says it is. What transpires in such a case
is that someone who has a mild inclination to believe, or has none at all but
wishes that he did, chooses to adopt courses of action, or even a systematic
way of life, that would be the natural expression in practice of the belief to
which he inclines if he did indeed hold it — though for him it is not yet this.
This mode of action has the effect, in time, of inducing the belief itself, and
thereafter, of course, of being its natural expression.[14]

It is worth stressing, before continuing, that if we accept that belief is
not directly voluntary, this gives no excuse for disregarding the fact that there
are indeed many deep-rooted obstacles to the recognition of truth on which
voluntary and sustained onslaughts need to be made. There are many real
temptations to error. These are all temptations to turn our attention away
from the evidence that could convince us, or to immerse ourselves in social
and intellectual environments that will sustain our comfortable illusions.
A proper assessment of them, however, is unlikely to arise if we misinterpret
the process that they obstruct.

THE PYRRHONIST STANCE

I return now to the evaluation of the Skeptic way as Sextus presents it. He
offers his account as an expression of the way things seem to the Skeptic
at the time of presentation. Thus understood, the Skeptic presents himself
as one who has an attitude which induces him to examine all the rational
arguments that are brought to support, or to undermine, the way things
seem, and which thereby leads him to suspend judgment with regard to all
of them; this in turn is followed by a cessation of all the anxiety associated

with the theories he has abandoned, and a life lived in conformity with the appearances that present themselves to him in his time and place – a form of life which is characterized by moderate affections rather than extreme ones. Such a presentation is thought to avoid charges of incoherence or impracticality.

I have argued thus far that although Sextus is correct in supposing that we are passive in respect of appearances (that we do not choose how things appear to us), he cannot say that we are able to admit that things appear to be thus and so, yet be wholly without commitment on whether or not they are. To admit that they seem to be thus and so to him is to say that he has a mild degree of belief that they are. If this is correct, then there is one respe respect in which Sextus seriously misrepresents the practical accommodations that the Skeptic makes. For these will be a matter of acting in accordance with mild beliefs that he himself has, as well as acting in accordance with beliefs (presumably stronger and more dogmatic ones) that his non-skeptical fellows have. So his distance from them is a matter of degree.

This is only part of the story. The Skeptic's actions are also due to the fact that "we cannot remain wholly inactive". Leaving aside for the moment the fact that this, for all its limp negativity, is an unabashed statement of a general policy, we can see that it is necessary for Sextus to add it because otherwise the appearances would be nullified as motives for action by the evaporation of all grounds for judging them true. To permit activity, the appearances, or on our analysis the mild beliefs, have to be seen as sources of actions which would otherwise not get chosen and done; to offer the appearances in answer to the criticism that Skepticism does not allow action is to concede that otherwise action would not take place, which is to admit that suspense of judgment would otherwise freeze us into immobility. I suggested earlier that we can discern the Skeptic way as having important resemblances to the way of faith, in which commitment has to contend with doubts. We can now see that the Skeptic way involves its own special kind of chronic conflict-state. It is a conflict between those mild beliefs on which action depends and an alleged suspension of judgment which manifests an inability to find any more grounds for what one thus mildly believes than one can find against it. The Skeptic is distinguished by the fact that his manner of life is one in which he sustains the habit of suspension by applying his philosophical dialectic to each belief in turn. What in fact the Skeptic is doing, then, is following a fourfold course. He (i) finds himself, by circumstance and tradition, inclined to believe that p; (ii) he reaches a stage, through philosophical enquiry, of feeling unable to hold that there are any grounds for p that cannot be matched by equally strong gounds for not-p; (iii) since this eliminates all intellectually-based inclination to believe p, and would thus far tend to inaction, he yields to the need for action by relapsing into the ungrounded traditional beliefs which he has purged himself of all desire to support by argument; so (iv) he acts on p, with a lesser degree of involvement than his fellows, who do not have the benefit of stage (ii).

While Sextus' own characterization of this fourfold course as beliefless conformity is incoherent, I do not think the one I have just given is. But even though this description is coherent, it by no means follows that the course it describes is free of inconsistency. On the contrary, there is a critical inconsistency from which the Skeptic way cannot be freed. In suspending judgment about p, I do not believe it. In yielding to custom and habit and believing it, however mildly, I do believe it. The Skeptic cannot, therefore, *simultaneously* suspend judgment about p and follow the appearance of p. He can, of course, alternate these, between the study and the market-place. There is nothing incoherent about setting out, as a matter of policy, to spend all the time one can in undermining all rational attempts to support or refute our beliefs, and then spending all the time one must in acting these beliefs out in daily affairs, in the open understanding that the beliefs one follows are mere products of custom and upbringing. One might well adopt a policy like this because one felt that the time spent in the study would keep the degree of involvement in our daily affairs as cool as possible, and make for a quiet life. It amounts to a general policy of believing as little as possible, in order to avoid being bothered or involved more than necessary. This is no doubt enervating, but is coherent enough. What would not be coherent would be saying, as Sextus appears to say, that the Skeptic has one consistent attitude while he believes and while he does not believe, and that this is an attitude of not believing. What he has is a policy, adopted because of the exigencies of practice and the supposed desirability of detachment, of believing only when one cannot avoid it for practical reasons.

For this is a policy, not just an inclination or groundless habit as Sextus' language suggests. He himself says that the Skeptic accepts the guidance of appearances because he cannot remain wholly inactive. But of course he could, and if he does not it is for a reason, presumably that it is undesirable to do so. Similarly the yielding to appearance, if it is indeed a matter of belief, would never yield to suspense unless the latter were induced by reasoning. Sextus says the Skeptic begins by reasoning to attain quietude through the discovery of truth, and comes in fact to experience it only after abandoning the quest; but for the reasoning to continue, it has to be the product either of the original mistaken intention or a wish to experience quietude anew. These considerations suggest that the Skeptic ways can only be correctly described as a policy. We can agree that the adoption of the policy is a matter of following appearances, but only if this is recognized to mean that the Skeptic adopts it in practice because of some degree of belief that it is the best way to follow.

Some concluding comments.

(1) We can now evaluate Hume's criticism of the practical possibility of Skepticism more accurately. He is, after all, right when he says that Skeptic suspense is impossible for anyone all the time, given any involvement in human activity. This is true even when we give due weight to the fact that the Skeptic can treat his beliefs in the market-place as lapses; for such supposed lapses are of the essence of the conformity which Sextus tells us the Pyrrhonian practices. It is therefore not correct to say that his conformity is undogmatic, if this means it is beliefless. It is not possible to envisage coherently an ideal Skeptic life in which such conformity would continue without lapses into belief. If we examine what the Skeptic does, rather than his own account of what he does, we find he follows a policy of permitting his inbuilt or environmentally-acquired tendencies to believe to have that degree of exercise which activity demands, and no more. For the retired scholar whose social involvements are at a minimum, this might be very little. For such a person we might reasonably say that he lived a life dominated by Skeptic doubt, though necessarily not wholly dominated by it. It is a matter of decision whether or not to say that such a person really doubts those propositions he has to conform to in practical affairs, but it seems at least reasonable to say that he does, since he doubts them more of the time than he believes them. If we say this, we can disagree with Hume when he tells us that the impact of the Skeptic's questions is only momentary or short-lived. After all, he has to urge us out into the world in order to dispel them, and the Skeptic has his own reasons for not following this advice.

(2) While we can disagree with Hume about Skeptical psychology in this respect, it is hard to accept that what Sextus says about himself and his fellows would be true for everyone in other ways. Two doubts in particular stand out. It is not clear that someone who conforms with local tradition while giving up all rational evaluation of it will be preserved by this means from immoderate attachment to what it supports. This will depend on the nature of the forces sustaining it in that tradition. It is also not clear that when one gives up the search for rational grounds for one's opinions, this in itself tends toward quietude. For some it might lead, instead, to intensified

anxiety, even to despair. We have the testimony of two such disparate thinkers as Pascal and Hume that this can be the result. In both these matters the likely truth is that Sextus may be right about himself, but wrong about others.

(3) Finally, nothing in all this complex discussion has shown that it is impossible to try to maintain suspense of judgment permanently and constantly about some *particular* subject-matter. This will be possible, presumably, if it is not a subject-matter to which one needs to attend at all in practice. For many, religion is now such a subject-matter, and they succeed quite well in maintaining a constant agnosticism about it by rehearsing appropriate arguments when others mention it, and avoiding all thought of it the rest of the time. Whether it, or any other suggested subject-matter can be avoided in this way, is a matter of one's environment. One cause of Conformist Fideism was the fact that its proponents did not live in an environment where such avoidance was practically feasible, and they did what was for them the next best thing.

THE CLASH WITH REASON

I conclude with some comments about the way in which Bayle describes and defends his fideist state of mind. I have included Bayle among the Conformist Fideists because it has seemed to me that his objective is, like that of Montaigne and Erasmus, to encourage a form of religious life that escapes doctrinal disputation and emphasizes right conduct rather than dogmatic orthodoxy. But since he is clearer than they are that the religious life requires *profession*, he inevitably confronts us more clearly than they do with the question of how far it is possible (without hypocrisy) to profess what you also say reason shows to have no grounds. Indeed, his position is harsher even than this, since he argues, as we have seen, that crucial Christian professions can be shown by rational demonstration to be false, yet the fideist makes them in full cognisance of this. Let us recall some of his words:

One may cry out that he is not sincere; and that our mind is not made in such a way, that it can accept as true that which a geometrical demonstration shows is completely false. . . . . Do we know the human soul sufficiently to declare that such and such a combination of views cannot be found int it? . . . For it must be observed that there is no contradiction between these two things: (1) The light of reason teaches me that this is false; (2) I believe it nonetheless because I am convinced that this light is not infallible and because I prefer to submit to the proofs of feeling and to the impressions of conscience, in short, to the Word of God, than to a metaphysical demonstration.

In trying to assess the state of mind that Sextus describes, the problem was to see how far it is possible for the apparently omnivorous suspension of judgment to coexist with acceptance of appearance and tradition. I have argued that what he describes in this way can only be coherently understood as a conflict of belief. The same is even more clearly true in the analogous state of mind that Bayle describes, particularly if we take with any seriousness the substitution of a judgment of falsity for a suspension of judgment.

Someone who knows the truth of the premisses of a demonstration and sees that they entail a certain conclusion, or who comes to see that a self-evident principle entails that conclusion, is not then in a position to ask himself whether he believes the conclusion or not. He already does. He may, of course, find this a very uncomfortable situation, since he may already believe something incompatible with what he has now come to believe. He is indeed free to relieve this discomfort by trying to undermine one or other of the beliefs he finds he has, by indirect means. One such means is the marshalling of philosophical arguments that suggest he does not really know what he began by saying he did know, or that the logic by which he arrived at the unwelcome conclusion from that earlier knowledge was faulty; philosophy is quite capable of reducing the amount of knowledge someone has and of shaking our confidence in the soundest arguments. But this, and all the other ways and devices we have for manipulating our beliefs are not able to free us from the beliefs we have without also undermining our assent to what entails them, if they are the conclusions of demonstrations. This means that if someone really is in the position Bayle describes, of seeing that a 'geometrical' demonstration shows the falsity of some article of faith, he is not at liberty not to believe that it is false. (The same is true, indifferently, if he merely *thinks* that some demonstration shows it to be false.) Now beliefs have many sources, including habit and tradition and preaching, and also competing processes of rational thought in which we cannot discern any failings. So it is entirely possible that although someone believes that an article of faith is shown by a demonstration to be false, this is an article of faith which he already believes. He is then in a state of conflict, because he believes two incompatible things.

Someone in this state can seek to make it tolerable in many ways. The most common way is probably that of attending to each belief only when one has to, and seeing to it that when one does the other is ignored – holding one, we might say, on Mondays, Wednesdays, and Fridays, and the other on Tuesdays, Thursdays, and Saturdays. Another and more sophisticated version of this procedure is that of deciding that since one of them must be false,

but one cannot yet see which, one must have a second-order policy of alternating between them until one of them destroys itself by generating falsehoods or contradictions. There are subtler, and potentially more dishonest,
ways. One is to assist the less attractive of the two beliefs to wither away by
avoiding circumstances that will draw attention to the reasons for it, and
seeking out circumstances which will require exclusive concentration on
those which support its competitor; the end-product of this process, it is
supposed, is the elimination of the conflict by the creation of a one-belief
mentality once more. But Bayle selects another subtle method.

We have seen that Bayle has special reasons for not looking away from
those demonstrations which he says show the doctrines of the faith to be
impossible. But he cannot recommend that we concentrate so exclusively
upon them that we lose our grip on the faith itself. Instead, he describes
the conflict in language which makes illegitimate but seductive use of what I
have earlier called the device of externalization. This device is commonly
used in coherent enough ways when we say that some desire or inclination
to which we yield is one with which we do not identify ourselves — so that
although we have it, and may act from it, at some deeper level we still reject
it. I have argued that we cannot properly understand inclinations toward
beliefs or opinions as inclinations which we can decline, since the necessary
gap between desire and decision does not exist in these cases. But Bayle
speaks as though it does. He speaks as though I can say "No" to my reason,
not merely in the sense that I can refrain from doing what it tells me I should
do, or do what it tells me not to do, through weakness or obstinacy of will,
but in the further sense that I can refuse to believe what it demonstrates to
me is true. He says that I can be taught that something is true by the light
of reason yet decide that the opposite is true because I prefer to accept what
I am taught by feeling, conscience, or the Word of God. This suggests some
process analogous to being advised in one way by my professor and the
opposite way by my minister and choosing to follow the advice of the minister. This language obfuscates the crucial fact that a person divided in this
way is someone who has two conflicting beliefs, and is not someone who
chooses one and does not have the other in consequence.

Bayle, it will be recalled, protests that his supposed sort of fideist is in a
state of mind which is "not at all the same as believing and not believing the
same thing at the same time". This, he says, is impossible. It is not impossible, and it is this state which he exemplifies.

Conflicts need not, of course, be *agonizing* ones. One way of making
them less agonizing is to describe them in language that conceals them.

Talk of recognizing rational demonstrations and then of abandoning reason to reject their results is one way of doing this. It does it in a particularly pernicious way: it conceals the need for a resolution of the conflict by describing it as though the conflict itself is a resolution.

SUMMARY

At this point I will attempt to sum up the major points that have emerged in this consideration of the early modern attempts to present Christian faith within the frameword of classical Skepticism.

Conformist Fideism is blatantly mistaken in attempting to present the transcendent commitment of faith in the idiom of Skeptical suspense. This error, however, reflects some deep similarities between the two traditions. Both are life-patterns which seek to free their participants from anxiety, and do so by yielding a mode of detached participation in life's affairs. This pattern has to be sustained by combating tendencies in the soul which are acknowledged to be present but are disowned. In the Skeptic's case these are tendencies toward belief; in the Christian case these are tendencies toward doubt. Hence the Skeptic's repeated reabsorption in the Dogmatic arguments and counter-arguments he might be thought to have left behind him serve the purpose of sustaining his overall stance of non-commitment in a way which parallels the Christian's regular participation in sacramental, prophetic, and apologetic reminders of his commitment. It is these similarities in what I have suggested we might call the salvific aspects of each tradition, which make the point of view of the early modern Conformists intelligible.

In order to assess the coherence of classical Skepticism and of some of its Fideist expressions, it has been necessary to explore the vexed question of the relation between belief and will. I have argued that belief is not itself voluntary, but is subject to voluntary control to an extent that permits moral judgments upon the beliefs people hold. This has permitted two historical judgments. The first is of Sextus. While correct in representing the effects of appearances as passive modes of consciousness, Sextus is not at liberty to suggest they are not beliefs. He is therefore misrepresenting his state of mind as one in which he yields to appearances belieflessly. His stance is rather one in which he yields to beliefs to which appearances incline him, but does so only on those occasions when a general policy of suspense is not possible in practice. In other words, he follows a policy of keeping his beliefs to a minimum by the rehearsal of philosophic arguments. His resultant manner of life is one which can best be described as a controlled conflict of beliefs which arises because on the one hand he follows appearances, and on the other has a general belief that no beliefs are better grounded than their opposites. This mode of life can be coherently described, and probably coherently espoused, however enervating it might seem to outsiders. But it is not coherently described by Sextus himself, when he claims the Skeptic yields to appearances while remaining unsullied by any beliefs whatever. The second historical judgment is of the version of Fideism we find in Bayle. He seems to espouse a profession of Christian doctrines accompanied by a declaration that these doctrines are false by the light of reason. I suggest that this is a misdescription of a conflict between contradictory beliefs. It is not incoherent to ascribe such a conflict to someone, even to oneself, but it is incoherent to suggest that by the abandonment of reason one resolves it. One can hold beliefs that fly in the face of reason, but if one holds that they fly in the face of reason one holds their contradictories too. To the Pyrrhonist the outcome of such conflict is suspense; but if the outcome is not suspense, the residual adoption of a Pyrrhonist framework, as we find it in Bayle, merely conceals the conflict and calls it peace. If by concealing it in this way a thinker reduces spiritual agitation, this merely shows that self-deception sometimes works.

NOTES

[1] On this see Burnyeat, 'Can the Sceptic Live his Scepticism?'

[2] The main argument is to be found in the Fourth *Meditation*. For a recent critique, see Chapter 6 of Bernard Williams, *Descartes: The Project of Pure Enquiry*, Penguin, London, 1978.

[3] See particularly the treatise on faith, *Summa Theologiae*, 2a2ae. 1–7; Volume 31 of the Blackfriars edition, ed. by T. C. O'Brien, Eyre and Spottiswoode, London, 1974.

[4] See propositions XLVIII and XLIV of part II of the *Ethics*.

[5] Hume's views on belief are scattered through Book I of the *Treatise* and the first *Enquiry*. See particularly Section I of Part IV of the former and Section V of the latter. There are good treatments of Hume's theories in H. H. Price, *Belief*, Allen and Unwin, London, 1969, lecture 7, and in John Passmore, 'Hume and the Ethics of Belief' in *David Hume: Bicentenary Papers*, ed. by G. P. Maurice, Edinburgh University Press, 1977.

[6] Or, as we equally easily say, *being inclined* to believe.

[7] Hume introduces the distinction between liberty of spontaneity and liberty of indifference in the discussion of freedom in Sections I–III of Part III of Book II of the *Treatise of Human Nature*. On the distinction and its history see Chapter VII of Anthony Kenny's *Will, Freedom, and Power*, Basil Blackwell, Oxford, 1975.

[8] See his essay, 'Deciding to Believe' in *Problems of the Self*, Cambridge University Press, 1973.

[9] The text of the Fourth Meditation that I have used here is on pp. 92–100 of *Descartes: Philosophical Writings*, ed. by Elizabeth Anscombe and Peter Geach, Nelson, London, 1966. I have learned a great deal about the complexities of Descartes' position on this matter from the essay 'Descartes on the Will' in Anthony Kenny's *The Anatomy of the Soul*, Blackwell, Oxford, 1973.

[10] H. H. Price, 'Belief and will', *Proceedings of the Aristotelian Society*, supplementary Volume **28** (1954), pp. 1–26.

[11] Arthur Danto, *Analytical Philosophy of Action*, Cambridge University Press, 1973.

[12] See the discussion of his famous 'Wager' argument below, Chapter 4.

[13] See my essay 'The Analysis of Faith in St. Thomas Aquinas', *Religious Studies* **13** (1977), 133–154.

[14] This is Pascal's recommendation at the conclusion of the 'Wager' argument, discussed below.

EVANGELICAL FIDEISM – I

PASCAL

> Pyrrhonism is the truth. For, after all, men before Jesus Christ did not know where they were, or whether they were great or small. And those who said the one or the other were guessing without good reason, by chance. And they always went wrong in excluding the one or the other.
>
> What you seek in your ignorance religion declares unto you.[1]

This fragment sums up Pascal's response to the Skeptical tradition. The Skeptic shows us that our search for meaning and consolation cannot be satisfied by reason, and so brings us to a point where we are enabled to accept the grace which alone can give us the faith that will satisfy us. Without the Skeptic's corrective, reason can only serve to inflate our pretensions and hide the realities of our predicament from us; yet if faith does not ensue, skeptical questioning can only yield despair. In articulating this complex judgment, the greatest of Christian apologists produces the most penetrating expressions of the Fideist tradition.

Pascal's projected *Apology for the Christian Religion*, of which we have the variously-arranged fragments known collectively as the *Penseés*, would not have been a philosophical work. Its aim was to lead its reader toward conversion, not philosophical enlightenment. The exact plan Pascal had in mind, and the place of this or that fragment in the whole work, is a matter of unending controversy, and the reader must study the fragments in one or other of a number of proposed arrangements. Any philosophical treatment of Pascal must proceed in full recognition of these difficulties.

The *Apology* was addressed primarily to Pascal's cultivated and freethinking contemporaries, who were assumed to be interested in the dramatic developments in the natural sciences and their implications, to possess some degree of philosophical sophistication, and to have been wearied by the bitter religious divisions that had plunged France into civil warfare. Such an audience would have acquired an inclination toward skepticism, and to a self-protective and superficial religious conformity. For such people the writings of Montaigne would have been a major influence, and it is clearly Montaigne from whom Pascal derives his understanding of Skepticism. Pascal is passionately convinced that neither the noble pretensions of rationalist philosophies, be they Stoic or Cartesian, nor the easy-going Conformism of Montaigne, can offer man an appropriate antidote to anxiety.[2] And the faith which alone can save them is a passionate surrender of the whole personality: a far cry from the social profession with which the Conformist is content. Pascal's most famous work after the *Penseés*, the *Provincial Letters,*[3] is an onslaught on the corruptions of that kind of wordly religiosity.

The first Part of the *Apology* would have been an analysis of the human predicament and of the errors of attempts to escape from it by unaided human effort. The purpose of the whole would have been to induce the reader to turn willingly to the revelation of God in Christ, which is the subject of the second part. It is Pascal's passionate contention that an honest understanding of man's predicament can only come from the standpoint that God's grace makes available to us in faith; but as an apologist he has to present this predicament to the reader in a manner that does not presuppose this faith beforehand. Man's need of God, as he puts it, has to be proved by nature itself, even though God reveals his answer in the Scriptures.[4] Only by the acceptance of this answer can man come to understand the real meaning of his predicament (that he is fallen) but many of the features of his predicament can be made obvious to honest observation, even for those supposedly comfortable souls who are his primary audience. In describing them Pascal has a double purpose: he is not only seeking to make his readers recognize the misery and corruption of the human condition, so that they acknowledge they have a plight which needs to be remedied, but also to undermine their contempt for religion by emphasizing those evils which the Christian revelation would lead us to *expect* if it were true. He is trying to effect a transition from a disdain of faith to a willingness to admit its claims are worthy of consideration.[5] The passages in which he describes the evils of the human condition are the best-known and most powerful in the *Penseés*. It is not surprising that some have rejected his description with a passion almost as great as his own, accusing him of misanthropy and life-denial.[6] While he indeed challenges our most fundamental evaluations of ourselves and our world, it is essential to remember that he seeks to present a picture of man that is not uniformly black, but dual. To him man is a creature whose wretchedness is a consequence of his own wilfulness and corruption, which frustrates his capacity for greatness and union with God, and cannot be redeemed without the acceptance of divine intervention. His wretchedness is due to his own choices, but is not something he can escape from by an unaided act of will, or by his own philosophical systems of self-improvement.

Man is afraid and anxious,[7] but instead of seeing this clearly and recognizing his very anxiety as a sign that he is great as well as small,[8] he tries to conceal his condition and persuade himself that things are not so bad.[9] He submits to forces within him that conceal reality from him: imagination,[10] custom,[11] and egocentricity;[12] he also deceives himself by manipulating his circumstances to provide diversions and distractions, so that he can avoid considering his real situation by absorbing himself in external trivia.[13] It adds up to this:

We run heedlessly into the abyss after putting something in front of us to stop us seeing it.[14]

These very devices, however contemptible and doomed to failure, are signs of the duality in man's nature. He cannot be the mere satisfied brute into which he tries to turn himself, for he is posed uniquely between the finite and the infinite, more accurately between the infinitely great and the infinitely small,[15] and his restlessness is a sign that he is aware of the special place that he has, though the forms it takes hide his real status from him. This status is declared by the Christian revelation:

All these examples of wretchedness prove his greatness. It is the wretchedness of a great lord, the wretchedness of a dispossessed king.[16]

But to recognize one's wretchedness, even to recognize one's capacity for greatness, is not itself to accept the understanding of it that the Christian revelation makes available, even though it may be enough to overcome fashionable contempt for it. It is not yet *listening to God*. If man were doing that, the many signs of God's presence in the world would not have escaped him. As it is, he misses them because he is not heeding them — as the Scriptures have also declared, in saying God hides from those who do not look:

It is true then that everything teaches man his condition, but there must be no misunderstanding, for it is not true that everything reveals God, and it is not true that everything conceals God. But it is true at once that he hides from those who tempt him and that he reveals himself to those who seek him, because men are at once unworthy and capable of God: unworthy through their corruption, capable through their original nature.[17]

This is what Scripture shows us when it says in so many places that those who seek God shall find him. This is not the light of which we speak as of the noonday sun. We do not say that those who seek the sun at noon or water in the sea will find it, and so it necessarily follows that the evidence of God in nature is not of this kind. It tells us elsewhere: *Verily thou art a God that hidest thyself.*[18]

Before there is a possibility of man's listening to God as he needs, he must not only acknowledge his tendency to succumb to the lowest elements in his carnal nature, but humble the pretensions of his reason.

One of the most famous of all passages in Pascal is one which singles out man's reason as a mark of his nobility.[19] Although man is only a reed, he is a thinking reed. All his dignity consists in thought. Taken alone, this has a rationalist flavour, and indeed it demolishes any attempt to interpret Pascal as one who disparages the proper exercise of our intellectual powers. But of course it cannot be taken alone, and it is of central importance to his apologetic procedure for him to show that reason in its turn needs to be humbled and subordinated, and its limitations recognized. What reason cannot do, any more than absorption in carnal concerns can, is provide us with a way out of the anxieties that beset us. Just as the Order of Body has its proper and essential role in our natures, but is commonly allowed to usurp roles that belong to the other two Orders, so the Order of Mind, though its existence is a mark of man's special dignity, is commonly inflated in importance and leads to its own forms of intellectual arrogance and pretension. When it does this, reason tries, vainly, to supplant the role of the heart.[20]

It is of course philosophers who are tempted to inflate the claims of reason in this way. They are typified for Pascal by the Stoics on the one hand, and Descartes on the other. The former represent vain moral aspirations, the latter represents vain speculative ones. The role of the Skeptic is the exposure, with reason's own tools, of the vanity of these pretensions − though the responses of the Skeptic to the results of his own destructive activity are as dangerous spiritually as the attitudes they replace.

In spite of sharing the admiration of his contemporaries for the moral uprightness of some of the great Stoic figures of antiquity, such as Epictetus, Pascal castigates the Stoics for their unnatural exclusiveness, which bars all but a select few from moral salvation, their spiritual pride, their unnatural refusal to recognize the weaknesses in us which make their way of life so hard to sustain, and their disregard of our physical needs (which leads them to accept and even to praise suicide).[21] A similar blend of admiration and rejection characterizes his judgments of Descartes.[22] A mathematician of genius himself, Pascal insists in his scientific controversies on a central role for observation.[22] More importantly for our purposes, he rejects Descartes' attempt to use reason to establish its own first principles and starting-points, claiming it is the heart and not the reason which teaches us these things. In the fragment which deals most clearly with this, he seems to express agreement with the Pyrrhonists that reason cannot prove the existence of space or the infinity of numbers, and that it is not possible for reason to refute the suggestion that we are dreaming, even though he does not agree with them that there can be genuine doubts on these matters.[23] He also insists on the emptiness of attempts by dogmatists like Descartes to demonstrate the reality of God by argument. There is a famous short judgment on Descartes himself: that he cannot forgive him the fact that he would have liked to do without God in his whole system, but that he was forced to allow him a flick of the finger to start the world moving.[24] Most of his comments on philosophical proofs of God are wider in their application, but their upshot is the same – that what such arguments yield is not the God of Abraham, Isaac and Jacob, but the God of the philosophers.[25] I do not find Pascal clearly stating, let alone attempting to demonstrate, the invalidity, or lack of philosophical soundness, of particular arguments; he emphasizes their uselessness, and their spiritual dangers. They are remote and complex, and even those who might be helped by them would always be concerned lest they forget some of the steps, so the help would not last.[26] Since God is a hidden God, and the self-important philosopher is not seeking him humbly but trying to use his existence for the purposes of his system of thought, he inevitably goes wrong in the assessment of the very facts which serve to reveal him to those who approach him in faith. At best he gets deism – "almost as remote from the Christian religion as atheism".[27] The deist can only sustain his doctrine by ignoring the corruption in nature on which Christianity insists, and pretending that nature *as it is* bespeaks God. This facile theory, which is an insult to the honestly enquiring intelligence,[28] merely presents a convenient excuse for those who do not want to know God to reject him,[29] and say he cannot possibly exist. For the very corruptions that hide God from us are counter-evidences when viewed with theoretical detachment. But in order to come to know God we must abandon this Cartesian detachment since it is arrogant presumption to sustain it on such a theme. Faith requires the heart – indeed Pascal tells us that faith is God perceived by the heart, not by the reason.[30]

So philosophical reasoning cannot bring man to God in faith. But it can still help to open him to it, and make him more likely to listen to God. The first way it can do this is by exposing reason's own weaknesses. This is the role of Pyrrhonism, typified for Pascal by Montaigne, from whom he borrows much of his account of human frailties and whose critique of man's intellectual powers he also accepts. But the Pyrrhonist, having done this, has not moved on into faith. Instead he has taken the breakdown of dogmatism as an excuse to adopt an easygoing reabsorption into the everyday, with at most a superficial conformity with religious practice. The proclamation of his intellectual limits does not yield a humility that opens him to God, but to a self-congratulatory indifference in which he wears his agnosticism on his sleeve with a smile. This is worse than the less reflective vanities of which philosophical systems were supposed to be a cure. We therefore find Pascal exerting great efforts to combat any suggestion that the Skeptical tradition can provide an antidote, or even a palliative, for the ills of the human condition.

He declares that the Pyrrhonian response to the breakdown of reason's search for ultimate truths is unnatural, intolerable, despicable, and imprudent. It is unnatural because the Skeptic way is impossible to live by. It is intolerable because the natural human response to the failure to find answers to the questions that concern us most deeply is not relaxation but despair. It is despicable because any examination of the attitudes of the easy doubter shows them to be no more than expressions of monstrous frivolity. And even though reason is unable to show us whether God exists, it can still be shown by rational calculation that we should set ourselves to accept him. It is this last, the famous Wager argument, that has attracted the most attention from philosophers; but all are closely connected, and have important philosophical implications.

(1) Pascal tells us that although the Pyrrhonist exposes the inability of reason to prove the most central and necessary human convictions, this does not show that the Pyrrhonist's alleged solution is possible for us. Our natures, in fact, make it out of the question for us to adopt the Pyrrhonist's stance consistently:

What then is man to do in this state of affairs? Is he to doubt everything, to doubt whether he is awake, whether he is being pinched or burned? Is he to doubt whether he is doubting, to doubt whether he exists?
 No one can go that far, and I maintain that a perfectly genuine Pyrrhonian has never existed. Nature backs up helpless reason and stops it going so wildly astray.[31]

His assertion here is similar, as indeed are many of his other comments at this stage, to what Hume says later about the unlivability of Skepticism. I have already attempted to indicate how far this long-standing criticism of Pyrrhonism is a sound one. What is novel here, and what appears in another form in Hume also, is the claim that our nature protects us from the ravages of Skeptic thought, and in so doing 'backs up helpless reason'. The Pascalian version of this claim depends on his doctrine of the Three Orders, on which I comment below. Clearly for him (and it is notoriously otherwise with Hume) nature can only succeed in protecting us in this way, as this same fragment proclaims so eloquently, if reason is humbled and gives place to faith:

Who will unravel such a tangle? This is certainly beyond dogmatism and Pyrrhonism, beyond all human philosophy. Man transcends man. Let us then concede to the Pyrrhonists what they have so often proclaimed, that truth lies beyond our scope and is an unattainable quarry, that it is no earthly denizen, but at home in heaven, lying in the lap of God, to be known only in so far as it pleases him to reveal it. Let us learn our true nature from the uncreated and incarnate truth. . . . . .

Listen to God.

(2) The doubts and questions of the Pyrrhonists are not only incapable of being sustained. At least as important is the fact that when the serious seeker after truth has to abandon the quest, his natural response is not the suspense and quietude of which the Skeptic speaks, but despair. This despair, as Pascal describes it, takes a very special form. Like the Skeptic, he does not see a world that is silent on whether there is a God to give our lives meaning or whether there is not. On the contrary, he is driven to desperation because there are such signs, but they are contradictory and inconclusive to the eye of reason. It is the very ambiguity which the Skeptic notices that makes Pascal respond in a fashion quite foreign to the Skeptic:

This is what I see and what troubles me. I look in every direction and all I see is darkness. Nature has nothing to offer me that does not give rise to doubt and anxiety. If I saw no sign there of a Divinity I should decide on a negative solution: if I saw signs of a Creator everywhere I should peacefully settle down in the faith. But seeing too much to deny and not enough to affirm, I am in a pitiful state, where I have wished a hundred times over that, if there is a God supporting nature, she should unequivocally proclaim him, and that, if the signs in nature are deceptive, they should be completely erased; that nature should say all or nothing so that I could see what course I ought to follow. Instead of that, in the state in which I am, not knowing what I am nor what I ought to do, I know neither my condition nor my duty. My whole heart strains to know what the true good is in order to pursue it: no price would be too high to pay for eternity.[32]

It is salutary to be reminded in this way that quietude is not the most likely result for most of us when one of our most fundamental impulses is frustrated. Even though the Skeptic has succeeded in seeing the manner of its frustration so clearly, Pascal is surely right to insist that his response is not the most obvious one. Perhaps the truth is that people differ, and that the Skeptic way is a psychological solution for some and not for others.

(3) Pascal, however, is by no means willing to leave it at that. He is fully aware that, in his own day (as now) many doubters appeared to be quite relaxed in their doubts. Some of the most passionate fragments,[33] including one of the longest,[34] are assaults upon this attitude, which he regards as absurd and monstrous. (I do not think that these passages are merely intended

to attack the unphilosophical good-livers of polite society; they apply primarily to those who follow the Pyrrhonian in *returning* to an unexamined life by shrugging off the claims of the infinite.) Pascal imagines someone reciting all the things he does not know about the human condition – whence he comes, where he will go, what his death signifies, and concluding from this that he should spend his days without further thought or concern for the answers! Such a person is of no use in life to himself or others. He is adopting a stance of heedless indifference to hide his inner fears – "nothing is more cowardly than to brazen it out with God". The facts of death and eternity and future gain or loss do not go away because we do not wish to reflect upon them any more, and declining to think about them is criminal folly. "Can we seriously think how important this matter is without being horrified at such extravagant behaviour?"[35]

(4) Pascal's most famous response to the Skeptic, however, is the 'Wager' argument.[36] This is an ingenious attempt to counter the unconvinced enquirer on his own terms, and does not depend, as the attacks on indifference do, upon asseverations of the madness of unconcern. For the reader who has followed him to the point of abandoning the rationalist prescriptions might reasonably feel that, for all its inadequacies, the life of everyday pursuits is the only viable alternative to the stresses of inconclusive argument. In the Wager argument Pascal tries to demonstrate that although we have to give up the claims of speculative reason, and admit it can do nothing, there is still a place for prudence: that acquiring faith can be demonstrated to be the only prudent course. The very equivalence of the arguments for and against God on which the Skeptic insists, produces a decision situation which can be shown to favor faith conclusively.

The argument is a sophisticated attempt to persuade someone inclined toward Skepticism to take instead the path toward faith. It has been discussed from many standpoints, and is usually rejected quite brusquely. Hacking, who has many good things to say for it, makes clear that it is the first substantial exercise in decision theory.[37] Like much of the material in the *Penseés*, it is addressed to the reader in the form of an imagined dialogue with him. It is common ground between the author and the reader in this argument that no appeal to faith, no argument that goes beyond our 'natural lights', is to be used, and that reason cannot tell us one way or the other whether God exists. The force of the argument depends totally on these two assumptions.

The author points out that God is said by Christians to be beyond our comprehension, and that they should not therefore be criticized merely because their religion lacks rational grounds. The unbeliever says that this does nothing to excuse those who *accept* what believers offer to them when there are no grounds to do so. The author says that if reason can tell us nothing either way, the question of God's existence is like a game of chance in which a coin is being tossed and we do not know, at all, which way it will fall. In such circumstances no one can be accused of irrationality if he bets that it will come down heads rather than tails. The unbeliever objects by saying that when there is no reason to choose one way rather than the other, one should not bet at all, but abstain from the wager.

Pascal's response is one of the springs of the 'existentialist' tradition: one does not have the choice of not wagering on the existence or non-existence of God. On this we are already committed to make a decision. ("Cela n'est pas volontaire, vous êtes embarqués.") Not wagering is equivalent to wagering that God does not exist. He then proceeds to examine the nature of the wager. What we have to put down as stakes (our reason and our will, the pleasures of this life) are finite; the prize if our wager is successful (eternal happiness) and the penalty if our wager fails (eternal misery) are both infinite; the chances of winning and of losing are (this is given) equal. In such circumstances someone who wagers that God does not exist gains nothing if he wins and loses everything if he loses; whereas someone who wagers that God does exist gains everything if he wins and loses nothing if he loses. So if the Skeptics are right and the arguments for and against God are indeed equal, this creates a situation in which it is evidently wiser to wager that he exists. It goes without saying that Pascal's point is not that an *attitude* of Pyrrhonian suspense is psychologically impossible, but that since we know that either God exists or he does not, even though we do not know which, this attitude is practically equivalent to a decision that God does not exist. It is also worth noting that when he says that he who wagers on God gives up virtually nothing, he presupposes his earlier judgments on the vanity and emptiness of man's pleasures and obsessions; but even if we do not share this estimate of them, the core of his argument is the relative triviality of this finite sacrifice compared with the infinite reward open to us if we stake it and succeed.

The hearer, though convinced of this conclusion, raises a deeper question: is he *capable* of wagering that God exists? For this amounts to *believing* that God exists, and he is so made, he says, that he cannot believe. Pascal's reply to this is resourceful. He does not suggest that someone convinced of the infinite possible balue of believing can then, by simple election, do it. He recognizes that since the argument his hearer has just accepted is a product of reason, his inability to act upon its conclusion must be due to other elements in his nature. It is his passions that prevent his believing. This being so, belief will be something that he can move toward by diminishing their power. Here he must follow the example of those who have gone before, and exercise that indirect control on his beliefs that so many others have exercised. What they have done is "behave just as if they did believe, taking holy water, having masses said, and so on". This course will make him come to believe quite naturally, by utilizing the known power of the mechanical and habitual elements in his personality to engender the belief that reason could not engender, but has shown it to be in his interest to have.

Pascal has taken over and transformed Montaigne's conformist prescription. Instead of using conformity to avoid commitment, he offers it as a way of inducing it. The very customs and habits which so often serve to keep men at a distance from God can be utilized to bring them to him, and neutralize those negative passions which they have served in the past. This is made clear in the next fragment:

Custom is our nature. Anyone who grows accustomed to faith believes it, and can no longer help fearing hell, and believes nothing else. . . .[38]

This argument has aroused much negative comment, and might in this respect be compared with the Ontological Proof of God's existence: philosophers feel it is somehow a professional obligation not to accept its cogency. But given certain assumptions which Pascal makes, I think it is irrefutable. Before turning to these, some ill-conceived objections can be dismissed. Both philosophers and theologians have said that it is morally disreputable to propose that one should arrange one's beliefs in terms of one's interests, and that it is almost blasphemous to suppose that faith could be the product of such a crassly prudential decision.[39] What is not fully understood by such objectors is that it is taken as given in Pascal's argument that reason can tell us nothing about whether God exists or not. Speculatively speaking there *are*, therefore, no grounds for decision. Given that a non-decision is a negative decision, self-knowledge dictates that the enquirer turn to prudential considerations as the only remaining considerations that there are. This might well be immoral if there were speculative reasons for preferring one selection to the other; but it is assumed that there are not, and if this assumption is correct, the objection is misplaced. Furthermore, Pascal does not say that the practices which one enters in pursuit of faith themselves constitute faith. They are merely those activities that someone who *has* faith engages in, and he proposes that someone who wishes to be of their number should engage in them as well in order to acquire it. The enterprise he proposes is only successful if real faith actually ensues. Believing as he does that faith is a gift of grace, he implies that someone seeking to acquire it may be granted it if he makes efforts to remove some of its obstacles. It seems to me theologically unacceptable for Christian thinkers to insist against him that someone wanting faith, even for prudential reasons, would be denied it by God. The crucial consideration here is that what the hearer of the Wager argument *seeks* is real faith, not simple conformity. There is also a simple answer for the Christian critic who feels that Pascal's understanding of God's requirements is too severe, and that belief is not a necessary condition for salvation: the answer that if there are several possible understandings of what the Christian God requires, then the urgings of prudence dictate that one immerse oneself in the one that is doctrinally the most stringent, since if that is sufficient for salvation, *a fortiori* the requirements of the less stringent creeds will be satisfied.

A minor, but more significant, difficulty can be found if we consider the short shrift Pascal gives to the sacrifice the intending believer would make if he followed his advice. He says these are negligible. Let us accept Pascal's very low valuation of wordly pleasures. But let us also look with some care at his swift dismissal of the Pyrrhonist's suggestion that one should refrain from wagering altogether. It may be true that if one says one is not wagering, what one gains or loses in the long term will be the same as if one wagered negatively. But in the short term the Pyrrhonist has something real to offer in competition with what the Christian offers. For in the short term both claim to provide an antidote to anxiety and distress. The Christian concept of salvation includes both this element of spiritual healing in this life, and the eschatological element of bliss hereafter. If one concentrates exclusively on the latter, as Pascal does in this argument, then he wins, and his judgment on the Pyrrhonian alternative is correct for the simple reason that no short-term gain bears comparison with eternal bliss or torment. But if one concentrates on the former, the contest is less uneven, since the Pyrrhonian is not offering vain pleasures, but the life of quiet and moderate affection which is supposed to ensue upon suspense of judgment. Pascal is taking it for granted that it is not quietude that will ensue; if he is wrong about this, then the Skeptic can retort that he is offering a likely short-term gain whose value is only trivial if viewed in the light of a long-term loss which, though greater, is agreed to be no more likely than not. What he gains by not wagering is finite, but still significant. While I do not judge this argument to be a strong one, it has some topical relevance. At the present day there are many informed unbelievers who reject the commitments of faith as more disturbing and demanding than

the more uninvolved mode of life that a scholarly agnosticism permits them
to live; they do this in the face of cosmic claims which they think are very
unlikely to be true, and are frequently under-emphasized by many Christians,
who often interpret salvation in purely psychological terms.[40]

The critical problem for the Wager argument, however, lies in Pascal's
assumption that there are only two alternatives that each of us has to choose
between in life's game of chance. If we make this assumption, then the arge-
ment is prudentially compelling. But we are not in this position. It is true,
indeed, that either the Christian God exists or he does not. But the latter
alternative is compatible with the existence of many other cosmic arrangements which may demand decision.[41] Indeed, there would seem to be infinitely many of them, since there is no theoretical limit to the number of
world-views that an imaginative philosopher could invent if he is not con-
strained by considerations of likelihood or evidence – which the Wager is
supposed to exclude.[42] In such a situation the laying of odds cannot even
begin.

Of course, with an infinity of equipossible alternatives no rational choice
could begin anywhere. Faced with this obvious truth, William James invented
the important but obscure distinction between a living and a dead option.[43]
A living option is one that, given one's time and place and one's knowledge,
one is in a position to consider seriously, whereas a dead option is one that
one cannot view in this way. The notion is clearly 'person-relative': what are
living options for some are dead for others. There may be many strong
reasons in favour of an option which is dead for me because I cannot know
about those reasons, and the option looks absurd to someone placed as I
am. The notion applies both to the choice between assertions or systems
that claim truth, and to the choice between courses of action that claim to
offer benefits. For all the inevitable emphasis upon the impact of culture and
environment and temperament which we must make when we discuss these
matters, it is clear that a living option is an option which I have some *inclination to believe* may contain the truth, or lead to the good; one to which I
judge it proper to assign some degree of likelihood, however low. The Pyrrhonian *says* his reflections have carried him to the point where all options
are dead for him; I have argued earlier that if he then goes on to say he will
be guided by appearances, he is adopting a stance at odds with this. Pascal
presents the Wager in a manner which appears to accept the Pyrrhonian's own
estimate of his position. But in assuming that *either* our world is governed by
the Christian God *or* our world is governed by none, so that each human
life ends with extinction, he is assuming that there is no third alternative

comparable in likelihood to either. If this assumption could be made, plus the assumption that neither of the two admitted options is more likely than the other, the argument could go forward as Pascal says, but not otherwise. In our own day and age, the number of potentially live options is increasing rapidly, as men's knowledge of the major and minor religious traditions of the world increases. In his own arguments for Christianity as opposed to Judaism and Islam, Pascal shows tacit recognition that the situation in his own day, though restricted, was not as clear-cut as the Wager requires. If we recognize that a rational agent would not arbitrarily restrict the range of options available to him, but would seek to learn of as many as possible in his own circumstances, it would seem clear that an argument like the one Pascal uses can only have relevance if a very small range of these have been selected as more likely than any of their alternatives, and if, in this process of selection, no considerations have emerged which make one of this small range appear more likely to be true than any of the others in the range. This is in itself unlikely, though not, perhaps, impossible. Only then however could the agent's reflection on his choices be unsulliedly prudential.

I shall now attempt to sum up Pascal's estimate of Skepticism, and his use of it, in his *Apology*. To be rescued from their fallen condition and submit to the revelation of Christ men need to be made conscious of the depths of their own depravity and the sources of their anxieties. Their traditional response to this is to try to put their trust in the power of their own reason, which is indeed a manifestation of their potential greatness. But reason does not serve this need, and only spins pretentious intellectual schemes which gloss over men's deepest defects and are unable to supply any power for radical change or any relief from anxiety. Reason in its turn must be humbled. Pyrrhonism serves to expose the emptiness of men's rational pretensions, by demolishing the dogmatisms that they generate. But in using reason to demolish itself, the Skeptic in his turn falls prey to arrogance, thinking that this negative achievement itself offers a viable solution to the human predicament. To some extent man's nature provides a built-in antidote to the Skeptic's vanity, by enabling us to form necessary convictions about everyday concerns and first principles in the absence of the proofs the Skeptic has shown to be impossible. But on the deepest question of man's relationship to God, the Skeptic's destructive activities can leave only despair in their wake; and Pyrrhonian indifference is monstrous and unnatural. Reason should not glory in its own self-destruction, but see that it must in its turn be humbled and give place to a receptiveness to revelation into which faith may enter. Indeed, the need for this can be demonstrated prudentially. When man consents to listen to what God may have to say to him, and studies the presentation of Christ in the scriptures, God will speak, not to his intellect, but to the heart; though when he does so, man will attain to a deeper understanding of his nature and of his former predicament as a result.

KIERKEGAARD

I have attempted in the course of this exposition to comment on Pascal's specific responses to Skepticism. But this can only go a short way toward helping us estimate the value of the form of Fideism which his great work presents to us, which has been enormously influential, for good and for ill. To do this I must go more deeply into the merits and defects of three of his most important contentions: his rejection of the 'proofs' of God; his famous doctrine of the Hidden God; and his doctrine of the Three Orders, together with the doctrine of the heart. Each of these has been a source of many subsequent apologetic arguments, some insightful and some confused, but all still fashionable. Before proceeding to do this, however, I shall add a short account of some similar arguments in Kierkegaard. No treatment of Evangelical Fideism could omit this. In Kierkegaard, beside claims which echo those of Pascal we also find another well-known theme, reminiscent historically of Bayle. While Pascal tells us that men, wishing that Christianity were false, elect to despise it and hide from it and to pretend it is easily refuted, he does not say, as Bayle does, that reason can prove it false. It is one thing to say that reason can do nothing to show it is true, and that to attain to salvation reason must be humbled and transcended; it is quite another to say that the claims of faith are absurd and contrary to reason. It is one thing to say that God is hidden, but another to say that he hides behind contradictions. The theme Kierkegaard adds is the theme of paradox.

There are many likenesses between Pascal and Kierkegaard, both in intent and in teaching. Each is an evangelist, not a philosopher, in spite of each having the capacity for deep philosophical insight and the ability to engage in philosophical debate. The evangelism of each takes on a peculiarly agressive form, which Denzil Patrick calls "an advocacy for the prosecution of the spirit of the age",[44] which does not only emphasize the universal corruptions that he sees as obstacles to faith, but judges more conciliatory forms of apologetic, such as the traditional proofs of God, to be themselves sophisticated attempts to avoid faith by subjecting it to the demands of human institutions. Each has caused his students to pay far more attention to the biographical details of his life than is thought to be necessary for the works of more conventional thinkers — this in line with the emphasis each places on confronting those students themselves with the relationship of what they read to their own personalities and needs. Each sees faith as the product of divine grace, not human effort, while holding simultaneously that barriers to it are due to the misuse of human freedom. Kierkegaard's threefold distinction of the aesthetic, ethical, and religious stages of man's life bears many likenesses to Pascal's doctrine of the three Orders; and his story of the divine incognito is very close to Pascal's doctrine of the hiddenness of God. To these and other resemblances we must add the fact that each leans upon the arguments of Skepticism, in all their perceived negativity, in order to make the positive, fideist, point that faith is vouchsafed to those willing to endure the humiliation of reason's pretensions.

I make no attempt here to produce any general estimate or overview of the vast and complex body of Kierkegaard's writings. I shall confine my comments to some aspects of his attempt to underline the essential discontinuity between faith and philosophical quests for meaning. The writings in which this theme is paramount are those works which are, inevitably, best-known to philosophical readers: *Fear and Trembling, Philosophical Fragments, Concluding Unscientific Postscript*, and *Training in Christianity*. The two most important for our purposes are the *Fragments* and the *Postscript*, which belong together and are written under the same pseudonym, Johannes Climacus (John the Climber). It is in the former, and much shorter of these two, that the most explicit use of Skeptical argument is found.

Kierkegaard's use of pseudonyms is a study in itself.[45] A pseudonymous author of a work by Kierkegaard must not, of course, be taken to be expressing the views of Kierkegaard himself, though the reader in encountering him will be experiencing one phase of Kierkegaard's evangelical strategy. In the case of Climacus in the *Fragments* and the *Postscript*, however, the general assumption that the views he expresses are his creator's own seems to be a sound one. What is not the creator's own, and what is not intended ultimately to be the reader's own either, is the attitude of analytical detachment with which, especially in the *Fragments*, the themes discussed are examined. Indeed, the whole thrust of Kierkegaard's thought is that objectivity has to be abandoned and transcended for faith to be possible, since faith is the truly human expression of involvement in one's existence before God — of what he notoriously calls subjectivity. What Climacus in the *Fragments* does is to make use of *philosophical* means to show why faith must be offensive to the reason. *That* faith is offensive in this way is the well-known burden of the panegyrics on Abraham in *Fear and Trembling*, where Abraham's assured willingness to go forth and sacrifice his son Isaac at God's command is shown to make no prudential or moral sense to the reason, so that attempts to liken it to such more readily intelligible phenomena as the sacrifices of the tragic heroes of antiquity make human sense at the cost of falsifying the mentality Abraham displays. In the *Fragments* Climacus, by trying to deal with speculative philosophical questions, comes by stages to demonstrate that faith makes no speculative sense, and that nothing that did make speculative sense could answer the questions.

In spite of the fact that the purpose of the exercise is a religious one, the exercise itself is philosophical. Since Kierkegaard is frequently approached with great suspicion, even hostility, by many philosophers, it is worth making this clearer by two analogies. The first one can be found in Kant. At the close of his *Groundwork of the Metaphysic of Morals*[46] he makes a typically insightful and pedantic remark: that while we do not comprehend the practical unconditioned necessity of the moral imperative, we do comprehend its incomprehensibility! This piece of heavy-handed wit is no doubt commonly read as one final blow to the endurance of the exhausted undergraduate as he ends his journey through Kant's argument, but it is the expression of a point of great importance, which in the Twentieth Century should be congenial to many philosophers: that philosophical understanding often comes, not when one gets an answer to a question, but when one comes to see why an answer to such a question must be unavailable. In Kant's case what he has in mind is in part the fact (as he sees it) that we cannot get an answer to the question of why something that we perceive as our duty is binding upon us; that any answer to such a question can only take the form of representing it as something other than the duty we have already perceived it to be. Kant may be wrong about this. But he is pointing out that philosophical enlightenment may merely consist in indicating where the boundaries of intelligibility have to lie. This is all that can fairly be asked, he says, of a philosophy which presses forward to the very limit of human reason.

A second analogy with Kierkegaard's procedure (or Climacus' procedure) in the *Fragments* is one we have already examined in Pascal – the Wager argument. This is indubitably philosophical, but it amounts to a use of philosophical techniques designed to show doubters, by means of their own thought-forms, that they should turn aside from the exhausted procedures of theoretical reason and tread the path of faith.

In both of these cases a philosophical procedure is used to show that we are entering an area where philosophical enquiry must come to an end, and why this must be so. Climacus rightly sees that such perception was part of the way of the Skeptics of antiquity, and he therefore makes use of Skeptical epistemology, some of it apparently augmented by Hume, at critical stages in his argument.

The style of the work is to some degree an exaggerated parody of the philosophical logic-chopping of Kierkegaard's own time. He is of course outraged by the practice, typified for him by Hegel and his followers, of treating the Christian revelation as though it were merely a poor man's substitute for a properly worked out philosophical doctrine. The outrage is here expressed initially as mild ridicule, designed to show how philosophers trivialize the most serious questions by expressing them in ways that seem perversely remote from ordinary human concerns. So the real subject of the work, namely the proper response to Christ, is expressed in terms of an old conundrum of Greek thought: How can the Truth be learned? A reality that Kierkegaard, as a Christian, believes has entered history at a particular time and place, is here approached in philosophical fashion as an abstraction. One of his purposes is to address those contemporaries who were puzzled by the fact that Christianity, which they wished to assimilate to the abstract Hegelian system, seemed to depend upon certain historical assertions about the life and death of Jesus. Historical events, unlike eternal truths, are contingent, not necessary, and so might well have been otherwise. They also seem to be much easier to accept for those close to them in time than for those who are much later in time — and surely eternal truths are equally accessible to all rational beings? What Climacus has to do is to show that this sense of the incongruity of philosophical speculation and Christianity is correct, but is incorrectly interpreted. It leaves out the most critical factor of all, the historical and individual situation of the enquirer himself — even though it nominally makes reference to it.

The question Climacus poses[47] is the question posed by Socrates (or at least the Platonic Socrates) in the *Meno* and elsewhere. The puzzle, typically tiresome to the philosophically uninitiated is: if you know the truth already, you cannot learn it, but if you do not know it already, you cannot recognize it, so either way learning is impossible. So something we all feel we are quite familiar with turns out to be conceptually absurd. The answer Socrates gives in Plato is the doctrine of Recollection: that the learner (taken here to be the learner of eternal truths such as those of mathematics or philosophy) is not ignorant before he begins, but has the truth within him. His historical situation has hidden it from him. What the teacher does is supply some reminder that will unlock the knowledge he already has. It follows from this, as Socrates saw, that the teacher does not *impart* knowledge, but serves as an accidental stimulus for the learner to recover it. (Our tradition of liberal education is based on this perception of the teacher's role – in particular our obsessive concern to distinguish teaching from indoctrination.)

Suppose, however, Climacus asks, that we ask how real or new learning is possible; how it could come about that someone came to learn the truth if it were *not* in him already? Clearly the role of the teacher will be all-determining. For the original dilemma makes it clear that without the truth being present already the learner will not know it when it is presented; so the teacher has to present it *and* enable the learner to recognize it. But this is the sort of transformation that no human can perform upon another. So a teacher of the truly ignorant must be a God. But it is impossible that God should have created the learner in such a manner that he would of himself be unreceptive to the truth when God presents it; so a situation in which the learner is thus unreceptive and needs to be changed by God must be one in which the learner has *made himself* unable to recognize it. So what God has to do in order to teach him is to remove the barriers that man has himself erected to what God wishes him to know. God has to restore his freedom to seek the truth, i.e. convert him. So the moment of real learning is a Moment of transformation of the learner. It is in this sense that Christianity is a historical religion, and at this Moment that the Eternal comes into time for him.

But how can God thus transform man without overwhelming him? How can learning thus conceived be something which the learner freely does? Such teaching can only be an act of total condescension (that is, love) on God's side; but why does this condescension not detract totally from the learner's freedom? Here Climacus tells the parable of the king and the humble maiden. The king loved the maiden and longed for his love to be returned. This would not be possible if the king pressed his suit in all his glory and rank, for it would be these and not he himself that won the maiden's response. Nor could it come about by the elevation of the maiden, for then it would not be she herself who responded. It could only come about by the king's descent to the maiden's level. So if God wishes to teach us, he must himself descend to the level of the humblest of us – the level of a servant. And such descent, if it is not to be deceit, must be real, not a piece of play-acting. So this teaching requires a miracle.

It is at this stage, after the Incarnation has been brought to the surface of an apparently philosophical treatise, that Climacus resorts to Skeptical argument. Its purpose is to show that philosophical speculation itself cannot bring us to knowledge of the presence of God. The placing of this argument is not accidental. If God must appear in the form of a servant for us to come to know him, he must appear in a form which permits us to ignore or over-look him if we choose. To the philosophical mind this naturally raises the question: can we not find some less ambiguous way of determining his presence than this?

Elsewhere Kierkegaard pours scorn on the motives of such an enterprise, which he sees as evasion of God's demands. In the *Postscript*, for example, he ridicules the arrogance he sees in it:

So rather let us mock God, out and out, as has been done before in the world – this is always preferable to the disparaging air of importance with which one would prove God's existence. For to prove the existence of one who is present is the most shameless affront, since it is an attempt to make him ridiculous; but unfortunately people have no inkling of this and for sheer seriousness regard it as a pious undertaking. But how could it occur to anybody to prove that he exists, unless one had permitted oneself to ignore him, and now makes the thing all the worse by proving his existence before his very nose?[48]

In the *Fragments*, however, the uselessness of proofs is argued on internal, philosophical grounds, even though the whole drift of the work is designed also to show that these barriers to philosophical success are to be expected theologically. As Popkin has pointed out, the arguments Climacus uses here are all to be found in Hume (and Kant).[49] In close congruence with the position Hume states most succinctly in the early passages of Section IV of the *Enquiry Concerning Human Understanding*,[50] Kierkegaard insists that matters of fact, as Hume expresses it, are not demonstrable, and that if the real being of something is stated in the conclusion of a demonstration it must already have been assumed in the premiss. Reason can deal only with concepts or essences on its own account. To pass from the realm of concepts to real existence is always, he says, a *leap*.[51] If we claim to discern God's mind at work in the glories of nature, either our inference is not conclusive, or we have already assumed God's real being and are interpreting nature accord-ingly.[52] Intellectual certainty, therefore, is something one cannot reach in matters of real existence. So the attempt to prove the existence of God, if genuinely beginning from supposed ignorance of whether God really is or not, Kierkegaard calls "an excellent subject for a comedy of the higher lunacy".[53]

So reason fails to provide any substitute for the sort of learning which God himself has to bring about miraculously. In showing this much, however, reason can see that the learning it seeks, if it comes about, is not merely miraculous in the sense that it is beyond human powers to produce, but also

that when God produces it he has to do this by becoming human himself –
the Eternal has to come into time and take on the very limitations he is
enabling man to transcend. It is this which Kierkegaard now refers to as the
Absolute Paradox.[54] Faced with it, reason may well refuse to submit to it.
This refusal in the face of the 'offence' can take the form of dismissing it
as absurd or impossible, or of trying to deny its reality by patronising it and
explaining it away as not really paradoxical after all – the common mode of
philosophical theology:

When the Reason takes pity on the Paradox, and wishes to help it to an explanation,
the Paradox does not indeed acquiesce, but nevertheless finds it quite natural that the
Reason should do this; for why do we have our philosophers, if not to make supernatural
things trivial and commonplace?[55]

If reason does not resort to these forms of 'acoustic illusion' to reject the
Paradox, but submits to it willingly, the result is faith. But in the remainder
of the *Fragments* Kierkegaard takes great pains to emphasize what faith is
and is not.

It is not any species of historical knowledge. In part he says this because
of the inevitable hesitancy and tentativeness attaching to historical assertion,
which involves interpretation of testimony, and hence uncertainty. But the
primary reason is that the intrusion of the Eternal, of God, into history,
cannot itself be a merely historical proposition, that could be rendered
probable by the use of historical methods.[56] If it were the case that faith was
a mere matter of assenting to a historical proposition about (say) Jesus of
Nazareth, a contemporary of that personage would have been in a better
position to have faith than we are two thousand years later; and Kierkegaard
is anxious to insist this is false.[57] For the divine incognito entails that a contemporary could (as many did) overlook the fact that it was God he was
encountering, and yet one of us today can, reading the testimony, recognize
it. So although the divine Teacher is a historical figure, he is also a *contemporary*[58] who makes the same demand on us as on those who lived in the
period of history he entered. So faith in him is not a form of historical
knowledge, any more than it is a form of demonstrable knowledge.

When the Skeptic sees that the knowledge reason seeks is impossible, he
resolves to doubt and withholds assent. Kierkegaard says[59] that this is an act
of will.[60] Just as this act of will is possible, so the opposite decision to accept
a proposition, is possible. We perform such an act when we accept historical
testimony on the evidence of our senses. We then have what Kierkegaard
calls belief or secular faith. When we confront the Paradox that the Eternal

has entered history we are faced with a claim that reason does not merely judge to be *unproven*, but to be *absurd*. For there to be an alternative to the Skeptic's way here we have to have what Kierkegaard calls faith in the eminent sense — an assent to the paradoxical. In purely human terms this will seem to be the sheer wilful acceptance of the logically impossible by an act of will. But it is an act of will which I cannot myself produce; I need to be a new being to do it. Hence he says that it is not, rightly understood, an act of will at all, for God himself enables me to accept what he teaches me.[61]

But this too is inaccurate. If faith is not a form of knowledge (either demonstrative or historical) and is not an act of will, it emerges that it is not belief in a proposition, but submission to a person. Its object is not what God teaches, as though God were a superior professor, but the Teacher himself. Faith is discipleship, which is properly described in the language of the emotions — 'that happy passion we call faith'.[62]

So what the *Fragments* tries to demonstrate is that the quest for meaning expressed in the Socratic search for knowledge can only be fulfilled in a personal transformation that is not a state of knowledge at all, but one of loving trust in God as he has appeared in human history. This transformation comes about through grace, not through intellectual endeavour. The Skeptic's refutations of reason's pretensions can help us toward such a transformation by freeing us from the search for misguided substitutes for it.

In somewhat more detail, but detached from the oddities of the text, Kierkegaard's view of faith and reason seems to me to be as follows. Man's ignorance of God is not the mere intellectual or sensory deprivation he may suppose, but is due to his corruption or sinfulness. This affects his thought-processes, so that he cannot come to know God through the exercise of his reason. If he ignores this and tries to 'prove' God for himself, he will fail. He will fail for two reasons. First, in seeking to attain to God through such a method, he is refusing to accept the real barrier for what it is. Second, he can only attain to empty conceptual truths by the use of reasoning, and only get uncertain results through sensory or historical observation, so he is inherently unequipped to discover a truth of such moment. This second reason for failure is one which the Skeptic recognizes; so from him we can learn the salutary truth that proof of God is impossible. He can also show us that in mundane matters we are required in practice to make a 'leap' beyond the evidence of the senses or of testimony. To make such a leap we require an act of will; the Skeptic in his turn exerts a contrary act of will — the will to doubt rather than assent. Assent in these matters Kierkegaard calls belief, or secular faith. In the case of knowledge of God, man is too corrupted to summon up any comparable act of will, since the length of the leap is so much greater.

This situation is one which only God himself can redeem. But to rescue man from his moral and epistemic predicament, God must act in a particular way. He has to transform man so that he is morally capable of accepting him; but he must do this in a manner which does not turn that acceptance into something else, such as fear or stupefaction. It must be a free recognition, a chosen leap. The mere presentation of a proof, however conclusive, would not do this, since it would do nothing to remove the corruption of man's nature. A dramatic revelation of God in his glory would not do this, for it would annihilate, not merely overcome, man's capacity to resist. So God must come himself to man in a form that man can reject. He must therefore come incognito, humbly. He must come in a form that invites recognition and submission but can equally easily be rejected and scorned. Hence the Incarnation in the form of a Servant.

This manifestation of God is paradoxical, and therefore an offence to the reason. The man who accepts the God-man and becomes his disciple, and thus has faith must, therefore, do so in the face of the paradox. This requires an even higher act of will than that which is required in secular faith. Hence Kierkegaard both speaks of it as though it is a human act of will, or a leap, and says that it is not an act of will. It is an act that only God can enable him to perform; it is not really the man's, but an act of God's grace in the man. This makes the language of passion the only appropriate language to describe it.

So the paradox of which Kierkegaard says so much emerges in two ways at least. It emerges because the only divine act that can save man is paradoxical in its nature, entailing that God becomes man. It also emerges as a necessary feature of what the disciple has to acknowledge, for his decision is the extreme example of a leap in the face of what Kierkegaard calls objective uncertainty – in this case a leap in the face of contradiction rather than in the face of mere inconclusiveness.[63]

I shall be considering the Fideism of Pascal and Kierkegaard together, in view of their many likenesses. But there are clearly two important respects in which they differ. The more obvious is that even though Pascal, like Kierkegaard, makes his argument culminate in the submission of the enquirer to the person of Christ, rather than in the acceptance of philosophical doctrines, and in doing this emphasizes that man's reason must be humbled and sacrificed, this is not presented by him as a grasp of paradox. His emphasis is on the transcendence of reason, not on collision with it. Allied to this there is another difference. Pascal rejects the Skeptic's path as one which our natures prevent us from following. Kierkegaard presents the Skeptic to us as someone who elects to hold back his assent by a sheer act of will, and presents the rest of us to ourselves as people who give assent by a contrary but similar act of will. His view of belief seems to be very close here to that of Descartes. So acceptance of contingent propositions is a matter of making a voluntary leap which the Skeptic declines to make. The miraculousness of the leap of faith comes from the fact that our spiritual legs are in this case not long enough without the help of God. It will be clear from previous discussion that I reject the voluntarist understanding of belief that Kierkegaard holds. If the notion of believing just by choice is unintelligible, so will be the notion of doing it by the addition of miraculous power. But it would be superficial to dismiss what Kiergaard says on this ground alone. Since we have seen reason to agree that we do have indirect control over what we believe, it is not impossible to represent what he says in a way consistent with this fact: that in ordinary circumstances we accept judgments about reality that exceed what the evidence requires, and we do this by allowing ourselves to be moved toward belief by factors which the Skeptic, more unnaturally, keeps at bay. In the case of our awareness of God, our temptations are all away from, rather than toward, acceptance, and God himself has to break the barriers down.

This makes Kierkegaard sound much less unlike Pascal; and indeed their differences here mask a key likeness. When Pascal says it is the heart that over-rules skeptical hesitations, and the heart which brings us to God, he is making an assimilation between secular and religious assent which parallels the assimi-lation Kierkegaard makes when he speaks of secular and Christian faith, and tells us they each involve a leap. For each, divine grace enables us to complete a process that is prefigured in our secular life, but which our corruption prevents us from experiencing in our relation to God. The Skeptic unwittingly helps us to break down some of the barriers that our corruption has erected. It is this common judgment on which I shall concentrate in what follows.

NOTES

[1] Fragment 691/432. (The textual reference here is to Acts 17:23.) References to Pascal's *Penseés* are to the Lafuma numbering, used by Alban Krailsheimer in his Penguin translation (Harmondsworth, 1966). The second number is that of the same fragment in the Brunschvicg ordering. The translations quoted, with the exception of the first, are from Krailsheimer. In interpreting Pascal, I have been particularly helped by the following

books: Roger Hazelton, *Blaise Pascal: The Genius of His Thought*, Westminster Press, Philadelphia, 1974; A. Krailsheimer, *Pascal*, Oxford University Press, 1980; J. H. Broome, *Pascal*, Barnes and Noble, New York, 1966; and Denzil Patrick, *Pascal and Kierkegaard*, Lutterworth, London, 1947, Vol. I.

[2] For Pascal's criticisms of dogmatic philosophies, especially Stoicism, it is useful to consult the *Conversation with M. de Saci*. An English version of this is available in *The Essential Pascal*, New American Library, 1966.

[3] English transation by A. Krailsheimer, Penguin, Harmondsworth, 1967.

[4] 6/60.

[5] 12/187.

[6] For a striking example, see Aldous Huxley's essay on Pascal in *Do What You Will*, Chatto and Windus, London, 1956. Comparable criticism from a Christian standpoint can be found in *Pascal's Philosophy of Religion*, by C. C. J. Webb, Clarendon Press, Oxford, 1929, Kraus, New York, 1970.

[7] 68/205.

[8] 114/397.

[9] 70/165b.

[10] 44/82.

[11] 419/419; 645/312. These fragments show that our dependence on custom may lead us into good paths as well as bad ones, even though the latter may predominate. The Wager argument, discussed below, depends on utilizing the good possibilities of habit.

[12] 627/150; 792/101; 597/455; 668/457. On these three 'deceiving powers' see Hazelton, pp. 83–92.

[13] There are a wealth of fragments dealing with this theme, which greatly exercises Pascal. See 133/169; 136/142; 139/143. The last ends with one of his most passionate outbursts: "Que le coeur de l'homme est creux et plein d'ordure".

[14] 166/183.

[15] See the magnificent 199/72.

[16] 116/398.

[17] 444/557.

[18] From 781/242. The text is Isaiah 45:15.

[19] 200/347.

[20] For an account of the Three Orders, see Broome, Chapters VI and VII, and Hazelton, pp. 116–23.

[21] 144/360; 146/350; 208/435. See the *Conversation with M. de Saci*, also Krailsheimer, *Pascal*, Chapter 3.

[22] The most famous example of this is his dispute over the vacuum. See, for example, Krailsheimer, Chapter 2.

[23] 110/282. See Broome, pp. 75–81.

[24] Fragment 1001.

[25] This famous phrase from his Memorial virtually reappears in the fullest fragment on this theme, 449/556.

[26] 190/543.

[27] 449/556.

[28] 781/242.

[29] See again 449/556.

[30] 424/278.

[31] 131/434. (I have substituted 'Pyrrhonian' for 'Sceptic', for the French 'Pyrrhonien'.)

[32] 429/229.

[33] 427–431/194, 195, 229, 431, 560.

[34] 427/194.

[35] 428/195.

[36] 418/223.

[37] Ian Hacking, *The Emergence of Probability*, Cambridge University Press, 1975, Chapter 8.

[38] 419/419.

[39] William James, for example, in the title essay in *The Will to Believe* (Longmans, London, 1897) says, "We feel that a faith in masses and holy water adopted wilfully after such a mechanical calculation would lack the inner soul of faith's reality; and if we were ourselves in the place of the Deity, we should probably take particular pleasure in cutting off believers of this pattern from their infinite reward".

[40] The case of Hume also deserves comparison here. See below, Chapter 6.

[41] I ignore the possibility that the former is also, since the Wager strategy could accommodate it.

[42] See Antony Flew, 'Is Pascal's Wager the Only Safe Bet?', *The Rationalist Annual*, London, 1960, pp. 21–25.

[43] See 'The Will to Believe'.

[44] Denzil Patrick, *Pascal and Kierkegaard*, Vol. I, p. xi.

[45] For a general overview of this and related questions see G. B. and G. E. Arbaugh, *Kierkegaard's Authorship*, Augustana College Library, Rock Island, Illinois, 1967.

[46] See page 131 of H. J. Paton's translation, *The Moral Law*, Hutchinson, London, 1950.

[47] Søren Kierkegaard, *Philosophical Fragments*, trans. David Swenson, p. 11.

[48] Søren Kierkegaard, *Concluding Unscientific Postscript*, trans. David S. Swenson and Walter Lowrie, p. 485.

[49] See Richard Popkin's essay, 'Hume and Kierkegaard' in *The High Road to Pyrrhonism*, pp. 227–236.

[50] See also Cleanthes' response to Demea in Part IX of the *Dialogues Concerning Natural Religion*.

[51] *Fragments*, p. 53.

[52] p. 52.

[53] p. 54.

[54] p. 59.

[55] p. 66.

[56] As Popkin points out, Kierkegaard agrees here, in the most literal way, with Hume. See the last paragraph of Hume's discussion of miracles in Section X of the *Enquiry Concerning Human Understanding*.

[57] He points out that even awareness of contemporary events requires an inference, or 'leap'.

[58] The contemporaneity of Christ and the disciple is the recurrent theme of *Training in Christianity*.

[59] p. 102.

[60] This is not, of course, how Sextus viewed the matter.

[61] p. 77. I am trying here to combine the arguments of Chapter IV of the *Fragments* with those of the Interlude. See Arbaugh, p. 141.

[62] p. 76.

[63] I think Popkin emphasizes the second of these considerations too exclusively.

CHAPTER 5

EVANGELICAL FIDEISM – II

My purpose in this chapter is to assess the judgments of Skepticism that we have found in Pascal and Kierkegaard. They are judgments which have had great influence on religious thought, and continue to do so. In essence, both Pascal and Kierkegaard tell us that the Skeptic, in undermining the philosophical pretensions of human reason, particularly the pretensions of dogmatic philosophers to provide intellectual backing for the Christian tradition, has unintentionally performed a service for faith. Their reasons for holding this can be divided, for convenience, into three. First, they have seen the Skeptic as a co-belligerent in a war against the traditional enterprise of proving the existence of God and of attempting to show, by philosophical means alone, that some of the major tenets of Christianity are likely to be true. Second, they have thought that the Skeptic, in stressing the ambiguity of our circumstances, and the intellectual uncertainty of God's presence, has drawn attention to something that is theologically to be expected, in view of the hiddenness of God. Third, they say that although the Skeptic sees our situation without God more clearly than those dogmatic philosophers who have tried to justify faith, he has not been able to provide the antidote to bewilderment and anxiety that he supposes. His very failure, however, should spur us to recognize that human nature has resources other than reason which enable us to conduct our secular affairs in spite of our uncertainties. It should also help open us to divine grace and so prepare the way for faith. In this way it will help us indirectly toward the assurance that we have been mistakenly seeking through the exercise of reason.

I shall comment on each of these in turn, bearing in mind the matters on which Pascal and Kierkegaard differ, as well as those on which they agree.

THE REJECTION OF PROOF

There is little in Pascal, and only a modest amount in Kierkegaard, by way of philosophical criticism of the traditional proofs of God's existence. Each is more concerned with the motives of such proofs, and with their alleged inutility, than with the details of particular arguments. It is also noteworthy that such criticism as there is does not show serious interest in the relevant discussions in Sextus. There is no reference to the elaborate attacks on proof, or the critique of indicative signs, or to the attacks on natural theology in Sextus or Cicero.[1] This is even true of Kierkegaard, whose philosophical arguments against proofs are to be found in Hume, and who refers to the Skeptics of antiquity solely in order to contrast their supposed will to withhold assent with the alleged free leap he finds in the stance of believers.[2] The influence of Skepticism on each of them seems at this level to be indirect.

The two most important fragments in Pascal which deal with the proofs do not make unadulteratedly philosophical points about them. The first[3] emphasizes the remoteness of metaphysical argument from human reasoning, and tells us that its complexity limits the value of the proofs to a very few people; and those few, says Pascal, would always be concerned lest, once the details had slipped from memory, they might be reposing confidence in a demonstration that had been unsound, so that whatever value a proof might have for them would only be fleeting. The whole thrust of the fragment is clearly to minimize the utility of the proofs, not to deny they might be philosophically sound. The complexity and remoteness of the proofs was, of course, fully recognized by Aquinas,[4] who inferred from it that God would not have left the majority without some alternative means of hearing those truths which the learned could discover by proving them, but did not think it showed they could not be proved. The remoteness and complexity of metaphysics is also shared by much of mathematics, whose utility Pascal would not question on this account. The worry that one might lose the assurance of a demonstration once it had receded from memory is also, I think, primarily an assertion that the intellectual watchfulness which philosophy requires is the antithesis of the assurance that faith provides. But there is also, undoubtedly, an echo of one of the questions that Descartes addresses in his Four Rules of Method and in his attempted refutation of the 'Malignant Demon' hypothesis: the question of how one can be sure of the cogency of a complex argument when the clarity and distinctness with which one conceives the constituent parts of it seem to depend on their relative simplicity. This worry, particularly characteristic of the *Cartesian* Skeptic, does indeed require a philosophical answer, and in drawing our attention to this fact Pascal, like the Pyrrhonian, is emphasizing the restless and inconclusive nature of philosophical debate. But this does not show that any particular proof is or is not cogent. It rather presupposes that some are, and gnaws at our confidence in our ability to recognize them.

The other and larger fragment[5] is also designed to emphasize that without Christ proof of God's presence in nature is 'useless and sterile'. But it, too,

makes the secondary point that when viewed with the detached eye of philosophy, nature does not speak of God unambiguously. It does speak of him,
but it is also full of corruptions; Christian faith makes these intelligible, but
in its absence they are counter-evidence. Hence the philosophical feebleness
and empty optimism of Deism, which has to sustain itself by ignoring them.
The point Pascal makes here is, at first glance, one which has been made
familiar to most philosophers in our time by Hume, in Part X of his *Dialogues
Concerning Natural Religion*. There he makes the skeptical Philo, in agreement on this matter with the orthodox Demea, say that the evils in the world
decisively refute the attempt of Cleanthes to establish the existence of the
Christian God by a supposed scientific appeal to the evidence. For although,
says Philo, it may indeed be possible to *reconcile* these evils with the omnipotence and perfect goodness of God, if these attributes are independently
established; if they are not independently established the presence of evils
in the world (even little ones) is substantial evidence against God's having
them. If the world *as it is* is all we have to go on, then it seems that God is
good in some ways and not in others, or is limited in power or does not exist.
Hume presses the point by making Cleanthes espouse a watery optimism that
denies the gravity of the very evils the Christian faith most emphasizes. In
spite of the close parallel here, I think that Pascal's point is more complex
than this argument of Hume's. Pascal says the failure of such arguments
leaves behind it a situation of *ambiguity*, over which he agonizes very particularly.[6] An ambiguous situation, as he conceives it, is clearly not properly
characterized by the disjunctive assessment that either this world is created
by a limited god or by no god at all. For Pascal the ambiguity is a *tense* one.
It is tense because there are signs that nature *is* the work of an omnipotent
and all-good God; and it is these signs, which are not adequately recognized
in the Humean resolution, which the evils we know of seem to contradict.
Although he might well agree that at the level of reason the alternatives are
what Hume says they are, he also seems to suggest that this leaves behind a
despair wich is not only a spiritual desperation, but also includes an *intellectual* dissatisfaction. For he says that the Christian doctrine of the Fall and
of the hiddenness of God are not only pointers to salvation, but make the
baffling scheme of things fall into place; that the understanding of man as a
deposed monarch living in a world where the presence of God can readily be
discerned by those who look, and can easily be ignored by those who do not
look, is an understanding which *explains* both the positive signs and the negative ones. If this is indeed what he thinks, then it means, roughly, that 'God
indeed does exist and man is a fallen creature' is a better explanation of our

world *as it is* than 'God exists' alone is. Clearly Pascal does believe this. But equally clearly he believes that only the heart and not the reason can teach it to us, and that only through submission to Christ can one come to accept it. How are we to interpret this?

There are two obvious answers, both correct as far as they go. First, Pascal no doubt would say that the explanation of our predicament as a fallen state is one that human reason could not, of itself, have *invented*; that it has, therefore, to be revealed to us. In that sense, therefore, it is *beyond* our reason. Many would think that human invention could indeed extend far enough to think up an explanation like this. But even if this is not so, it is important to see that even though we might be quite unable to invent an explanation of some fundamental features of our world, once an explanation has been offered to us we might still be able to recognize quite clearly that it was the correct one, and made sense of those features in a way that nothing we could have invented would have done. It is also important to notice that some philosophical theologians would say that God's existence can be proved by an *a priori* argument like the Ontological Proof, or by some version of the Cosmological Proof, without the evils in nature being explained; and that the explanation of those evils can be provided subsequently by revelation.[7] Second, Pascal would also say that only when God reaches the heart are we genuinely willing to *acknowledge* the evils, especially the evils in ourselves, that the explanation of our predicament includes; that only when we are ready to repent of our corruption are we in a position to understand it. I suggest that this would not show there is no proof of God's presence or of our need for him; only that grace is needed for us to accept it. I comment further on this theme below. In the meantime, it is enough to say it is no surprise to find that Pascal's rejection of the proofs is an equivocal one:

It may be that there are such things as true proofs, but it is not certain.

Thus that only proves that it is not certain that everything is uncertain. To the greater glory of Pyrrhonism.[8]

Kierkegaard's philosophical critique of the proofs needs little comment here, largely because of its derivative character. He follows Hume and Kant in saying that there can be no demonstration of existence by reason; that all existential judgments are contingent, and that there is consequently a 'leap', or logical gap, between them and any premises from which we argue to them. A similar gap must exist between any historical evidence and any claims about God in history. In addition, as Popkin has made clear,[9] he adopts, at least for the occasion, a radically skeptical view about all knowledge of contingent truths. Since they all involve a leap beyond the evidence, any assurance we may feel about them must come from a sheer act of will, a kind of act of which the leap we take in faith is an extreme instance. He then dismisses the moderate or probabilistic skepticism favoured by the Academics and by Hume. He thus seems to admit only two kinds of assent to propositions: the assent given to necessary truths, which he insists are merely conceptual in character, and that given to contingent propositions, which require a voluntary leap, or logically unwarranted inference. He at least seems to reject the reality of an intermediate assent to propositions which are more likely than their alternatives. His position, then, seems to be that the assent given in faith is, on the one hand, of the same voluntary character as that given (in his view) to secular contingent truths. He thinks this point is reinforced by the skeptical thesis that, since all contingent truths carry us beyond their evidence, there is no good reason for holding that some are more probable than others. On the other hand, he holds that the assent given in faith is unique and requires a miracle, not because it differs in degree from secular inferences (for they do not differ from each other) but because it is a leap into a paradox rather than a leap over a gap. Faith involves assent to something absurd, not merely assent to something devoid of logical guarantee; but of course both secular assent and faith are indeed devoid of such a guarantee.

Whether or not this is a correct reading of his view about secular contingent truths, there is no doubt that he rejects, with vehemence, any suggestion that God's presence could be rendered probable. (In telling us this he seems to take it for granted that the notion of probability does have a legitimate use in other places, but we may disregard this.)

The offended consciousness holds aloof from the Paradox and keeps to the probable, since the Paradox is the most improbable of things. Again it is not the reason that made this discovery; it merely snatches the words from the mouth of the Paradox, strange as this may seem; for the Paradox itself says: Comedies and romances and lies must needs be probable, but why should I be probable?[10]

This is the appropriate point to note that throughout the complexities of his argument, Kierkegaard, like Pascal, never abandons the traditional assumption that faith requires certainty. His rejection of proof is a rejection of the attempt to locate this certainty in the logical necessity of 'eternal' truths. The certainty that can be found there is, as Hume told us, bought at the price of emptiness and abstraction from existence. The certainty of faith resides elsewhere: in the nature of the passion with which the paradox is grasped, a passion which can only be ours through a miracle. So the alleviation of human disquiet which philosophers have sought in the quest for eternal truths must come from the passionate reception of the paradox – which is, of course, the person of the God-man himself. This is why there can be no place for the tepid and hesitant stance we take toward what we judge to be probable. The adoption of a Pyrrhonian skepticism, or what he thinks is a Pyrrhonian skepticism, rather than an Academic skepticism, is intended to make such suggestions epistemologically unavailable as well as theologically obnoxious.

But neither Pascal nor Kierkegaard is primarily interested in the detailed reasoning by which Skeptical argument undermines attempts to prove the being of God by reason. Each is primarily interested in showing us that the attempt to do so is an obstacle to faith, not a step toward it; and that it is the Skeptic who helps us toward faith, whether he wants to or not, by showing us that the attempt is doomed to failure. They hold this because they think that what separates man from God is man's own corruption, not the absence of evidence or rational grounds. Even the despair that Skeptical reasoning can lead to is a harsh but real benefit to us, because it can serve to make us aware of the need to break down this barrier, and cease refusing to heed God.

Their other attacks on the enterprise of proof are corollaries of this basic position. (a) In trying to prove God by reason, men are engaged in an undertaking that asks for objectivity and detachment, whereas to come to God they have to abandon this attitude, which is appropriate only in science or mathematics, and engage themselves as living, 'existing' individuals whose salvation is at stake in the immediate moment. (b) Adopting the detachment necessary for proof is something men do in order to postpone or avoid this individual involvement. (c) Indeed, undertaking to prove God results from arrogance and presumption, the very antithesis of the humility needed to turn to God. This shows itself in the way philosophers are even prepared to use God to fill vacant intellectual corners in their systems. (d) Faith is in any case a relation to the person of God himself, not intellectual assent to dogmatic propositions. (e) Trying to prove God, therefore, is an attempt to do for ourselves what can only be done by God's grace. As usual, Pascal sums it all up in one powerful sentence:

What are we to conclude from all our darkness but our unworthiness?[11]

All these secondary condemnations appear in a different light if the fundamental judgment on which they depend is mistaken. I shall now try to show this.

I begin with two analogies. Pascal is best known for his attacks on the superficial pleasure-seeking with which he thinks men distract themselves from their predicament rather than confront it and pay the price necessary to change it. His examples are such familiar activities as hunting hares, playing cards and ball-games, and the like. He sees them all as pathetic yet blameworthy, since they hide reality and their satisfactions are fleeting. Even if this judgment on human play is sound, it would not be made more compelling if Pascal had said, to reinforce it, that such objectives as killing hares, scoring goals, or trumping were beyond human powers. It is of their essence that they should be attainable, though with some effort; if this were not so their pursuit would not serve the purpose he thinks he has uncovered.

Another, and somewhat closer, analogy. People who are addicted to drugs or alcohol are often known to resist evidence from their families or their doctors that they are undermining their physical health. Even if they are willing to consider this, they may still resist the suggestion that they are indulging their habit in order to avoid confronting unpleasant realities in their professional or personal lives. If they subsequently escape their addiction, they will admit these things freely. It would be odd, however, to say that because they were unwilling to *recognize*, or *acknowledge*, these facts about themselves, such facts can never be made clear by anyone, or to anyone, who has not escaped from addiction. Indeed, two familiar phenomena would be impossible if this were true. One is the case of the addict who undertakes treatment just because he has been convinced of the need to do so by the very facts that others have placed before him. The other is the case of the informed smoker, or the medically-trained drug-addict, or the neurotic who has been enlightened about his state and goes no further than boring his acquaintances with repeated self-diagnoses.

I do not wish to place great weight upon these analogies, but I think they suggest some obvious points in the present context. From the fact, if it is one, that men are prevented from coming to know God by their own corruption, it does not follow that God's existence and his will to save them cannot be proved. If it is man's corruption that keeps him from God, this would more likely be manifested in their refusing to accept proofs than in their labouring to invent them. Someone who does not want something to be true is likely to resist any claim that it has been proved to be true. And if someone else suggests to him that it *cannot* be proved, he is likely to be relieved and confirmed in his negative attitude, not shaken from it.

The only context in which a Skeptical evaluation of proofs is likely to emancipate him from his attitude of rejection is one in which the attempt to prove the existence of God, or some other Christian doctrine, is itself an undertaking which manifests the very corruption in which he is enmeshed. Like any other human activity, it may be corrupt in this way. Both Pascal and Kierkegaard suggest some corrupt motives that might be at work, and perhaps a dose of Skepticism would cut some of them down to size. But one must surely say that sometimes the attempt to prove the existence of God has not been undertaken from such motives as these. When Pascal thinks about dogmatic philosophers and their attempts at proof, he thinks too readily of Descartes. When Kierkegaard talks about rationalistic philosophers, he thinks too readily of Hegel. It may be fair to say that these two thinkers were reasoning about God only in order to fill gaps in their systems, though I am not certain that it is. But there are natural examples that do not fit this understanding. I cannot see that it fits the two cases of St. Anselm and St. Thomas Aquinas. These are usually taken to be men of faith, who still thought it worth while to prove the existence of God.

These two cases might remind us that someone who produces what he claims is a proof of the existence of God need not be in the same spiritual situation as someone who hears it or reads it. *Prima facie*, someone who hears it might come closer to God because of it, even though the person who produces it might be doing so in order to fill some gap in his philosophical system, or even, like perhaps Cicero in the *De Natura Deorum*, or Hume in the *Dialogues Concerning Natural Religion*, in order to go on to produce a refutation of it. Similarly, someone might produce a proof of God as an act of devotion, like Anselm in the *Proslogion*, or from missionary motives, like St. Thomas in the *Summa Contra Gentiles*, yet a reader might be distracted by the intrinsic interest of the argument away from his spiritual needs and spend his time on points of logic instead. And all of these possibilities are consistent both with the alleged proof's being a successful one, and with its being a bad one.

These considerations suggest that if our corruption keeps us from God, this does not show any philosophical argument for God to be unsound. At most it shows that such arguments may be irrelevant for many evangelical purposes, and will carry their own spiritual risks. It is possible that immersion in Pyrrhonist arguments may turn some toward their real spiritual needs and away from these risks. But the reality of these risks, and the fact, if it is one, that people deny or doubt God because of their own corruption, are quite independent of the correctness of Pyrrhonism. Any advantages that Pyrrhonism might have in turning us toward faith could be obtained if Pyrrhonism were false.

I think, however, that the case against Pascal and Kierkegaard on this point is stronger than this: that if our spiritual situation is as they describe it, then it is not merely unnecessary for Pyrrhonism to be true — it would be quite surprising if it were true. To show this, and to place the previous considerations on a more formal footing, I shall now discuss the concept of proof itself.

Let us look at what is involved in proving something; and more particularly at what thinkers who have tried to prove the existence of God, or have tried to prove the truth of certain Christian doctrines about God, have considered themselves to be about. The concept of proof is used in more than one way, and it is important to be sure that we are using it in the way that is appropriate for assessing their arguments, and the criticisms levelled against them by Pascal and Kierkegaard.[12]

(1) To begin, arguments that are offered as proofs of God are arguments from premisses. They are what I have called indirect proofs, in contrast with the sort of proof one might try to give by pointing out some fact one has been insisting on to one's hearer's sensory observation. One might call that a direct proof.

(2) Secondly, they are supposed to proceed from premisses that can be stated without stating the conclusion they are designed to establish. A supposed proof that failed to meet this requirement would commonly be dismissed as 'circular'. (It was largely through arguments suggesting this requirement is impossible of fulfilment that the Skeptics sought to undermine confidence in the possibility of proof.)

(3) Thirdly, the premisses must be true.[13]

(4) Fourthly, they must be *known* to be true. To adopt this as a condition of proof is to make it clear that we are defining that use of the word 'proof' in which it characterizes an action that someone performs, rather than the set of sentences or propositions he utters in performing it. Clearly the latter use of the world is also quite proper and quite common; indeed it is the more natural one to adopt when discussing proofs in logic or mathematics. In such a use, one might well come across a proof in an old manuscript which is in fact successful but can no longer be seen to be successful because no one now knows whether its premisses are true, though in fact they are. Given the particular concerns of Pascal and Kierkegaard, it seems better to define that use of the term in which proof is an act which someone performs, or tries to perform. I suggest it cannot be performed successfully, unless the premisses that are offered are true and are known to be.[14]

We now have a difficult question: known by whom? There are two roles involved in the action of proving. There is the role of the *speaker* (or writer), who states the premises and points out that, and how, they support the conclusion, and there is the role of the *hearer*, who apprehends the statements that are the premises and their relation to the conclusion, and then accepts or rejects it. One and the same person can, of course, perform both roles. (A good deal of what Pascal and Kierkegaard, especially the latter, say about proofs of God, applies only when this is so.) Most commonly both speaker and hearer will know that the premises are true. But this does not seem to be necessary. For example, a professor may invent an argument whose premises he does not believe, and draw a conclusion from them, just as an example in a logic class; and a student may hear the professor do this, but happen to know that the premises are true. Then the professor may have proved the conclusion to that student accidentally. But if we allow this we must say that there can be no proof unless the person who plays the role of hearer knows the premises to be true. So far, then, a successful proof is one in which there are premises which can be stated without stating the conclusion, which are true, and which are known to be true at least by the hearer of the proof.

(5) Obviously there must be more. The premises and the conclusion have to be related in a suitable manner. One such manner is that the premises entail the conclusion, so that someone who has accepted them but rejects the conclusion is guilty of inconsistency or self-contradiction. A proof that meets this standard is a successful deductive argument. But are all proofs deductive? It seems clear that some who have offered proofs of God have not supposed this. This is particularly true of those who have used the so-called 'Design' argument for God's existence. Cleanthes, in Hume's *Dialogues*, thinks that the evidences of order in nature, plus the experience of human intelligence behind designed artefacts, together prove that God's intelligence is at work in our world; but he does not give any sign of supposing that it follows from these facts on pain of self-contradiction;[15] and although Cleanthes is a fictional personage, he is usually taken to be typical of a well-known style of argument. If he is, there are many who have thought that a conclusion can be proved without being established deductively. Now such a view would be foolish if all it meant was that a conclusion is proved if it can be shown to be probable on the basis of its premises, for it would eliminate the very necessary distinction between showing something to be probable and proving it. So if there are non-deductive proofs there must be some relationship other than the deductive one between their premises and their conclusions which is not captured by the mere concept of probability. I have suggested the concept of *overwhelming* probability. This is difficult, if not

impossible, to analyze. But it is at least a beginning of an account of its character to say that if someone says that some premisses, p and q, make a conclusion, r, overwhelmingly probable, they imply that anyone who agrees that p and q are true but reject r is guilty of irrationality, even though he is not guilty of logical inconsistency: that even though 'p and q, but not r' is not self-contradictory, it is unreasonable to believe it or even entertain it seriously. It is clearly possible, and not uncommon, to restrict the word 'proof' to deductive arguments. But it is also common enough to use it in a less restricted way, to include arguments that establish their conclusions by showing them to be overwhelmingly probable. I shall follow this more permissive usage. Adopting it does not commit us to the view that there *are* any arguments on any subject-matter which establish their conclusions as overwhelmingly probable in this way, only that an argument that did so would properly be called a proof. Historically, skeptical thinkers have used the concept of proof more restrictedly, since they have wished to argue that the absence of entailment in an argument is itself a ground for doubting whether its conclusion has been established. When Sextus, therefore, discusses whether any truths can be shown to be overwhelmingly probable by evidence (which of course the Skeptic does not accept) he does so not under the heading 'Does Proof Exist?' but under the heading 'Does the Indicative Sign Exist?', proof being assumed to be deductive.

(6) If we adopt this more permissive use of 'proof', however, we must note that it is *logically* possible for a conclusion to be rendered overwhelmingly probable by premisses known to be true, but yet to be false. 'Proof' is a success-word, so that it is not logically possible to prove a false statement. So we must include in our definition of what a proof is the explicit requirement that the conclusion of a proof is itself true, a requirement which would not have to be explicit in this way if proof were defined as deductive.[16] Such an explicit requirement might well raise the prospect of more skeptical queries about how one could ever be sure that a proof had been given in non-deductive cases; but I do not think these are germane to our present concerns.

(7) To sum up so far: we have a proof, or a successful attempt at proof, when we have a true conclusion in an argument which begins with premisses which are true and are known by the hearer of the argument to be true, which can be stated without stating the conclusion, and which either entail it or make it overwhelmingly probable. It is clearly also necessary that the hearer understand that the premisses support the conclusion in one of these two ways. From this it follows that if the hearer rejects the conclusion of such an argument he is being irrational in doing so, since for someone in his

position the conclusion has been placed beyond reasonable doubt. Put more briefly, it has been proved to him even though he rejects it.

The elucidation of such a state of mind is difficult.[17] We might even be tempted, if we adopt a view about belief and will like the one I supported in Chapter 3, that someone in the position described here cannot really reject the conclusion of a proof, but can only pretend to do so. But this is too simple. It is likely that someone in this position will give ambiguous signs, which will suggest both that he does know the conclusion to be true and that he does not. We would naturally speak of self-deception in such cases, and say that he 'knows very well' that the conclusion is true, but will not acknowledge it to himself or to us. Perhaps, following our previous analysis, we can say that he does believe the conclusion (because he cannot do otherwise) but since he already has incompatible beliefs, or hates it, he tries to cast doubt on it, in order to shed it before it takes hold. In some sophisticated cases a hearer may see, during an argument, where it is leading him, and while secretly realizing he has no escape, may retreat into questioning the premises which he has previously conceded that he knows to be true, or into questioning the soundness of the inferences from them. In these ways people may, out of fear or sloth or hostility, seek to reject what is proved to them. The fact that such devices are irrational or self-deceiving is what is critical here. The fact that people resort to them does not mean that the conclusion they are resisting has *not* been proved to them. Proof, in other words, does not guarantee knowledge. It merely places hearers in a position where the only barriers to it are the self-imposed barriers of irrationality and self-deceit.

There are other situations in which perversity can frustrate a speaker's intent of proving something to a hearer, in a more straightforward way. These occur when a speaker, or more likely a writer, selects certain premises which a potential hearer, or group of hearers, know to be true, and draws from them a conclusion which is entailed by them or rendered overwhelmingly probable by them, and which they have the ability and opportunity to see to be established by them in this way; but they do not seize the opportunity that they have, because they do not wish to have such a conclusion proved to them. They will then have frustrated his intention to prove it to them, and he may end up having proved it only for himself. But we can say that he has *provided a proof* for them,[18] because if they had attended to it, it would have placed its conclusion beyond reasonable doubt for them. They would, in such circumstances, be perverse in not knowing the conclusion. Their perversity would be a consequence of the fact that had they attended and then refused to accept the conclusion, it would have been irrational or self-deceiving on their part to do so. One term we have, of course, for a person's willingness to attend to an argument in circumstances like these, even though he does not welcome its possible conclusion, is objectivity.

It is less important for our purposes, but important theologically, to realize that a speaker or writer may provide a proof for a group of hearers in the way we have described, but they may be prevented from attending to it by circumstances, not perversity. They may not have the necessary leisure, or may not know his language or technical vocabulary, even if they have the requisite intelligence. Since in such cases it is lack of opportunity that would prevent his being successful in proving his conclusion to them, they could not fairly be blamed for his failure. So it is not surprising that Aquinas, for example, insists that although it is possible to prove God's existence, for most people God has provided other means of making himself known — namely revelation.[19]

The conditions of proof that I have outlined so far apply to proofs of any subject-matter. But I must now comment on a special feature of proofs of the existence of God, and of other Christian doctrines. It is tacitly assumed in most discussions of these proofs that their premises must not 'include' or 'presuppose' the existence of God. This requirement is not the same as our second condition, that the conclusion must not be stated when one states the premises; for one statement can be 'included' or 'presupposed' in an-other, on some natural understandings of these words, without being stated when that other is stated. For example, if a theologian were to argue from the premiss 'All men are sinners' to a conclusion such as 'All men have cut themselves off from God' or 'Only God can rescue humanity', the logic of such an argument might be impeccable, and in the case, at least, of the second conclusion, stating the premiss would not involve stating the conclusion. But the premiss does include or presuppose God's existence, even though no one stating it *states* that God exists. For the concept of sin is a theological concept: necessarily there are no sins if there is no God. If someone were to try to prove God's *existence* from the premiss that men are sinners he might well be greeted with impatience, even though his argument met all the conditions I have laid down for proof. Readers might say he was wasting their time. He might not be, however. If they were people who knew that God existed already, then he would be proving something to them that they already knew. This is not necessarily pointless, because it might show them how things they knew were related to one another, and had unsuspected logical relation-ships. Proofs might deepen our understanding of things we knew before we encountered them. But if the audience to whom the proof was addressed was one consisting of persons who did not previously know that God existed, then it might be pointless to offer *them* an argument whose premises could not be known to be true by someone who did not have this knowledge. Such a proof would fail, of course, by our fourth condition, so ruling it out does not require the addition of an eighth condition of proof. But it is an important feature of the traditional theistic proofs that God's existence not be presupposed in their premises. I have expressed this by saying that the premises must not include theistic statements, which I define as statements which one could not know to be true without knowing that God exists.[20]

I return to the criticisms of the enterprise of proof which we find in Pascal and Kierkegaard. They are based on an insistence that the barrier between man and God is man's corruption and perversity. If this is true, it does nothing whatever to show that the enterprise of proving God's existence must fail.

If men are held back from God by perversity, it does not show there can be no proofs. It only shows that if there are, men will refuse to accept them. They might do this either because God's existence had been proved to them and they irrationally or self-deceivingly rejected it; or they might do it by refusing to attend to arguments which would, if they heeded them, place them in a position where it *would* be irrational to reject it.

If this is true, something else follows. Skeptical criticism is thought by those who use it to undermine the pretensions of reason to prove conclusions, including conclusions about God. If the Skeptic is right, we can never have confidence in reason's power to place any conclusion beyond reasonable doubt. How could the Skeptic's success be thought to be a contribution to faith, even an accidental one? For it would *undermine* the claim that what keeps men from God is their own perversity, by suggesting there is another cause – their intellectual incapacity. It would give us a good reason for doubting whether God exists. If the Skeptic were right, it might still be true that God does exist and that men are kept from him by their own corruption; but it would also be true that no one has yet placed God's existence beyond reasonable doubt. But to concede that is to concede that unbelief has never been exposed as irrational. So what the Skeptic does, if anything, is to provide an *excuse* for not committing ourselves to God. If the Skeptic is wrong, and there are proofs of God, then this shows that many who reject them are being irrational to do so. The sort of irrationality one finds here is deliberate, and this reinforces the judgment that their rejection of God is perverse. The Skeptic gives us a reason for thinking their rejection might not be perverse but conscientious.

So if men are kept from God by their own corruption, it is logically possible that Pyrrhonism is true; but it is not what one would expect.

If someone says there can be no proofs of God, he is saying that there are no true non-theistic statements from which God's existence follows or which render it overwhelmingly probable; or that even if there are, we cannot know them to be true; or that even if there are such statements and some people can know them to be true, no one can see that God's existence follows from them or is rendered overwhelmingly probable by them. Such a position is not proved, or even rendered likely, by holding that men are prevented from knowing God by their own perversity. On the contrary: if this is what it means for proof of God to be unavailable to us, then we are in a situation where denying God's existence is never unreasonable. Men can indeed deny something out of perversity which it is also reasonable to doubt, but if it is reasonable to doubt it, it does not have to be perversity that makes someone reject it. So if the Skeptic demolishes reason, he does not make the claim that unbelief is due to sin more likely, but less likely.

I will now comment more briefly on some of the secondary attacks on proofs of God that Pascal and Kierkegaard make.[21]

(a) The sort of objectivity required for a speaker to prove something to someone is the willingness to recognize relationships between evidence and conclusion, and to see that certain standards are satisfied when one is offered to support the other. It may be that a potential speaker is so absorbed in facts that constitute the conclusion that he regards it as a waste of time to exercise objectivity in this way. It may also be that he is so hostile to the possibility that they might be facts that he will not consider seeing whether there are any premises which serve to prove them. In these cases he cannot prove them. But neither positive nor negative attitudes to a fact *need* prevent someone from proving it. Nor would the fact that he summoned up the objectivity necessary to prove it show that he did not have a particular attitude toward it. Even if we judge objectivity, as I have described it, to be an attitude quite other than the humility and joy that faith requires, it does not follow that such humility and joy cannot be the motives which lead someone to *take up* the attitude of objectivity in order to prove the existence of God to others. (Consider the attitude of detachment a parent might assume towards a wayward child's offences in order to train the child. It would be absurd to insist that such assumed detachment could not be due to love.) Even if a speaker undertook to prove some truth quite frivolously (not realizing at the outset that it *was* a truth, for example), the objectivity he would need to complete his argument efficiently might lead him, and certainly could lead his hearer, into a new seriousness. As far as the hearer of a proof is concerned, the objectivity necessary for him to recognize that a conclusion has been proved to him is the willingness to concede that it is supported in the required manner by its premisses and that he knows these premisses to be true. His hostility to the conclusion may prevent him from summoning this degree of objectivity; so, in a way, might the eagerness he has for it to be true, since he might say "Yes" to the argument when the premisses do not support it adequately. On the other hand, neither might prevent it, and both could generate it. He might hate the conclusion so much that he insisted on the best possible grounds for it, but then be forced into accepting it because this insistence made the speaker do a better job of supporting it. Or he might want it to be true so badly that he left no stone unturned in seeking out incontrovertible grounds for it. If, in Kierkegaard's language such hatred and such yearning are properly called manifestations of subjectivity, these can generate success rather than failure in the enterprise of proof.

(b) It may indeed be true that some thinkers have set about producing supposed proofs of God, and others have set about reading them, in order to avoid dealing with the problems within themselves that are really keeping them from accepting him. There are many culpable forms of procrastination, and this can undoubtedly be one of them. Philosophy is a fertile source of devices to use in the service of indecision – especially perhaps today, where our self-consciousness about the distinction between first- and second-order questions provides another opportunity for distancing from urgent human problems if we abuse it. But it cries out for demonstration that all those who concern themselves with the proofs of God do so for this reason, or that concerning themselves with the proofs of God must always contribute to the postponement of their decisions. I see no plausibility in ascribing such motives to Anselm or Aquinas, or to all of their readers.

(c) Proving God's existence may be presumptuous, or it may not. This is a question about the motives from which a particular speaker undertakes to do it. Perhaps Pascal was right to see this presumption in Descartes, and perhaps Kierkegaard was right to see it in Hegel and his followers. But although this should lead us to be suspicious about this or that thinker's credentials, and should make us *wonder* about his likelihood of succeeding, it proves nothing about proof *per se*, even if we ignore the fact that more creditable motives can be found in other cases. For one thing, something the speaker does for discreditable motives might still serve to lead the hearer into real knowledge, and might even make the speaker himself take the topics of his thinking more seriously. For another, it is not even obvious that when a philosopher introduces God to fill an explanatory gap in his system, his motive is mere professional efficiency. A natural counter-example is Berkeley, whose theories of perception and causality seem to require God. Some readers think that the fact that they require God for their completion shows they are weak. But this was not how Berkeley saw the matter. He saw it as a merit in his system that it showed we cannot understand these fundamental phenomena of human existence without ascribing them to God's agency. He was doing philosophy from a religious motive. And why not?

(d) Faith is not (that is, it cannot be equated with) assent to dogmatic propositions. This is a recurrent theme in theology, particularly since Luther. Faith is most commonly said to be trust in God — *fiducia* rather than *fides*. This is clearly the core of Kierkegaard's argument when he tries to show that what philosophers have sought in eternal truths they can only find through submission to the divine person, a submission which can in turn only come through miraculous divine action. This is less radically opposed to the classical Catholic understanding of faith than it is commonly supposed to be — as we might well imagine from the fact that Pascal holds a similar position. In formulating the Catholic view,[22] Aquinas does understand faith to be assent to truths about God, but he also insists that the truths to which assent is given in faith do not include any that are learned through reason; that the assent is available to us only through supernatural grace; and that faith is incomplete (unformed, as he expresses it) if the believer does not also manifest the related supernatural virtues of hope and charity. But this point must be deferred for the present.[23] Let us, for the moment, ignore it and assume that the contrast is complete, so that faith is as distinct from assent to propositions as Kierkegaard says it is. Where does this carry us? If it is true, it certainly shows that faith is not the immediate intended outcome of a successful proof, for this outcome is the placing of the hearer in a position where, if he attends and is rational, he will assent to its conclusion. Faith, on this view, is not the same as this assent, whether we call the latter belief or knowledge. But it would be hard to support the suggestion that those who have tried to prove God's existence have thought that it is. They have at most thought it would assist men toward faith by showing it to be reasonable, or by showing that the Church, which proclaimed it, had intellectual credentials. This it would do, they have thought, by showing that the being to whom submission was demanded really existed and was righteous toward us. This has been well expressed by E. L. Mascall:

One of the grounds on which traditional theism has refused to base belief in God simply upon the fact of revelation is that revelation itself needs rational justification. To accept something on the authority of revelation is to accept it because one is convinced that God has said it; and this involves a previous conviction of the existence of God. . . . To say that a man's conviction of the existence of God is based upon reason is not to say that he must be capable of setting it out in the form of a technical and logical argument; it does, however, mean that before he can accept anything upon the authority of God, he must first of all have been convinced that there is a God and that God has spoken.[24]

This way of puting it assumes the Thomistic understanding of faith as the assent to truths that come from God. But the same point can readily be made if one views faith solely as trust in God: such trust presupposes the conviction that there is such a being, and that he invites us to trust in him.

Now if God's existence could be proved to someone, and he then did not take steps to change his attitudes so that he could place his life in the hands of such a being, he would be acting perversely. There is no doubt that human beings could be like this. But such behavior would not only be perverse; it would be monstrously *foolish* into the bargain. Human beings could be like that too. This gives us a reason why such a person would resist the process of proof, and would want it very much to fail: he would be vain of his rationality, as we all are, and would not want to be exposed as foolish. Such a person would welcome the Pyrrhonist as an *ally*, since he would give reasons for supposing that the most rational of us could not succeed in the process of proof. Pascal goes to great lengths to convince someone who believes that neither God's existence nor his non-existence can be proved, that he is foolish not to try to trust God in spite of this. It is hard to see why, if he is right to do this, Pyrrhonism could be an ally for faith. For if it can be shown that someone who does not think he can discover whether there is a God is unwise not to act as if there is, it is surely much more obvious that someone who has had God's existence proved to him would be foolish not to do so!

So even if faith is quite distinct from assent to propositions about God, it is hard to see why proving such propositions should hinder it. While it would not itself be faith or produce faith, this would be because those to whom God's existence was proved would refuse to act on it. It would expose them as foolish as well as wicked. The Skeptic would show them not to be foolish in such an obvious way, and so would provide them with an excuse for their reluctance.

(e) Even though faith is not the same as assenting to a doctrine, the fact that it could only come to us through grace would not show that a philosopher who tries to prove a doctrine is seeking to do for himself what grace alone can bring about. For he would be trying to do something quite distinct.

His attempt would only amount to this sort of presumption if he *confused* the possession of faith with the assent to those doctrines he was trying to prove. This could happen, but there is no reason to suppose it must happen, or that it has happened in any actual case. For even those, like Aquinas, who have thought of faith as the assent to doctrines, have not thought that it was assent to those doctrines that they felt they could prove.

THE HIDDENNESS OF GOD

The insistence on God's hiddenness is perhaps the most important legacy of Evangelical Fideism, and its influence is deep and continuing. This influence is in many ways a healthy and necessary one, both in theology and philosophy of religion. Here I have the limited purpose of showing that it cannot sustain the anti-intellectual purposes for which both Pascal and Kierkegaard seek to use it. Both seek to infer that God's hiddenness confirms the Skeptic's rejection of human reason as a proper source of knowledge of God. In dealing with the matter of the traditional proofs, I have argued that their criticisms confuse questions about the epistemological grounding of beliefs with questions about the non-epistemic forces that are also at work when we adopt them or reject them. I shall argue similarly here, and can therefore be briefer.

The doctrine of the hidden God in the *Penseés* is both positive and negative.[25] Positively it teaches that God discloses himself when and where he chooses, and that when he chooses to disclose himself he still discloses himself as mysterious and transcendent. He may, of course, choose to disclose himself in the most unlikely or unexpected corners of human experience, as well as in such things as the glories of nature. Negatively it teaches that God may also choose to conceal himself, even though he is a God of love and consolation, in the face of human pride and corruption. This will mean that one and the same phenomenon will sometimes serve to reveal him to some people and hide him from others, since some will be truly seeking him and others will have made themselves incapable of finding him. Among the latter group will be many presumptuous thinkers who have sought to prove his presence, solely in order to satisfy their desire for intellectual aggrandisement. They are seeking him in the wrong way, or rather not really seeking him at all, and for them the rigors of Skeptical doubt and frustration are a healthy corrective. The doctrine is thus a theological response to the *ambiguity* of human experience, which the negative critiques of the Pyrrhonist can serve to make clear to us. It provides a limited but real explanation of that ambiguity, by showing it to be what one would expect if the Christian proclamation is true. So Pascal applies it both to the signs of God's presence in nature and to the signs of his presence in the revelatory events of the Scriptures.[26] Kierkegaard, of course, concentrates his attention on the latter, emphasizing that even someone close in time and space to the Jesus of history could easily, through his own attitudes, fail to recognize him as God. As the story of the prince and the maiden tells us, if it were impossible for us *not* to recognize the presence of God, our response to it would not be the response of faith and love which God seeks.

In one respect, Kierkegaard in the *Fragments* appears to go much further than Pascal does. Pascal talks as though the signs of God are indeed there, but reason in the grip of corruption is unable to recognize them. Kierkegaard seems to say that there *can be* none, that even to the eye of faith God's revelation does not make clear sense. Not only is the divine teacher paradoxical, but the recognition of him is,[27] since it involves perceiving that which presents itself in a total disguise. While these differences are real and serious, and the one position is not merely a hyperbolic repetition of the other, both have the same claim at their core. It is this claim that I wish to concentrate upon at this stage in the argument. The claim is that man, by his own corruption, has cut himself off from God, so that God alone can restore him; God elects to do this for those who have some willingness to turn to him, but stays hidden from those who do not. These latter include those who seek to reach God through their own rational powers rather than turning to him to rescue them.

An important part of this claim is its assertion of human freedom. The insistence on the necessity for divine grace leads readily, especially in Pascal, to a predestinarian view of the origins of faith – so that if men do turn to God, this turning is itself to be credited ultimately not to them but to him. But in spite of this (and the notorious theological difficulties to which it leads) it is clear that at the human, or psychological, level, both claim that men's corruption is what keeps them from God, and that he reveals himself to those who recognize this and *choose* to turn to him to rescue them from it. Hence there can be no clear sign of God for those who do not make this choice. Philosophical routes to God lead nowhere. Pyrrhonists can show us that this is so. The doctrine of God's hiddenness shows us why.

In order to assess these claims, I wish to introduce a technical expression, which I think will give the reader no difficulty in the light of the earlier remarks about the nature of proof. I wish to speak of *probative phenomena*. A probative phenomenon would be a fact which is known to a hearer, and which, when stated either alone or in conjunction with other facts already

known to the hearer, would prove to him either that God exists or that some
other theistic statement is true.

We can add the following in the light of our earlier discussion,

(1) A hearer made aware of such a phenomenon and its implications can
only deny the theistic conclusion to which it points through irrationality or
self-deception.

(2) A phenomenon that is probative for one person might not be probative for another, in that its probative character might depend on the other
premises with which the statement of it has to be combined, and these latter
might not be within the knowledge of a particular hearer.

(3) Nevertheless, a phenomenon might be probative for a whole community or generation, or at least those members of it with a certain level of
intelligence and experience, since they might all know the fact in question
and the other facts on which its probative character depended, and have the
ability to see its implications when combined with them.

(4) If they rejected the theistic conclusion it established, and did not do
so because they lacked a speaker to present the proof to them, they would
either be guilty of irrationality or self-deception, or be guilty of a wilful
refusal to attend to what a speaker had said or written for them. Such responses would be foolish and probably perverse.

(5) None of these conceptual points shows, of course, that there are, or
have ever been, any probative phenomena — or that there have not.

(6) A Pyrrhonist will not admit there are any probative phenomena, and
will undermine all confidence that we can come to know of any.

(Before proceeding, I should say parenthetically that someone who believes there are probative phenomena is not necessarily denying that all
knowledge of God comes through revelation. Proof and revelation are commonly contrasted, usually because proofs are assumed to begin with premises
that human beings have been able to discover for themselves by observation
or reasoning, whereas revelation is available only from God himself. The
concept of revelation is far too vast a subject to explore here. But if one is
willing, for example, to consider some historical events to be revelatory, then
if those events were known to have occurred by some hearers, and were
events that were quite unexpected but yet in accord with the purposes of
God as these were understood by some believers, then these events might be
probative phenomena as I have defined these. For it might be irrational to
accept that they had occurred and deny some theistic statement, such as the
statement that God cared for his people. They would be different from the
sorts of phenomena that philosophers usually offer in attempted proofs of

God's existence, in that no one without some prior convictions about God's purposes could have predicted that these events would ever happen. But if they were known to have happened, I see no *a priori* reason to suppose that they could not be *both* revelatory *and* probative. In such circumstances an unbeliever, presented with the proof for which they provided the premises, would be most likely to resist it by denying that they are known to have taken place. He would say this just because they would be probative if they *were* known to have taken place. This is of course the general tactic of resistance which Hume recommends us to adopt toward miracle-stories.[28])

I return now to Pascal and Kierkegaard. In the language I have just introduced, they tell us that since God hides himself in the face of human corruption, there are no probative phenomena. The Skeptic, in making us despair of finding any, is therefore performing a service for faith. I wish to show that this is a bad argument.

If God hides himself in the face of human corruption, he may hide himself from human beings who are in the presence of probative phenomena. Our previous arguments suggest several kinds of circumstance in which their corruption might keep him hidden from them when such phenomena were present. Their corruption might hinder them from heeding the presence of these phenomena. It might hinder them from drawing from these phenomena the conclusions they proved. And it might affect some of them so that they drew the conclusions but did so with such reluctance that they did not submit themselves to God and allow their knowledge of him to change their lives. In all these cases they would be responsible for God's remaining hidden from them, for they would be keeping faith at arm's length.

The last of these possibilities is one I have emphasized too little hitherto. I have proceeded in my earlier arguments too much as though someone accepting that God's existence, or some other theistic truth, is proved to him, must act upon it. I cannot enter here into a detailed discussion of the relation between belief and behavior, but it would be counter-intuitive, and also contrary to Christian understandings of human nature, wholly to follow Socrates in holding that what a person believes or knows has to be judged from what he does rather than what he says, for this notoriously obscures the distinction between having a belief and being ready to act upon it, and forces us to construe all weakness of will as a sign of ignorance. Yet both Christianity and common sense make it necessary for us also to be able to distinguish between what someone says, even to himself, that he believes, and what he really does believe, thus making it necessary to question whether assent can ever be wholly 'notional' either.[29] This suggests that assent to a proof of God would entail some personal change, but that this could be confined to a mere discomfort at the foolishness or moral weakness involved in not making a serious effort to act upon it. We might find someone who responded like this taking steps to conceal from himself the real implications of what he had acknowledged. One way of doing this might be to join an undemanding church organization that let him participate in cosy and received practices that could serve as a specious sign of involvement and lull him into complacency. This is the sort of conventional Christianity which a Pyrrhonist might incline to. It is certainly the sort of conventional religiosity which Kierkegaard attacks most heatedly.[30] Another way would be to adjust his understanding of the moral demands to which he saw he was subject so that they did not interfere much with his wordly preferences. This is the sort of behavior which Pascal ascribed, no doubt unfairly, to the Jesuits of his day, and attacked in the *Provincial Letters*. These are ways in which people who encountered and recognized probative phenomena might circumscribe their assent to them and try to ensure that God stayed hidden from them.

Hence there is no good reason to think that the hiddenness of God would show the Skeptic to be right when he questions the reality of probative phenomena. God could be hidden when there are conclusive reasons to believe in him as well as when there are not. If there were such reasons, it would be clearer that this was due to human perversity than if there were no such reasons. So the hiddenness of God would not make the Skeptic an ally of faith, even an unwitting one.

I can now consider the form which the argument from God's hiddenness has most commonly taken in recent years. What appears here is implied in all that Pascal and Kierkegaard say about this theme, but it is still worthwhile to look at more recent presentations. It is claimed that the existence of probative phenomena would be inconsistent with the *freedom* man has to accept God or reject him. If his presence were unambiguous and evident we would be overwhelmed by it, and forced into submission through awe or fear, rather than drawn to it in a free exercise of love. A well-known expression of this argument is to be found in an essay written by Alasdair MacIntyre in 1957:

Suppose religion could be provided with a method of proof. Suppose, for example, as was suggested earlier, that the divine omnipotence was so manifest that whenever anyone denied a Christian doctrine he was at once struck dead by a thunderbolt. No doubt the conversion of England would ensue with a rapidity undreamt of by the Anglican bishops. But since the Christian faith sees true religion only in a free decision made in faith and love, the religion would by this vindication be destroyed. For all the possibility of free choice would have been done away. Any objective justification of belief would have the same effect. Less impressive than thunderbolts, it would equally eliminate all possibility of a decision of faith. And with that, faith too would have been eliminated.[31]

This passage assimilates two quite distinct things. One is the coercion of human beings into submission by some dramatic and frightening sign. The other is the acceptance of what has been placed beyond reasonable doubt. If freedom is destroyed in the first, it is not in the second. There are all sorts of ways in which we can reject what is placed beyond reasonable doubt for us. The most MacIntyre's argument shows is that if our freedom is to be preserved, God will not make himself known in ways that are frightening or overwhelming. It does not show he would not permit his presence to be placed beyond reasonable doubt.

John Hick's views on this matter are well-argued and influential. One expression of them is the following:

We must ask: why should God want to present himself to his human creatures in such an indirect and uncertain way instead of revealing himself in some quite unambiguous fashion that would permit no possible room for doubt as to his reality? Perhaps the answer is that God is leaving men free in relation to himself. Perhaps he has deliberately created an ambiguous world for us just in order that we shall *not* be compelled to be conscious of him. But why not? . . . . God, if he is known to exist, can only be known as the One who makes a total difference for us. For he is known as infinitely higher than us, in worth as well as in power, and as having so made us that our own final self-fulfilment and happiness are also the fulfilment of his purpose for us. I cannot know that such a Being exists and be at the same time indifferent to him. For in knowing him I know myself as created and dependent, a creature on the periphery of existence, whose highest good lies in relation to the divine centre of reality. And so if the man who comes to be conscious of God in this way is to remain a free and responsible personality, the knowledge of God must not be forced upon him, but on the contrary, it must depend upon his own willingness to live in the presence of a higher being whose very existence, when we are conscious of it, sets us under an absolute claim.[32]

My response to this passage is the same as to the passage from MacIntyre. In addition, however, I should say that Hick himself supplies material for an answer in his own concept of 'cognitive freedom'[33] – his term for our ability to exercise control over certain of our beliefs. He recognizes that we can fend off unwelcome knowledge. But this does not show that when we do, the false opinion we cling to has to have any intellectual justification. (It of course may, but it is not necessary that it should.) For what we persist in denying may be provable to anyone in our situation who will attend. He also acknowledges[34] that 'notional' assent to a proof of God might be possible without faith following upon it. But this implies that I *can* "know that such a Being exists and be at the same time indifferent to him" — if I lull myself with sufficient persistence.

There are two points to make in conclusion of this section. First, I have followed Pascal and Kierkegaard in concentrating on the proofs of God. But both insist, of course, as Christians, that God has made himself known in the person of Christ, and that it is only through acknowledging him *there* that man can come to God in faith. My concern here is with the restricted question of whether they have given any reason to suppose that skeptical attacks on human reason are of service to faith. I might seem to have evaded this issue by not speaking directly to what they say about the specific claim that God has disclosed himself by entering history.

Both hold that in entering history as a human person God entered in a way that permitted rejection of him. It does not follow from this, though it may be true, that those who rejected him as he thus appeared in history would have to have rational grounds for doing so — let alone, as Kierkegaard claims, that they would have to have logically conclusive grounds for doing so. Aquinas thought that the Church's claims about Christ are beyond what reason can show to be true, but that we can approach them with a previously-demonstrated knowledge that God exists and is perfect and governs the world in his providence; so there would be strong grounds for accepting the further claims about Christ, though not conclusive ones — so, presumably, there would be some sort of case for rejection. Both he and Pascal are anxious to indicate how the internal evidences of scripture and prophecy point to Jesus as Messiah, though Pascal is of course emphatic that we can readily reject their implications. We should note here that the Gospels contain stories of events which, if they occurred, are candidates for the status of what I have called probative phenomena, though they would have to be probative *revelatory* phenomena, since reason would have had no grounds to expect any of them beforehand without prior theistic knowledge. If this would be the right classification for them, then Kierkegaard is mistaken in saying there is no difference between the status of the contemporary witnesses of Jesus and that of later readers of the scriptures who learn of these events only through reports. For although the former would be as well able to reject Christ as the latter, they might be less able to do so *rationally*.

However this may be, I would maintain that the hiddenness of God does not, even in relation to these central historical claims of the Christian tradition, give us good reason to suppose that faith must be devoid of rational support. It is not requisite for faith that when the Greeks dismiss it as foolishness they have to be right.

My second, and concluding point arises from this. It is true that in spite of the apparent probative phenomena I have referred to, the New Testament seems repeatedly to reject men's demands for signs – "If they hear not Moses and the prophets, neither will they be persuaded, though one rose from the dead."[35] But this rejection probes men's motives in demanding signs, and interprets this demand as a symptom of chronic unwillingness to accept God. This unwillingness, we are told, would not go away if the sign were given. But the very fact that the text says that men would not be presuaded by something that puts God's presence beyond reasonable doubt indicates that there is no theological necessity for his presence *not* to be beyond reasonable doubt. For even if it were beyond reasonable doubt, doubt would continue. So freedom and epistemic distance are not necessarily connected. If they have been thought to be, this again is due to confusion between questions about the epistemological grounding of beliefs and questions about the non-epistemic forces at work when men accept or reject them.

FAITH, REASON, AND THE HEART

Although a comprehensive account is out of the question here, I must begin this section with a brief outline of Pascal's doctrine of the three Orders (of body, mind, and charity) and the closely-related doctrine of the heart.[36] The three Orders represent three realms or levels in which life is lived, and it is clear that they stand in an ascending scale of value. Each has its own proper objects – physical things, intellectual constructions, and spiritual relationships. Each corresponds to a particular human faculty or group of powers – the senses and desires, the reason, and the heart. Each is the realm of certain human responses – fear and desire, intellectual enquiry and assent, and love and faith. Each dominates in a particular group or type – the rich and powerful, the scientific and philosophical, and the saintly. While Pascal speaks of spiritual progress as an upward movement through the lower two Orders to the third, each clearly has a proper and real place, since man has a body and an intellect as well as a spirit. Progress would therefore appear to be from a condition where the lower faculties dominate to one where they are suitably subordinate to the heart.

The doctrine of the heart is central, profound, but only partly developed. It is clear that the heart is as capable of corruption as other faculties. Indeed, in our fallen state the heart is hollow and full of filth.[37] It will only guide our lives as it should when God speaks to it and man responds in faith, and only then will the other human faculties play their proper roles in our life.

But even in our unregenerate state, the heart, not the senses or the reason, is our innermost personality. One of Pascal's most famous observations tells us that the heart has its reasons of which reason knows nothing.[38] This is of course a rejection of Descartes' definition of the self as a thinker, but it does not equate the self with feeling, as some think it does, or even with instinct — for the heart is said to have *reasons*, an almost Freudian observation. For our present purposes, however, it is most important to note that Pascal says[39] the heart is a source of *knowledge*. This is knowledge which the Skeptic is right to say reason cannot prove, but wrong to say we do not really know. Pascal's examples are 'first principles' such as the knowledge that space has three dimensions, or that the series of numbers is infinite. Reason has to presuppose these, and cannot prove them. The same is true of our knowledge that we are not dreaming. It is because the heart teaches us these things that Pyrrhonism is not, to Pascal, a real possibility for human beings. We must also note that he says[40] that we have no assurance that we are awake rather than asleep without *faith*. His position would seem, then, to be that in addition to the religious faith that can only come to us when God is known by the heart, there is also a secular faith in which the heart teaches us truths which reason cannot prove, but must assume to be true to advance our knowledge or guide our affairs.

We can compare this with Kierkegaard's claim that both secular faith and Christian faith involve a 'leap', the former being a leap that is possible for the human will, and the latter requiring a miracle for the will to perform it. The two positions share a common assumption: that our commonsense beliefs are incapable of proof by reason. They also share the view that our natures enable us to overcome this in practice; to Pascal this happens because the heart gives us knowledge of fundamental principles which reason can take for granted, whereas in Kierkegaard it happens because the person of commonsense performs an act of will to overleap the gap that reason cannot bridge — an act of will which is the counterpart of the Skeptic's supposed will to suspend judgment. The third thing on which they agree is that the same power in our natures should enable us to turn to God, but does not do so because of the depth of human corruption. Only grace can bring about our release from this self-imposed incapacity. Kierkegaard repeatedly insists that such an act of grace is miraculous, underlining this by his claim that what one accedes to in faith is paradoxical.

We can discern here two similar versions of what I have called the Parity Argument.[41] It is alleged there is an analogy between many of our common-sense convictions and faith in God, an analogy which is marked by the use of the word 'faith' for the former also. It is said that the Pyrrhonian attacks on reason can reveal the lack of rational justification for the former, and it is implied that it must therefore be non-intellectual factors alone which hold men back from the latter, since both kinds of faith are in the same state epistemologically.

This argument is very popular. How often one hears that faith is needed for all the day-to-day dealings of life! And how often it is inferred that only obstinacy can stand in the way of our showing a similar faith in God! Few arguments are more facile and irritating. Nevertheless, the Parity Argument should not be dismissed too quickly.

I have argued earlier that if God exists and only human corruption stands in the way of our recognizing him, it would be surprising if the Skeptical assessment of grounds for belief in God were true. For if they were true, they would provide an excuse for hesitation, since they would show that it was not irrational. The Parity Argument suggests a counter to this. If God exists, and, however surprisingly, Pyrrhonism *is* true, and its Skeptical hesitations apply both to religion and to common sense, there would have to be some special factor, other than our inability to support it by argument, which kept us from religious faith *if* we were not also held back from common sense beliefs, since they could not be supported by argument either. This might well be the corruption that the Christian doctrine of sin imputes to us. There is an obvious appearance of inconsistency here, which would have to be accounted for. It would only exist, of course, if Pyrrhonism were true, and undermined common sense as well as faith. But because this argument can be mounted if it is true, we can see some reason for the apologist to welcome Pyrrhonist arguments – if only to make a virtue of necessity when proofs of God fail him. If we are prepared to say our natures or our circumstances force us to disregard Pyrrhonist argument at the common sense level, why do we not say the same about them at the religious level?

I would like to consider some possible responses to the Parity Argument as I have presented it.

(1) There is first the response of the Pyrrhonian. He would embrace neither secular faith nor religious faith, remaining instead with appearances and suspending judgment both about common sense and about religion. The Conformist Fideist response is a special variant of this, available to a Skeptic who lives in an environment that has conditioned him to easy participation in religious rituals. Of course, neither of these responses preserves

the reality of faith. But since, within limits, Pyrrhonism seems to be practically viable, this form of response evades the charge of inconsistency without entailing religious commitment.

(2) Let us suppose, however, that we follow the urgings of common sense and commit ourselves to its principles. Is rejection of faith then inconsistent, given that we do not claim to have rational justification for those principles? The common-sense unbeliever might well respond as follows. Both Pyrrhonism and faith are radically at odds with common sense, and there is no better case, therefore, for dubbing common sense 'secular faith' than for suggesting it could be a form of Skepticism. This is, if anything, supported by the analogies we were able to draw between Skepticism and faith earlier,[42] for these depended on contrasting both of them with common sense living and thinking. Common sense just *is* that field of beliefs which the Pyrrhonist recommends we hold back from and the religious believer urges us to exceed. It is unatural to do either. The commitments of common sense are effortless — in this sense it is very misleading for Kierkegaard to have suggested they need an act of will; for it takes effort only to hold back from them or to go beyond them.

This is all true. But the Parity Argument can at least account for it. The effort we have to exert *not* to yield to common sense is taken as indicative of the falsehood, or at least the non-viability, of Pyrrhonism. The effort we have to exert to exceed it in the direction of faith is held to be a sign of corruption. When the latter is removed, faith becomes as natural in the religious sphere as in the secular.

(3) The force of the Parity Argument is of a very restricted kind. It suggests only that the commitments of faith are in no worse a position in relation to reason than those of common sense. It is vital to recognize that precisely the same argument could be mounted in defence of a theoretically indefinite number of systems, theistic or not, which offer liberation from some alleged disease of the soul, and are prepared to say that unbelief is a symptom of that disease. The Argument does not offer a reason for accepting any, or a reason to prefer one to another. All it does, and this is not wholly negligible, is suggest that if the commitments of common sense are groundless, restricting oneself to them is arbitrary.

(4) An opponent of the Parity Argument who tries to defend himself against this charge is best advised to find characteristics of secular common sense which distinguish it from faith in a way that provide some rational ground for not moving from the one to the other. One way of doing this is to say that the commitments of common sense are in some way indispensable,

whereas those of religious faith are not. Another is to say that the demands of faith are psychologically damaging in ways that those of common sense are not. A third is to suggest that the commitments of common sense entail intellectual consequences that undermine the claims of faith, so that the two kinds of commitment are inconsistent with each other. We find all three lines of argument in David Hume, whose philosophy of religion is in part an attempt to combine some of the legacy of Pyrrhonism with an emphatic rejection of religious faith, and thus to neutralize the Parity Argument. In the next chapter I examine his views.

A note in conclusion. It would be cowardly to say nothing about the distinctively Kierkegaardian thesis that faith requires us to embrace Paradox. I do not think that anything I have said above need be modified if 'paradox' does not mean, or at least include, 'self-contradiction'. If it does mean this, however, then Kierkegaard's position is identical for the most part with that stated by Bayle, and the criticism I have made of Bayle applies to Kierkegaard also.[43] Saying that something is paradoxical, in this sense, is logically equivalent to saying it can be demonstrated to be false (or to be false by the light of reason, as Bayle puts it). If I have argued correctly, one cannot judge this of what someone claims and not believe that what he claims *is* false. This does not mean, however, that one cannot *also*, through prior conditioning or later transforming experience, believe it. What then follows is a conflict of beliefs. This conflict need not be agonizing. It can even seem speciously liberating if its true nature is concealed. One can live with it quite readily if one misdescribes it. One way of misdescribing it is the way Kierkegaard and Bayle choose: the way of talking of one belief as the product of one teacher, reason, and the other as the product of another teacher, grace. This is self-deception, but it can be effective. For it looks like a commendable exercise of freedom to choose what is offered by a higher teacher and turn away from what is offered by a lower. But as long as one believes that what is offered by the higher is *self-contradictory*, one can only *say* that one has turned one's back on what reason teaches. One can keep reason's instructions at the notional level, but not eliminate them. If faith requires that one do this, it requires that one must make commitments while at the same time also holding them to be false. Faith that requires this is a form of self-deception – and self-deception is a misuse of reason, not an escape from it.

NOTES

[1] The attack on indicative signs is to be found in PH II, 97–133, and M VIII, 141–229. The discussion of proof is at PH II, 134–192. On natural theology, see PH III, 2–12 and M IX, 13–194 – and the whole of Cicero's *De Natura Deorum*.

[2] While not unperceptive, Kierkegaard's treatment of Skepticism is not first hand or free of errors. See the notes by Niels Thulstrup to Chapter III and the Interlude in the *Fragments*.

[3] 190/543.

[4] See the *Summa Contra Gentiles*, I, 4.

[5] 449/556. See also 781/242.

[6] 429/229.

[7] In the interim, that is to say, we would merely understand that there *has to be* some explanation.

[8] 521/387.

[9] See the essay 'Hume and Kierkegaard' already cited, and the paper 'Kierkegaard and Skepticism' in the volume of essays entitled *Kierkegaard*, ed. by Josiah Thompson, Doubleday, New York, 1972.

[10] *Fragments*, p. 65. See also Thulstrup's notes to this passage.

[11] 445/558.

[12] What follows immediately is a brief presentation of a position I first worked out, more fully, in *Problems of Religious Knowledge*, Macmillan, London, and Seabury, New York, 1971. See particularly Chapters 2 and 3.

[13] I omit here the special case of *reductio ad absurdum* proofs, which could be said to proceed without premises altogether. See *Problems of Religious Knowledge*, p. 27–28.

[14] I have assumed throughout that the premises and conclusion of a proof are *statements*. (See the second condition.) In the alternative use of 'proof' they could be sentences or formulae.

[15] This is partly because he follows his creator in thinking that *no* matter of fact can be demonstrated in this way.

[16] I foolishly missed this in my earlier discussion. I am indebted here to Professor Robert A. Oakes.

[17] *Problems of Religious Knowledge* p. 32–35.

[18] Presumably this would be a proof in the more restricted sense, which illustrates the relationship between the two senses.

[19] See *Summa Contra Gentiles* I, 4, *Summa Theologiae* la, 1,1.

[20] On the assumption that all Christian doctrines are theistic statements in this sense, if anyone should seek to prove one of them without first proving that God exists, while beginning with non-theistic premises, he might, in principle succeed if we admit that someone might come to know the conclusion of his argument and the existence of God simultaneously. I cannot explore this here, however.

[21] See above, pp.

[22] *Summa Teologiae* 2a2ae, 1–7.

[23] See Chapter 8.

[24] E. L. Mascall, *He Who Is*, Longmans, London, 1954, p. 27.

[25] For a fine treatment of this theme see Hazelton, *Blaise Pascal*, pp. 122–128.

[26] This is the basis of his doctrine of figurative meanings. See, for example, 501/659, 502/571.

[27] See *Fragments*, p. 81.

[28] *Enquiry Concerning Human Understanding*, Section X. I discuss the concept of a probative revelatory phenomenon in *Problems of Religious Knowledge* pp. 94–99 and 107–111.

[29] The term comes from Newman's *The Grammar of Assent*.

[30] In *Training in Christianity* and *Attack Upon Christendom*.

[31] Alasdair MacIntyre, 'The Logical Status of Religious Belief' in *Metaphysical Beliefs* ed. by MacIntyre, SCM Press, London, 1957, p. 209.

[32] John Hick, *Christianity at the Centre*, SCM. Press, London, 1968, pp. 55–56.

[33] He introduces the term in his *Faith and Knowledge*, Cornell University Press, Ithaca, 1966, p. 127.

[34] See his *Arguments for the Existence of God*, Macmillan, London, and Seabury, New York, 1971, pp. 105–106.

[35] Luke 16: 31.

[36] Here again, see the studies by Broome and Hazelton.

[37] 139/143.

[38] 423/277.

[39] 110/282.

[40] 131/434.

[41] See above, Chapter 2.

[42] See above, Chapter 2.

[43] See above, Chapter 3.

CHAPTER 6

SKEPTICISM, PARITY, AND RELIGION:
THE CASE OF HUME

> To be a philosophical sceptic is, in a man of letters, the first and most essential step towards being a sound, believing Christian.

This is the most explicit endorsement of Skeptical Fideism on record. It comes from Philo's concluding speech in Hume's *Dialogues Concerning Natural Religion*. It is remarkable because Hume is almost universally (and certainly correctly) judged to be an anti-religious writer and secularizer. Admittedly Philo is a character Hume creates, and Hume is therefore not saying this in his own person; but it is most common today, and I think it is right, to read the *Dialogues* as though Philo speaks for Hume himself throughout the work. To explain how Philo comes to say this as the book ends is a major task of Hume interpretation.

Hume interpretation is not my major concern here, and I have made what contribution I can to this aspect of it elsewhere.[1] My task is rather to see what Hume can teach us about the relationship between faith and Skepticism. To do this, I shall first try to outline the place Skepticism occupies in Hume's system, and evaluate what he says about it. I shall then try to use this to determine how his very influential criticisms of religion are affected by the particular form of Skepticism I think he adopts, and to evaluate the complex response he develops to what I have called the Parity Argument.

SKEPTICISM AND NATURALISM IN HUME'S PHILOSOPHY

On the surface no two thinkers could be more different from one another than Pascal and Hume. Certainly their objectives are exactly opposed, each adopting commitments that the other passionately rejects. But there are instructive parallels too, and their attitudes to the Pyrrhonian tradition bring these out most clearly. Both would agree that Skepticism exposes the emptiness of rationalist philosophical systems. Both would also agree that this emptiness extends to the realm of natural, or philosophical, theology. Both find the Pyrrhonian suspense of judgment a practical impossibility. Each finds the Skeptic's omnivorous doubts and questions deeply disturbing, and sees Pyrrhonism, therefore, as leading to anxiety and despair, not tranquillity.

And each finds instinctive resources in human nature which protect us from that anxiety by committing us to beliefs which make human life possible. They divide, however, at this point. One minor difference is that Pascal is prepared to say that these beliefs, in secular cases, constitute knowledge, whereas Hume speaks only of natural *beliefs*. The major difference is that Pascal urges us to conquer the wretchedness we find in the human life we enter by opening ourselves to faith; but Hume, thinking that faith, too, is another, needless source of anxiety and distress, holds that only by confining ourselves to secular concerns can peace of mind be a real possibility for us. He is quite aware that stopping short of religious commitment in this way opens him to charges of inconsistency, and it is one of his continual concerns to avoid this.

Hume is not only accused of inconsistency, like any other philosopher. He is also quite often thought to be guilty of *frivolity*. Certainly Pascal would not have been slow to accuse him of it. There is much in the ease and elegance and irony of his style that seems to support this judgment if one is minded to make it. But the judgment is mistaken. What such a perception of Hume misses is that when he seems to make light of things that others treat with solemnity, this is not the manifestation of temperamental frivolity, but something quite opposite. It is the deliberate application of a doctrine. The doctrine is that of the impotence of philosophical reasoning. Hume's central philosophical message is that we should not take philosophy itself too seriously. And this message comes to us from someone who is temperamentally inclined to do this. When we gaze at the fat and complacent-looking figure who stares at us from Allan Ramsay's portrait and think of all the stories of the charming and irreverent and clubbable Hume, it is too easy to imagine that the famous irony comes from a temperamental immunity to philosophical anxieties. There is plenty of evidence that this was not so. The *Treatise of Human Nature*, which was completed by the time he was twenty-six, is a work whose pages fairly glow with the excitement of intellectual innovation. In order to write it, Hume had to undergo financial hardship and emotional stress. He reveals the extent of this stress in one of his most famous letters, written to an unnamed physician in 1734, not long before his departure for France, where the *Treatise* was finally written. The letter does not seem to have been sent, but it was, significantly, kept by Hume all his life.[2] In it he tells how his mental exertions had produced the 'Disease of the Learned', a 'coldness and desertion of the spirit', accompanied by such psychosomatic symptoms as 'scurvy spots' on the fingers, 'wateriness in the mouth', and a sudden ravenous appetite which seems to have been the initial cause of his famous corpulence. At the close of the letter he tells us of his resolve to deal with these distresses by a period of activity in business. This activity was a failure, but the same pattern of anxiety and attempted release finds expression in the famous passages with which he concludes the first Book of the *Treatise*. Here he tells us, in prose in which I find no trace of irony, that his philosophical perplexities have led him into such melancholy and isolation that he fancies himself 'some strange uncouth monster', and is 'in the most deplorable condition imaginable'. He continues:

Most fortunately it happens, that since reason is incapable of dispelling these clouds, nature herself suffices to that purpose, and cures me of this philosophical melancholy and delirium, either by relaxing this bent of mind, or by some avocation, and lively impression of my senses, which obliterate all these chimeras. I dine, I play a game of backgammon, I converse, and am merry with my friends; and when after three or four hours' amusement, I would return to these speculations, they appear so cold, and strained, and ridiculous, that I cannot find it in my heart to enter into them any farther.[3]

At the personal level, therefore, Hume sees himself as one of a minority who have a predilection for philosophical thought. Unfortunately this predilection leads only to bewilderment and despair, for philosophy cannot answer the questions that it forces us to ask. The only cure for this despair is a recognition of the limits of philosophy and an absorption in common affairs and human society. Fortunately this release is available, for the philosopher does share a common human nature with the rest of mankind, and a reasonable apportionment of his time will be enough to ensure that the resources of our common nature will overcome the distempers that philosophy generates. It is interesting that Hume had a special venom in reserve when he criticized what he calls the 'monkish virtues' of the ascetic and the solitary. Such persons cut themselves off, by policy, from those very natural and social resources which serve as the corrective to theory and dogma.

So the fat and cheery Hume of tradition is real enough, but as a self-conscious *persona*. He is the deliberate achievement of a man who knows better, not less well, than his opponents what a hard taskmaster philosophy can be. Such a *persona* has to be deliberately sustained. Hume sustained it by his social proclivities, by extensive achievements in areas outside philosophy itself, such as economics and history, and by a refusal to engage in controversy with those who assaulted him in print; but, above all, he sustained it by systematic theory. Much of this theory consists of his psychological exploration of the imagination, including the doctrine of association of ideas. I can only concern myself here with the way he applies this body of theory to take the measure of the Skeptical tradition.

There are still well-informed philosophers who find it odd that anyone should even suggest that Hume is not a Skeptic. To most students of philosophy the two paradigms of Skepticism are the Descartes of the first *Meditation* and the Hume of the fourth and fifth sections of the first *Enquiry*. But it has come to be quite widely held that Hume's views, rightly understood, are not Skeptical at all.

The former opinion is the one held by many of Hume's own contemporaries, particularly Reid and Beattie, and presented at length by T. H. Green in his introduction to the Green and Grose edition of Hume's Philosophical Works.[4] It is taken as nearly self-evident by many students because they are confined in their studies of Hume to the first book of the *Treatise* and to Sections IV—VII of the *Enquiry Concerning Human Understanding*, of which it is the most natural and obvious reading. The attendant understanding of Hume represents him as the thinker who drew out the implications of Locke's 'Way of Ideas' and showed how it leads inexorably to unanswerable doubts about induction, perception, and self-identity. The latter opinion of Hume is due primarily to the work of Norman Kemp Smith, who represents Hume as a *naturalist*: someone whose main objective is to reveal those forces in human nature that govern our factual beliefs, out emotions, and our moral lives, and to show the inadequacies of rationalist interpretations of them.[5] As seen in this interpretation, Hume becomes a common-sense philosopher, not a subverter of common sense; for he represents all of us, himself included, as inescapably committed by our very natures to certain beliefs and to certain emotional and evaluative responses to our physical and social environment.

The basis of a solution is surely that the Reid—Beattie interpretation and the Kemp Smith interpretation are not incompatible. If Hume's objective is to reveal the sources of our beliefs and evaluations in human nature, it is a perfectly proper part of such an inquiry to argue that these beliefs and evaluations do not result from our having discovered good reasons for them, and are unaffected by the subsequent revelation that no good reasons for them exist. Such a conclusion would imply that one should seek their causes elsewhere. Conversely, if Hume decides that our most basic beliefs concerning matters of fact are beliefs for which there are no good reasons, it is perfectly consistent with this to go on to ask what it is about us that makes us hold them nevertheless, and whether it is possible for us to suspend them or abandon them. I would suggest, then, that Hume is both a Skeptic and a naturalist: that he does say that our basic beliefs about matters of fact are devoid of rational justification, that he offers us detailed accounts of how we come to hold them and why we cannot abandon them, and that these accounts are

applications of a general understanding of human nature that is applied elsewhere to our emotional lives and to our moral and social evaluations. Hume's
Skepticism is not something incompatible with his naturalism. It is an integral
part of it.

So far I have been arguing that Hume's Skepticism is closely integrated
with his naturalism, but I have not said much about the nature of either. I
now must do this, for one of Hume's best-informed interpreters, Richard
Popkin, has identified them.[6] He reminds us that one of Hume's overt concerns is to define the relationship between his own Skepticism and that of
the Pyrrhonians; and he argues that Hume, partly through misinterpretation,
arrives at a position that is in fact merely a consistent version of theirs. While
I find this illuminating, I do not think it is quite right.

Hume does indeed seem to misinterpret Pyrrhonism — if we take this to be
the views of Sextus. At least he ignores the practical accommodations Sextus
allows the Skeptic, and the natural assent to appearances. But I do not see
this as a fundamental misunderstanding. For Sextus's position still requires
an inner suspense of judgment about the conformity of appearances to reality,
and it is precisely this that Hume says we are not at liberty to exercise. "Nature, by an absolute and uncontrollable necessity has determined us to judge
as well as to breathe and feel."[7] He does not say that the Pyrrhonists' *arguments* are unsound; he even adds some of his own. But he insists that the
suspense of judgment they recommend is beyond us. We cannot even say,
with Sextus, "Yes, I realize that there is no good reason to suppose that my
sensations are veridical, but I will do what comes naturally and act as though
they are". Neither the plain man nor the philosopher can refrain from believing that they *are* veridical. We cannot make our assertions *un*dogmatically.

So I think that the form of Skepticism Hume *does* adopt; though it is
very close indeed to what Popkin finds in Hume, is more at variance than
Popkin thinks it is with the views of Sextus. The Humean Skeptic, according to
Popkin, recognizes the psychological impotence of Pyrrhonian arguments and
dogmatizes where it is natural to do so, in full recognition of his dogmatism
and of the groundlessness of it. He also accepts that nature does, for some of
us, encourage doubts and uncertainties at least for short periods, so that one
is still following nature if one engages in the attendant suspense of judgment
if one can. So the Humean Skeptic is hesitant and dogmatic by turns, as
nature encourages him. Such a thinker is bound to oscillate between a more
suspenseful mood while he is doing philosophy, and a more dogmatic mood
when playing backgammon. But he will follow nature more consistently than
the classical Pyrrhonian, who will be trying to suspend judgment in the most

unnatural way, both in his study and out of it. That way is not the way to *ataraxia*, but to madness.

This sort of Skeptic, alternating from nature between suspense and dogmatism, is indeed the Hume of the seventh, and concluding, section of Book I of the *Treatise*: the Hume who is openly and endearingly, and I think unironically, torn between Skeptical doubt and common-sense dogma. But there is one respect in which Popkin is superficial. He says that the classical Pyrrhonian will not achieve *ataraxia* by suspending judgment, because the attempt to suspend judgment constantly is unnatural. This may be so; but it does not seem to me to be this that Hume sees as the undesirable feature of Skeptical doubt. He regards it as independently disturbing, even when it is the result of the indulgence of a natural inclination to philosophize. That sort of inclination *is* natural, but it is also hazardous. We have seen evidence that Hume did find philosophical perplexity conducive to exhaustion and melancholia. He says this, again, more or less, in the *Treatise*:

But what have I here said, that reflections very refined and metaphysical have little or no influence upon us? This opinion I can scarce forbear retracting, and condemning from my present feeling and experience. The *intense* view of these manifold contradictions and imperfections in human reason has so wrought upon me, and heated my brain, that I am ready to reject all belief and reasoning, and can look upon no opinion even as more probable or likely than another. Where am I, or what? From what causes do I derive my existence, and to what condition shall I return? Whose favor shall I court, and whose anger must I dread? What beings surround me? and on whom have I any influence, or who have any influence on me? I am confounded with all these questions, and begin to fancy myself in the most deplorable condition imaginable, environed with the deepest darkness, and utterly deprived of the use of every member and faculty.[8]

Consequently, I think that it is not the unnaturalness of Skeptical doubts but their capacity to produce anxiety that makes Hume say the wise Skeptic will keep them in their place. In the *Treatise* this seems mostly to amount to a decision to indulge in philosophy only when so inclined, and to escape from its tribulations into social life when they become too much. But this recognition of the hazardousness of philosophy leads him in the first *Enquiry* to a more formal attempt to limit Skepticism, by limiting the subject matter of philosophical reflection as well as the psychological occasion of it. I refer, of course, to the introduction there of the concept of *mitigated Skepticism*, which Hume recommends to us as a mode of thought whose virtues can be made obvious to us if we have learned humility about the powers of our reason from indulgence in the Pyrrhonian variety.[9]

Hume characterizes mitigated Skepticism in three ways. First, it embodies a humility about the powers of reason, which may be a fruit of the study of Pyrrhonian arguments against it. Second, it 'confines itself to common life', and its decisions are 'nothing but the reflections of common life, methodized and corrected'. Finally, he deduces from this restriction that the Skeptic will confine himself to 'abstract reasoning concerning quantity or number' and 'experimental reasoning concerning matter of fact and existence'. This counsel of humility leads him to his final famous peroration about commiting writings that are more ambitious than this to the flames.

I will try at this point to summarize what I take to be Hume's overall position with regard to Skepticism.

(1) He agrees with the Pyrrhonians that the beliefs of common life and the constructions of divinity and school metaphysics are devoid of rational justification.

(2) He disagrees with the Pyrrhonian Skeptics in their recommendation that the philosopher should in consequence withhold assent from the beliefs of common life and the constructions of divinity and school metaphysics alike. He has at least three reasons for saying this. (a) It is psychologically impossible for us *not* to assent to the beliefs of common life. (b) The Skeptical attacks on these beliefs, though admitting of no answer, also produce no conviction: so not only is the assent to those beliefs something we are unable initially to withhold; it is also something that cannot subsequently be withdrawn. (c) Even if the assent could be withheld or withdrawn, to do so would produce not the inner calm and unperturbedness the Pyrrhonian pursues but the very anxiety he is seeking to avoid. In this respect, the questioning of the Skeptic is in the same position as the constructions of the theologian and the metaphysician. Consequently, one is as hazardous to our peace of mind as the other.

(3) The result of this is a recommendation to indulge our propensity to philosophical thought, if we personally have such a propensity, to the minimum. This recommendation takes different forms. (a) In the *Treatise* it amounts to a recommendation to indulge in philosophical speculation only on those occasions when we are minded to do so, and even then to treat it as a pastime in which nature has disposed us to participate. Its hazards are to be dealt with by making sure that we also participate actively in those social pursuits that will distract us from the rarefied doubts and wonders that beset us in our studies. (b) In the *Enquiry* this on-again-off-again policy is replaced by the positivist recommendations of mitigated Skepticism: instead of trying to contain philosophy by rationing the amount of time we spend on it, we should contain it by confining its subject matter, so that it is critical and

descriptive, not revisionary or speculative. Philosophy, thus understood, would become the journeyman study of those processes of reasoning we must use in common life and in science, where we presuppose and do not question the regularity of nature, the reality of the external world, and the identity of the self, and do not attempt to get above ourselves by treating of God, freedom, and immortality. Examples of this sort of activity would be his own comments on how we should estimate probabilities or judge of causes and effects.

The most obvious criticism of what Hume says concerns the consistency of mitigated Skepticism. How can he recommend that we confine ourselves to the reflections of common life, when their presuppositions are as incapable of rational justification as the pretensions of metaphysics? Surely Hume should either indulge both or reject both? How can Skepticism consistently *be* mitigated?

I think Hume's answer is as follows. Although it is true that the natural beliefs of common sense and the speculative constructions of metaphysics and religion are alike devoid of rational justification; and although it is also true that human nature admits within it forces that make it natural, in some manner or other, to engage in both; the forces that impel us to adopt the beliefs of common life are found in all men, whereas those that lead us into metaphysics or into religion are found only in *some* men. Metaphysics is a relative rarity, indulged in only by philosophers. Religion is not a rarity in the same way, but the forces that produce it are *pathological* forces, such as the superstitious fear of the unknown, and fortunate men in civilized communities can be free from them. So the real reason for restricting philosophical thought to the affairs of common life is that our pursuit of those affairs is the result of beliefs that none of us can avoid having, whereas the fancies of the metaphysician and the theologian can be avoided with a bit of luck and judgment. The difficulty is that even though some men are incurious about metaphysics and are free of superstitious anxiety, it might still be impossible for *other* men, such as you or I or Hume, to avoid wondering about the origin of the world or the immortality of the soul. Even though some commitments may be universal and some not, it might still be that those who are committed to the latter are as unable to avoid their commitment as they are to avoid the commitments that everybody else makes. Our inabilities may just vary; and the cautious advice of the mitigated Skeptic may be advice that can be taken only by those who do not need it.

So the mitigated Skepticism of the *Enquiry* accords less well with Hume's philosophical psychology than the quasi-Pyrrhonism of the *Treatise*, however much Hume the positivist and secularizer may wish to resort to it.

I have so far suggested that Hume rejects the way of classical Pyrrhonism for three reasons.

(1) He does not think we are able to withhold assent from the beliefs of common life.

(2) He does not think that anything Pyrrhonists may say can enable us to *withdraw* assent from these beliefs once we have acquired them.

(3) Suspense of judgment leads not to peace of mind but rather to anxiety.

I have little to say about the third of these propositions. It seems to me that the effect of philosophical perplexity upon human nature is unlikely to be uniform, and that Hume may be right about its effect on some people and wrong about its effect on others. But for his opinion to be based on experience (as I have suggested it is), and for it to form the basis of a recommendation that we indulge ourselves in philosophy in modest doses, it is obviously necessary to modify the doctrine that we cannot withdraw our assent to the beliefs of common life. If we could not do it at all, we obviously could not be distressed by doing it, or be urged to do it only in moderation. What Hume has to say, and does say, is that those who can be afflicted by philosophical doubts can be spared their distressing consequences because these doubts are only short-lived and cannot survive the transition from the study to the world outside.

I turn now to the other two contentions. Hume has a moderately complex argument, I think, in support of the claim that we cannot *not* assent to the beliefs of common life.[10] I suggest that it goes as follows. There are no good reasons in favor of the beliefs of common life. Hence we do not hold those beliefs because we have such reasons. The only reasons that have been offered are all bad ones; they are known only to the philosophers who have invented them; and the philosophers themselves have held the beliefs they have attempted to justify before inventing their reasons. Hence not only is our assent to our natural beliefs not dependent on our having good reasons for them; it also is not dependent on our having bad reasons for them that we think are good. Therefore, we hold these beliefs not for reasons at all, but only because of *causes*, such as laziness, custom, or habit.

I think this argument is unsuccessful.[11] Hume is clearly right in insisting that philosophical arguments have no share in the genesis of our natural beliefs, but he does not succeed in showing that *reason* has no role in their genesis. Even if we agree that we have no good reasons for them, it might still very well be the case that we *thought* we had good reasons. To prove that to be untrue Hume would have to show, as he realizes, that the only reasons that have ever been thought of are those that the philosophers have thought of. But this is very implausible, even on Hume's own accounts of the origins of our beliefs. What Hume calls custom or habit is manifested in our inferences from the past to the future: right or wrong, surely our doing this is something that we *think* to be rational? Our belief in the distinct and continued existence of our perceptions may be due, as he says, to the constancy they show and the fact that assuming their continuance makes it easier to anticipate them: but right or wrong, surely we *think* this basis is rational? And our belief in personal identity may be due to our confusing successions of related perceptions with continuous unchanging ones, but surely the ascription of identity in such circumstances is *thought* to be rational when we make it?

Hume's argument in support of the claim that our assent to the beliefs of common life cannot be *withdrawn* is, I think, this. The Pyrrhonian Skeptic shows us quite successfully that there are no good reasons in favor of these beliefs. But since these beliefs are not there because we have ever thought there are such reasons, we are naturally unaffected by the revelation that no such reasons exist. The Pyrrhonian's arguments are unanswerable, but they are also impotent, or 'vain'.

I think this, also, is a bad argument. Even if it were true that my beliefs are not due to my thinking they have good reasons, it by no means follows that when I am shown that they have no good reasons, they will remain unaffected. The discovery of their lack of epistemic respectability may nullify all the causes that have produced them. There is, in any case, some clear evidence that the encounter with Pyrrhonian arguments does at least have some shock value: even if we are no more rational than Hume says we are, we at least mildly aspire to be. Hume's recognition of this fact appears in his qualification, already noted, of the doctrine that Skeptical doubts are ineffectual. He says instead that they produce only a 'momentary amazement and confusion' and that involvement in daily affairs destroys their effects.

I have already argued that the classical Skeptic's repertoire can respond to this.[12] Given that philosophical questioning can undermine common sense beliefs for shorter periods, it would be possible to sustain these doubts deliberately for longer ones. We might here depart from a life of natural inclination; but this would not prove the Skeptic's doubts were 'vain' ones.

Neither the classical Pyrrhonist nor Hume describes the possibilities correctly. Sextus fails in his attempt to describe the Skeptic way as one where he yields to appearances without belief; what he actually describes is a way that can only be followed consistently as a pattern of deliberate and sustained minimizing of belief. This is a pattern, however, which Hume has not shown to be an impossible one. Since he admits that some of us have a tendency to engage in philosophical questioning and reflection, he has himself to admit that they can make inroads into our natures. *His* policy is the very different one of minimizing and circumscribing these inroads, since he thinks that they lead to anxiety and not to peace of mind. As he represents the matter, we are all protected from this anxiety by nature, which equips us with certain fundamental beliefs which do not have their source in reason and cannot be dislodged by it. As long as we do not permit our contrary tendency to do philosophy to get out of hand, we can avoid the doubts and the worries without effort. While he has failed to show that those who want to follow the Skeptic way cannot do so, he is clearly right to say that most people find it easier to indulge their natural tendency to dogmatize. In this he is a 'Common Sense' philosopher.[13]

But thinkers who set store by the plain man's repertoire of convictions are usually concerned to do more than ward off skeptical doubts. They commonly want to head off metaphysical speculation. Hume is no exception. But, more importantly for our purposes, he also wishes to undermine most, if not all, of our religious predilections. His reason is very clear. Just as he does not see the Skeptic's questions as leading to peace, but rather as leading to its opposite, so in his view religion does not calm and solace the soul as its adherents tell us it does, but rather feeds on fear and generates anxiety, self-deception, and fanaticism. So many of the criticisms that Skeptics have made of religious dogmas are criticisms Hume welcomes, and adds to himself. The Skeptic is right to stand aloof from *these* commitments. So his defence of common secular beliefs against the Skeptic, and his attack on religious faith, have a common central purpose: that of preserving the inner calm and moderate affection which both these perceived enemies threaten, yet claim to preserve. But even though we can discern a common objective here, it does not follow that the system of thought he develops to sustain this purpose can be consistent. For while it is logically straightforward for someone who tries to suspend judgment about common secular beliefs to do the same thing about religious beliefs, it does not look consistent for someone who espouses the former while admitting they have no rational foundation, to attack the latter *because* (he says) they have no rational foundation. Hume seems wide open to the Parity Argument, at least when it is wielded by anyone who holds that our natures have as much need to believe in God as they have to believe in the regularity of nature or the reality of the external world.

This problem is one which Hume seeks to answer throughout his career. In the course of trying to answer it, he makes fascinating use of the Skeptical Fideist tradition. I have already touched upon his answer above, and will now try to describe it more fully, to assess it, and in so doing to assess the Parity Argument itself.

SKEPTICISM AND RELIGION

It is widely agreed that one of Hume's major achievements is the destruction of the philosophical credentials of natural theology. This achievement can stand on its own, without the need of special reference to the rest of his philosophical system. The two most famous of his anti-religious writings are the Section, 'Of Miracles' in his *Enquiry Concerning Human Understanding*, and the *Dialogues Concerning Natural Religion*. In the former he shows that testimony to miracles cannot be used successfully as the source of premises for theistic conclusions, since if the truth of such conclusions is not taken for granted at the outset, the evidence in favour of the testimony can never be strong enough to establish miraculous events beyond reasonable doubt. In the latter work, without doubt the greatest book in English in philosophy of religion, and arguably the greatest on its theme in any language, he systematically exposes the weaknesses of the Argument from Design, presented as an attempt to establish the existence of the Christian Deity on the basis of observation and analogical reasoning. In the former case he shows that theistic conclusions cannot be established using the standards of secular history. In the latter he shows that they cannot be established using the standards of natural science. In neither case does he suppose that he has shown them to be false, although it is clear enough that he does not believe them. He recognizes that if the existence and providential care of the Christian God is presupposed, then we may claim to find signs of his presence in history and nature. His argument is that if we do *not* assume this beforehand, we have no good grounds to infer it from the evidence before us.

This, of course, is very like what he says about our secular natural beliefs. When the Skeptic challenges them, we cannot rebut his criticisms and prove to him that the same effect must follow from the same cause, or that we are right to believe in the distinct and continued existence of objects of perception, or that we retain our identity through the whole course of our lives. If we presuppose these things, we can make progress in science, history, and social relationships, but our experience in these realms will not provide philosophical justification for the beliefs it presupposes. All that can be done is to give accounts of the way in which our natures come to supply us with

these presuppositions. Hume offers such accounts, none of them at all com-
plimentary to us, since they make the genesis of these indispensable beliefs
a matter of habit, laziness, and intellectual confusion. (As argued above,
however, the fact that this last element is present indicates that 'reason', at
least in the form of *bad* reasoning, does have a key role in their genesis.) It
is of course just as well for us that we do not depend on our ability to produce the sort of argument the Skeptic asks for, since we cannot manage to
function without presupposing what he questions. The view Hume takes of
these beliefs, then, might well be called a Darwinian one: they are indispensable for our survival, and it is our good fortune that nature supplies them. He
never says this shows them to be true: that would be to confuse truth with
the need to believe, and in spite of being accused of confusing philosophy
with psychology, Hume is always aware of the difference between them.[14]

How far does the parallel extend to religious beliefs? In two respects it
is close enough. These beliefs cannot get adequate philosophical justification:
neither the *a priori* arguments of metaphysicians, nor the *a posteriori* mode of
argument embodied in the Argument from Design, are sufficient for this. And
yet it is also, I believe, recognized by Hume that if one presupposes the
existence of the Christian God, with his omnipotence, omniscience, and love,
many traditional theological inferences, and many religious interpretations of
nature and history, can readily be made. It is these inferences and interpretations, above all, that he wishes to prevent. How can he do this? There are
several ways in which he tries, and his defence against the Parity Argument
consists of all of them together.

(1) He recognizes that his account of the *origins* of our religious beliefs
has to be one which does not present them as benign natural provisions that
make human life possible, but shows them to be pathological hindrances to it.

(2) He attempts to make clear that even if one presupposed the being of
God in the way we presuppose the reality of an external world, this would
not legitimize the specific teachings of the Christian church as these were
known to him: something he can only show, of course, if he can prove that
any theistic presupposition we make is *not* a presupposition of the being of
the *Christian* God.

(3) In order to reduce the likelihood of specifically Christian teachings
being adopted by his readers, he has to address, in some manner, those who
do not see religion as the negative force he judges it to be, but consider it to
be the cement of the social fabric. To bring them, in practice if not theory,
to his side, he has to get them to accept a distinction between the revealed
religion he despises and a harmless or 'true' form he can live with. It is in the

second and third of these defences that Hume draws upon the tradition of Skeptical Fideism.

1. Hume's account of the origins of religion is to be found in *The Natural History of Religion*, a pioneering work in the comparative study of religions. It is noteworthy that he begins the book by distinguishing carefully between religion's 'foundation in reason' and 'its origin in human nature'. The *Natural History* is of course about the latter question; and Hume piously asserts (since it is *not* what the work he is engaged in is about!) that we all know that 'the whole frame of nature bespeaks an intelligent author' and shows the obvious truth of the 'primary principles of genuine theism and religion'. What he really thinks about what the whole frame of nature bespeaks we have to go to the *Dialogues* to see. But by emphasizing this distinction here he is able to indicate that actual religious belief and practice have sources quite different from the arguments that philosophers base on their observations of nature, and may even contain many features at odds with it — that actual religion and the so-called 'natural religion' of the philosophers are very different things. When he turns to the origins of actual religion in human nature, he makes the following important claim:

The belief of invisible, intelligent power has been very generally diffused over the human race, in all places and in all ages; but it has never perhaps been so universal as to admit of no exception, nor has it been, in any degree, uniform in the ideas, which it has suggested. Some nations have been discovered, who entertained no sentiments of religion, if travellers and historians may be credited; and no two nations, scarce any two men, have ever agreed precisely in the same sentiments. It would appear, therefore, that this preconception springs not from an original instinct or primary impression of nature, such as gives rise to self-love, affection between the sexes, love of progeny, gratitude, resentment; since every instinct of this kind has been found absolutely universal in all nations and ages, and has always a precise determinate object, which it inflexibly pursues. The first religious principles must be secondary; such as may easily be perverted by various accidents and causes, and whose operation too, in some cases, may by an extraordinary concurrence of circumstances, be altogether prevented. What those principles are, which give rise to the original belief, and what those accidents and causes are, which direct its operation, is the subject of our present enquiry.[15]

We have first, then, a somewhat hesitant suggestion that religion may not be universal, so that some men may not have it in any form, and a further claim that religious beliefs are so varied that even if everyone had it in some form, it must be due to secondary causes (we would probably say environmental factors) rather than be an inbuilt instinct, since the latter would produce greater similarity of religious attitudes than we find. Hume tells us that religious beliefs differ from the secular natural beliefs in being less than universal and in being far more diverse in their manifestations. Hence they can be prevented without violating the fundamental bent of our natures in the way this is violated by Pyrrhonain doubts about our secular commitments. In other words, reason does not have to be *subordinated* to religious beliefs in the way it has to be subordinated to our secular natural beliefs, for scientific enquiry and social life to proceed.

The detailed account of the origins of religion that the *Natural History* offers is designed to reinforce this judgment, and to show, indeed, that actual religion is a hindrance to intellectual enquiry and social life — so that those who can (like Hume's readers, of course) take advantage of some 'extraordinary concurrence of circumstances' to be free of it, should do so. The core of the story Hume tells is that real religion, unlike the philosophers' natural religion, is polytheistic, and is not founded upon a recognition of the orderliness of the physical world, but upon fear in the face of extraordinary or alarming phenomena, which are ascribed to personal deities who need to be appeased. In some cultures this form of religion gives place to monotheism, not because of rational argument, but because the momentum of worship causes some devotees to try to win the favour of one deity by exaggerating his powers and proclaiming his supremacy. This development has results which Hume says are undesirable, and make primitive polytheism look better by comparison. Monotheism generates intolerance. It also causes two other very great evils. One of these, which comes from the need to ascribe all things to the one God while endlessly proclaiming him to be good, is the sacrifice of intellectual integrity and the perversion of reason in the service of hypocrisy and self-deception. The other, which comes from the constant need to emphasize the deity's infinite superiority to ourselves, is the cultivation of 'the monkish virtues of mortification, penance, humility, and passive suffering, as the only qualities which are acceptable to him'. This reference calls to mind a more famous passage in the *Enquiry Concerning the Principles of Morals*:

And as every quality which is useful or agreeable to ourselves or others is, in common life, allowed to be a part of personal merit; so no other will ever be received, where men judge of things by their natural, unprejudiced reason, without the delusive glosses of superstition and false religion. Celibacy, fasting, penance, mortification, self-denial, humility, silence, solitude, and the whole train of monkish virtues; for what reason are they everywhere rejected by men of sense, but because they serve to no manner of purpose; neither advance a man's fortune in the world, nor render him a more valuable member of society; neither qualify him for the entertainment of company, nor increase his power of self-enjoyment? We observe, on the contrary, that they cross all these desirable ends; stupify the understanding and harden the heart, obscure the fancy and sour the temper. We justly, therefore, transfer them to the opposite column, and place them in the catalogue of vices; nor has any superstition force sufficient among men of the world, to prevert entirely these natural sentiments. A gloomy, hairbrained enthusiast, after his death, may have a place in the calendar; but will scarcely ever be admitted, when alive, into intimacy and society, except by those who are as delirious and dismal as himself.[16]

So we may sum up the relevant themes in the *Natural History* by saying that religious belief, though very common, is not natural and instinctive the way our secular natural beliefs are; that, unlike those beliefs, it can be dislodged or at least avoided by education and training; and that it has its origins in fears and anxieties and leads to the prostitution of men's rational faculties and the deliberate cultivation of miseries which hinder the smooth development of scientific understanding and civilized social intercourse. We may call this the *psychological* part of Hume's response to the Parity Argument.

2. The extended presentation of Hume's views on the epistemological status of theism is of course to be found in the *Dialogues Concerning Natural Religion*. I cannot attempt to do justice to its arguments here, but can only comment on those aspects of it which seem to embody Hume's response to the Parity Argument. It is well known that the *Dialogues* are formally modelled on Cicero's *De Natura Deorum*, and that, like Cicero, Hume does not appear in the work in his own person. Its three characters are Cleanthes, who represents the partially secularized theists of Hume's day who wished to support their religious convictions by arguments analogous to those of science; Demea, who represents conservative orthodoxy; and Philo, said to be a 'careless' skeptic, whose major role is that of critic of the Argument from Design as Cleanthes presents it. Hume's biographer E. C. Mossner has suggested that Cleanthes is modelled on Joseph Butler and Demea on Samuel Clarke.[17] Anders Jeffner has suggested that Philo is modelled on Pierre Bayle, which is at least as plausible.[18] Since Norman Kemp Smith's study of the *Dialogues*, most readers agree that Philo speaks for Hume, at least in most of the work, and I shall assume this.[19] (It is consistent with Jeffner's suggestion, at least for the most part.) To assume this, however, is not to solve all problems of interpretation, since Philo appears to change his position in the final part.

The first eleven of the twelve parts are devoted to Cleanthes' presentation of the Design argument and Philo's responses and objections (Demea's contributions, though not insignificant, are peripheral.) The argument Cleanthes presents is simple: nature is a vast and intricate machine, and since experience teaches us that such orderly contrivance and adaptation as machines exhibit is due to designing intelligence, the universe must also be due to such intelligence. "By this argument . . . do we prove at once the existence of a Deity, and his similarity to human mind and intelligence." Cleanthes frequently repeats this argument, but never qualifies it or adds to it significantly. Philo's (i.e. Hume's) objections can be summarized with extreme brevity and compression as follows.

(a) The analogy between machines and the physical universe is very strained, since it is a comparison of parts to the whole, and the universe is self-evidently a unique object. In any case only some of the examples of order and adaptation of which we know are *observed* to be due to the work of intelligence, not all of them (Parts II–III).

(b) The alleged similarity of the divine mind to human minds, if real, has theologically awkward results. It suggests that the divine mind is also housed in a body; that the created world is, like human artefacts, the result of a series of trials and errors; that it may be created not by one, but by a committee of minds; or that God may be mortal as we are, so that his world may survive him (Parts III–V).

(c) The analogy of the world to a machine is no better than the analogy of the world to an organism, for example. So we could mount an equally plausible argument in favour of the world's having God as its soul, or having been brought into being by sexual generation, or even randomly (Parts VI–VIII).

(d) The evils in the world cast doubt on the omnipotence of God, or on his moral attributes. Perhaps, if we knew of these independently, we could reconcile them with these evils; but without this, we have to recognize that the evidence we have does not suggest that the world is the creation of a being who is all-powerful and all-good, but at most something less than this (Parts X and XI).

All these arguments make it clear, in Hume's view, that if we use our reason in natural theology the way we use it in science, we do not get orthodox results. We cannot, by this route, establish the existence of the Christian deity. Let us assume that he has shown this. In the context of Hume's system, this means that if we assume the secular natural beliefs, as in his view we have no choice but to do, then even though we are thereby enabled to conduct the investigations and reasonings of natural science, and engage in moral decisions, no warrant is provided to accept the claims of those who contend that the world in which we are thus enabled to function is ordered by an all-wise and all-good deity. So the belief in such a deity is not only not indispensable for science and social life; it does not even have the support science can give to its own theories about causes and effects in nature.

Now this conclusion, enormously powerful and influential though it has been in general debate about the value of natural theology, looks irrelevant to the Parity Argument. This verdict is confirmed by the pains Hume takes from Part I onwards to show that the criticisms Philo makes of Cleanthes' argument do not depend for their force on accepting Pyrrhonian Skepticism, and that in spite of some inclination to Pyrrhonian (which is sharpened by the temptation to tease Demea), Philo is merely showing that Cleanthes' argument fails by the standards of evidence that Cleanthes himself says he is following. (In Hume's language, Philo's critique is only an application of *mitigated* skepticism.) The point of the Parity Argument, however, is that this cannot consistently be used to block acceptance of Christian theism: a point which Philo's arguments, even if successful, do not seem to touch.

I am sure that Hume is aware of this, and that the philosophical part of his response helps us to understand the puzzling change in Philo's speeches in Part XII. I have discussed the interpretation of Part XII at length elsewhere, and must refer to those discussions for support of the exegesis I shall offer here.[20] The change, which is formally unheralded, consists in the fact that, having refuted Cleanthes so successfully, Philo speaks as though he has never doubted that the orderliness of nature shows it to be intelligently designed. I think that Norman Kemp Smith fails to show Philo's statements on this matter to be wholly ironic. But if they are not, they represent a major concession to Cleanthes, since they seem to confirm his central contention. What sense is to be made of this?

It is very tempting to suggest that Hume is reluctantly admitting that some form of theism is an inescapable natural belief that his own philosophical critiques cannot dislodge, just as his scrutiny of causal inferences cannot dislodge our convictions of natural regularities. But the position he has taken in the *Natural History* looks inconsistent with this; and in any case Philo speaks as though the conviction he retains is one that is generated by the very contemplation of orderly phenomena that Cleanthes uses in his argument. However this may be, Philo certainly seems to think that his own counter-arguments are unable to destroy the conviction of an intelligent cause of the order in the world. But it is equally significant that he does *not* concede that this conviction must extend to the *nature* of this intelligent cause, in particular to its *moral* character, and he does not concede that we can draw any practical conclusions from it about how we should act. What he concedes, in other words, is the vaguest possible deism.

There is an argument within this. Just as our inescapable tendency to infer from causes to effects has to be supplemented by observation and reasoning before it can generate specific beliefs about what detailed regularities we find around us, so any inbuilt or acquired commitment to the being of an external intelligence can generate no specific beliefs about the divine nature or purposes, by itself. It has to be filled out by observation and reasoning, and Hume has shown that these fail entirely to supply what is required. So Hume's philosophical defence against the Parity Argument is to concede what it urges, but to insist that it can only carry us to a vague and thoroughly unreligious desim at the best. He does not so much deny there may be natural religion, as assert its unreligiousness. So he does not so much reject the Parity Argument as try to render it religiously unproductive. He accepts part of Skeptical Fideism and deflects it. We may call this his *philosophical* response.

3. We can now turn to what I shall call the *tactical* defence Hume uses against the Parity Argument. To begin, it is not clear at all that Hume, as distinct from Philo, really accepts the minimal desim of Part XII. But what is clear is that Hume, who valued social harmony, is willing enough to concede this deism formally in preference to adopting the abrasively unbelieving stance of such thinkers as the French *philosophes* of his time.[21] For this enables him to live in social and moral accord with the secularized, moderate theologians that Cleanthes typifies. He perceives that their domesticated theism does not generate any practical consequences that cannot be derived from a knowledge of human nature and an adherence to convention — from what we might now call secular humanism. So he is content to pay lip-service to a vague theism that is verbally similar to theirs. He can live like the Conformist Fideist in relation to the conventional religion they stand for — by adopting a stance of beliefless affirmation (which Philo calls 'a plain, philosophical assent'). Hume makes this clear by having Philo and Cleanthes spend much of Part XII debating the differences between what they call 'true' and 'false' religion — in decoded parlance secularized religiosity and real faith. He goes so far as to have *Cleanthes* describe what true religion is:

The proper office of religion is to regulate the heart of men, humanize their conduct, infuse the spirit of temperance, order, and obedience; and as its operation is silent, and only enforces the motives of morality and justice, it is in danger of being overlooked, and confounded with these other motives. When it distinguishes itself, and acts as a separate principle over men, it has departed from its proper sphere, and has become only a cover to faction and ambition.[22]

So true religion has no independent morality or doctrine. Hume was perceptive enough to see that a religious belief that seeks to commend itself to men of letters by supposedly scientific arguments that he can discredit will in time become nothing more than the domesticated nondenominational uplift with which we are all familiar today. To this, the most exacting Skeptic can conform with impunity.

But this tactic of formal conformity can only work, especially in an age like Hume's when atheism was still generally considered unthinkable, if believers like Cleanthes do not fully recognize that the consensus he and Philo have is wholly remote from the traditional doctrines they suppose themselves to be defending. Philo has to commend true religion to Cleanthes in a way that consolidates its doctrinal emptiness while underplaying, or even concealing it. To do this he adopts the language of the Evangelical Fideist. In his final speech he tells Cleanthes that the man of letters should be persuaded of the inability of reason to do more than show us there must be divine intelligence, so that he will then refrain from expanding upon this by philosophical means in the way the 'haughty dogmatist' does. Instead he will 'fly to revealed truth with the greatest avidity'. So the reduction of natural theology almost to zero is, after all, a boon to faith! Hence the sentence quoted at the start of this chapter, which is the last sentiment that Philo expresses. The endorsement of Fideism is of course only verbal. It is being parodied to serve an accommodation which is designed to help real faith wither away.

HUME AND THE PARITY ARGUMENT

How good is Hume's response to the Parity Argument? The Argument, it will be recalled, applies to someone in very specific philosophical circumstances. He must be someone who agrees, as Hume does, with the Pyrrhonist tradition that at least some of the fundamental philosophical commitments of secular common sense are without rational foundation. He must, however, decline to follow the Pyrrhonist in espousing suspense of judgment with regard to them; instead, he will yield to our natural tendency to believe them. The Parity Argument suggests to such a person that he is inconsistent if he refuses to yield also to the demands of religious belief merely because he considers that it, too, does not have a rational foundation.

Manifestly the Argument does not apply to someone who rejects religious belief and secular common sense together, as Sextus does. Nor does it apply to someone who holds that our common sense beliefs are philosophically justifiable, and the claims of religion are not. Hence someone who is prepared to say that he is sure there *are* justifications for common sense, even though he does not know, or perhaps care, what they are, also evades the Parity Argument, though those who know the literature may not be so sure that any case that has been made for common sense is stronger than those that have been made for the existence of God. How well does Hume, to whom the Argument does apply, answer it?

(1) I begin with what I have called his psychological response. It divides naturally into three parts. (a) He claims that none of us can avoid committing ourselves to common sense beliefs, but some of us can avoid committing ourselves to religious beliefs, since some have actually done this. I have already suggested that this argument is dubious. At least the classical Skeptic is a plausible counter-example to the first assertion. Sextus writes in a way designed to answer such a charge, and even if his answer contains major difficulties, I have suggested it can be amended in a way that yields a satisfactory response. With regard to the second assertion, even if we agree that some can avoid religious commitments, we do not thereby concede that those who *have* them could have avoided them. But what, in any case, is the point of making or contesting these two assertions? Presumably this: that the charge of inconsistency could not be made to stick if it should turn out that the beliefs the common sense unbeliever like Hume accepts are beliefs he cannot avoid accepting, whereas the belief he rejects is one he *can* avoid accepting. But the charge could surely still stick in these circumstances. If someone is accused of inconsistency in accepting *p and q* but rejecting *r*, and the reason for the accusation is not that *p and q but not r* is itself inconsistent, but that the reason he has for rejecting *r* applies equally to all three, then it is not a convincing defence to say that one is only able to control one's beliefs about *r*, and not one's beliefs about *p* or *q*. It is an adequate defence only if the reasons for rejecting *r* are *good* reasons. But if they are, they will, *ex hypothesi*, be good reasons for rejecting *p* and *q*, and what the argument will in fact produce for us will be an excuse for accepting *p and q*, rather than a reason for rejecting *r*. I think some excuses could be found in Hume for reading him this way, and even that if this were what he meant, it would be a satisfactory answer to the Parity Argument — always provided we agreed that no one can reject common-sense secular beliefs even though there are good reasons to do so. But if we do not read him in this way, and take him to be rejecting religious belief because there is no good reason *for* it, then the fact that we *can* reject religious belief, yet cannot reject common-sense beliefs, is not a

sufficient answer. For in rejecting religious belief, he is behaving in a way that is indeed inconsistent with his behaviour at the common-sense level; he is not acquitted of the charge of behaving inconsistently merely by the fact that he is at liberty not to! For his behaviour to be more than merely inconsistent, there has to be some special reason for rejecting religious belief — such as the principle that one should, where one has control of the matter, only assent to what has philosophical justification: a principle which Hume, who thinks that we are better off *not* being able to reject common sense beliefs, could hardly subscribe to.

(b) But it would be superficial to leave the matter here. For Hume undoubtedly thinks our secular natural beliefs are unavoidable in a more interesting way than this. He thinks we cannot proceed to think or talk about scientific or moral matters without presupposing them. The clearest statement of this is the following:

> Thus the sceptic still continues to reason and believe, even though he asserts that he cannot defend his reason by reason; and by the same rule he must assent to the principle concerning the existence of body, though he cannot pretend by any arguments of philosophy to maintain its veracity. Nature has not left this to his choice, and has doubtless esteemed it an affair of too great importance to be trusted to our uncertain reasonings and speculations. We may well ask, *What causes us to believe in the existence of body?* but it is vain to ask, *Whether there be body or not?* That is a point which we must take for granted in all our reasonings.[23]

No such thing holds for religious belief; we can function in everyday life and science without it. We do not have to take God's existence for granted in all our reasonings. Let us accept this. What it shows, if it is true, is a very important fact about the status of religious belief. But it is not clear that it is relevant to the Parity Argument. For the basis of that argument is that the secular natural beliefs and religious belief are alike in lacking rational justification; and I take Hume to be saying that we have to presuppose the natural beliefs *in spite of this*, but not the beliefs of religion. I assume, that is, that he is not offering their practical indispensability as itself a *justification* of the secular natural beliefs, but merely as a sign that we are fortunate to have a built-in tendency to accept them. If this is the right way to read him, then the inconsistency the Parity Argument complains of is unaffected, and the best we can get is an additional excuse for not resisting the secular belief — that such a resistance would create a hindrance to daily business. Certainly the fact that rejecting religion does not hinder daily business does not show we are consistent to reject it while adhering to common sense.

But even if we decide to read Hume as offering us a *justification* for our secular natural beliefs when he points out that they are indispensable in practice, his response to the Parity Argument can still be answered. The response would then depend, of course, on the fact that religious belief is not indispensable in the same way for daily business and natural science. But it *is* essential for *religious* actions and reasonings. In both the secular case and the religious case there is a system of thought and action which can only go forward if the basic beliefs on which it depends are presupposed. Let us agree that we are unable, in either case, to find independent justification in philosophy for the basic beliefs that are required. In the secular case the system is nevertheless activated by natural forces within us which seem to be outside our control, so the lack of independent justification presents no practical hindrance to our daily lives. In the religious case the lack of external justification does act as a practical hindrance to some, since the forces in our natures that impel us toward religious life are increasingly easy to deflect in our day, even by philosophy. But there is still a clear *inconsistency* in permitting this lack of external justification to deflect them. If the Parity Argument is redeployed in this way, I cannot see that Hume has answered it, unless of course he falls back on the remaining psychological objection that he has — the human undesirability of the religious life itself.

(c) We can see Hume and Pascal as offering starkly opposed evaluations of the lives of faith and of secular human society. What one says about the one, the other says about the other, and with passion. It is here that Hume's careful equanimity deserts him. While Pascal tells us that consolation can only come from yielding our lives to God, and not from the distractions of human society, Hume tells us the very reverse. To him the anxieties of the serious thinker can have no remedy but those very distractions (even those very games), whereas the religious life takes root in those anxieties and sharpens them. No doubt most would say that Pascal paints too dark a picture of human society, and Hume too dark a picture of religion. It does not seem practical to try to settle such a question in the way John Stuart Mill suggests we tell which pleasures are the most satisfying, by looking for a jury of experienced participants,[24] for we would always suppose their verdicts to depend on their wider commitments. But it is interesting to note that Pascal's melancholy account of the human condition is offered to the reader of his Apology as one that can be recognized to be correct even by those who do not share the faith from within which he composed it. Perhaps it is possible to compare it with Hume's contrary characterization of polite society, both in his informal asides and in his formal ethical writings, as best satisfying the needs of our natures. Even though most such comparisons would be made from committed positions, perhaps this need not be so, and we do have here a point of departure for an undecided enquirer. It is not part of my purposes here, however, to comment on the outcome of such a comparison.

(2) I turn now to what I have called Hume's philosophical response. I have suggested that Philo's concession in Part XII of the *Dialogues* can be viewed as embodying a philosophical rebuttal to the Parity Argument, and that it consists in yielding to it (or at least not openly resisting it) but denying that any doctrinal or practical consequences flow from this. His ground for saying there are no such consequences is that the evidence is ambiguous and can be used to support one fanciful cosmology as readily as another. Just as our natural custom of inferring from the same cause to the same effect commits us to nothing about what actual causes and effects there are until experience supplies the particulars, so conceding there is transcendent mentality tells us nothing about its nature or demands; and in this case experience cannot supply the particulars that are necessary.

Hume's concession is not the empty one he imagines. It is effective, in my view, against the natural theologians like Cleanthes who wish to make particular theological claims on the basis of observation and analogical reasoning. Here Joseph Butler is the historical paradigm, since his *Analogy of Religion* was an attempt to show those who were prepared to concede a vague deism, but no more, that experience does supply us with facts that justify particular Christian commitments as well. Hume's *Dialogues* are an attempt to demonstrate that Butler is wrong about this. If the arguments of Parts I to XI are sound, they do indeed show that experience and analogical reasoning do not support one theology more than another. It is common ground between Hume and the natural theologians that this is where we must look for help; and Hume has condemned to eternal vagueness and vacuity anyone who concedes there is nowhere else to look. But (without of course meaning it) he has himself suggested there is somewhere else: revelation. He makes this suggestion in a way that makes it plain he does not think any is yet to hand; but the studies of comparative religion that he himself helped to begin have by now made many think that our problem is not that none is to hand, but that there may be too much.

Would the fact that there are so many purported revelations defeat the Parity Argument? I think not. Indeed I think that by making the philosophical move he has made here, Hume has shown us a way of lessening its most obvious weakness — that it seems to make a case for too many unsupported beliefs. If the Parity Argument is intended, alone, to lead us into accepting some particular theological system, then Hume's rebuttal, especially if augmented by an awareness of the varieties of the world's religious systems, can only support total arbitrariness. Suppose, however, it were taken merely to be a partial case for yielding to the tendency we might have to presuppose *some* form of transcendent intelligence rather than none, leaving the selection of *which* form to accept to the application of some other principle? In our own day there are many who feel the pull of just this inclination. Dissatisfied with purely secular styles of life (leaning in fact more toward Pascal's view of society as we find it than to Hume's) they look to see which of the wide range of religious systems available to them is the most satisfying and rational alternative. Some even suggest it might be possible to produce a world-wide theology composed of elements from each.[25] This may seem a long way from faith as traditionally understood; but it is one step toward it, and one, I think, which Hume's concession to the Parity Argument permits. It is only prevented if one insists with Hume that the standards of secular life and science be used to determine the specific form such crypto-religious commitment takes. Hume is on strong ground in saying that if one does insist on this, no real religious specifics will emerge.

(3) Finally, Hume's tactical response. There is no doubt that even though Hume naturally failed to perceive the impact of comparative religious studies, he saw with precision the future of secularized Christianity. As humanist unbelief has freed itself from the aggressive hostility of a Holbach or a Bradlaugh, it has been met more than halfway by the toothless religiosity of what he has Cleanthes call 'true religion'. When faith is not believed to have its own sources of doctrinal commitment, it becomes only verbally different from polite agnosticism, and uses the same methods for determining its practical choices as are employed by secular social agencies or political movements. This is undoubtedly a part of what Hume means by saying that the disagreements between Cleanthes and Philo are 'entirely verbal' ones. There is still a mild vestigial reluctance, left over from the days when faith was more often real, to accept that the accord is as close as it is, however. Hume foresaw this too, so in addition to the Conformism he creates for Philo, he provides a mock Evangelical Fideism to edify Cleanthes. We have to remember, however, that this part of the debate goes on in the absence of the one character whose faith can be assumed to be genuine. Although he is not much of a thinker, we can be sure Demea would not have been taken in.

NOTES

[1] The general reading of Hume I shall adopt is worked out in Terence Penelhum, *Hume*, Macmillan, London, and St. Martin's Press, New York, 1975; and in 'David Hume, 1711–76: A Bicentennial Appreciation', *Transactions of the Royal Society of Canada*,

Vol. **XIV**, 1976. Te specific interpretations of the *Dialogues Concerning Natural Religion* that I offer here are explained and defended in 'Hume's Skepticism and the *Dialogues*', *McGill Hume Studies*, ed. by D. Norton, N. Capaldi and W. Robison, Austin Hill Press, San Diego, 1979 (from which some of the first part of this chapter is excerpted) and 'Natural Belief and Religious Belief in Hume's Philosophy', *Philosophical Quarterly*, 1983.

[2] See *The Letters of David Hume*, ed. by J. Y. T. Greig, Oxford University Press, 1932, Vol. I, pp. 12–18; also E. C. Mossner, *Life of David Hume*, Edinburgh University Press, 1954, Oxford 1970, Chapter 7.

[3] *A Treatise of Human Nature*, ed. by L. A. Selby-Bigge, Oxford University Press, 1888, repr. 1968, p. 269.

[4] Hume, *Philosophical Works*, ed. by T. H. Green and T. H. Grose, 4v; published by Longmans Green, London, in 1878, repr. Scientia Verlag Aalen, 1964.

[5] Norman Kemp Smith, *The Philosophy of David Hume*, Macmillan, London, 1941, repr. 1964. See also his articles 'The Naturalism of Hume', *Mind*, 1905.

[6] Richard H. Popkin, 'David Hume: His Pyrrhonism and His Critique of Pyrrhonism', *Philosophical Quarterly*, Vol. I, 1951; reprinted in V. C. Chappell (ed.) *Hume*, Doubleday, New York, 1966.

[7] *Treatise*, p. 183.

[8] *Treatise*, pp. 268–9.

[9] See *Enquiry Concerning Human Understanding*, in *Hume's Enquiries*, ed. by L. A. Selby-Bigge, 2nd ed. 1962, p. 161 ff.

[10] I draw on many passages, but especially on the arguments of *Treatise* I, 4, 2.

[11] I am indebted here to some comments of Mr Gary Colwell.

[12] See above, Chapters 2 and 3.

[13] For some perceptive comments on Hume's relation to the 'Common Sense' school of Reid and his followers, see David Fate Norton, *David Hume: Common-Sense Moralist, Sceptical Metaphysician*, Princeton University Press, 1982. This is the fullest and most balanced treatment to date of the question of what sort of skeptic Hume is.

[14] Here again see Norton, Chapter 5.

[15] *The Natural History of Religion*, ed. by H. E. Root, Adam and Charles Black, London and Stanford University Press, 1956; p. 21.

[16] In *Hume's Enquiries*, p. 270.

[17] E. C. Mossner, 'The Enigma of Hume', *Mind* **45**, 1936.

[18] Anders Jeffner, *Butler and Hume on Religion*, Diakonistyrelsens Bokforlag, Stockholm, 1966.

[19] See the lengthy interpretative introduction to his edition of the *Dialogues*, Nelson, Edinburgh 1947, repr. Bobbs-Merrill, Indianapolis, n.d.

[20] See 'Hume's Skepticism and the *Dialogues*' and 'Natural Belief and Religious Belief in Hume's Philosophy'.

[21] There is an interesting story (see Kemp Smith's edition of the *Dialogues*, p. 37–38) that Hume visited Holbach and remarked that there were in his opinion, no genuine atheists – only to be told that there were seventeen sitting at table with him.

[22] *Dialogues*, ed. by N. Kemp Smith, p. 220.

[23] *Treatise*, p. 187.

[24] See his *Utilitarianism*, Chapter II.

[25] See, for example, John Hick, *God and the Universe of Faiths*, Macmillan, London, 1973, or Wilfred Cantwell Smith, *Towards a World Theology*, Macmillan, London, 1981.

CHAPTER 7

FIDEISM AND SOME RECENT ARGUMENTS

EVANGELICAL FIDEISM – A RECAPITULATION

The Evangelical Fideist is not a Skeptic, but sees the Skeptic as providing an important service for faith by making it clear that it cannot depend on reasoning. In faith, rightly understood, we turn aside from attempts to allay human anxieties through intellectual reflection and dogmatic speculation. The Skeptic helps us to do this by exposing the intellectual baselessness of our fundamental secular beliefs as well as that of the commitments which faith embodies. I have examined some aspects of the thought of the two great Evangelical Fideists, and have assessed their positions under three main heads.

(1) Pascal and Kierkegaard alike reject, with contempt, traditional attempts to prove the existence and attributes of God. Their primary objection to these attempts is that what keeps men from God is their own corruption. I have argued that if this is true, it does not show that proving God's existence is impossible. It rather shows why men who had conclusive reasons for believing in God might still not do so. If the Skeptic is right in doubting the power of reason to provide such reasons, he makes it less likely that unbelief is always due to such perversity, and cannot, therefore, be judged to be an ally of faith – even an unwitting one.

(2) The second major argument, or group of arguments, that Pascal and Kierkegaard use to show that faith can only exist at reason's expense, depend on the doctrine of the hiddenness of God: the doctrine that in the face of human sin, God elects to reveal himself to those who seek him and to hide himself from those who do not. I have argued that if this is true, it shows that God could remain hidden from those who did not seek him, even when they were provided with conclusive reasons for believing in him. It therefore does not imply that there could be no such conclusive reasons; rather the reverse. I have also argued that the presence of such reasons would not impair human freedom to choose God or to reject him.

(3) A third group of arguments stem from analogies which Pascal and Kierkegaard seek to draw between faith and common sense. These analogies are used in various versions of what I call the Parity Argument. The previous two groups of arguments depend, in the last analysis, only upon accepting

146

skeptical criticisms of specifically theistic claims. The Parity Argument, however, depends also upon agreeing that the Skeptic is right in arguing that the fundamental convictions of common sense are devoid of rational justification. If then addresses itself to the unbeliever who makes the secular commitments but declines to make the religious ones, and suggests to him that he is guilty of inconsistency. If one accepts the two preconditions of the Parity Argument, it has some apparent strength, though such strength as it has can be mustered in support of many alternative religious positions. The examination of Hume's philosophy of religion in our last chapter was undertaken because Hume does concede these preconditions, but maintains a wholly secularist stance in religious matters, and we can accordingly view many aspects of his estimate of religion as attempts to respond to the difficulty that the Parity Argument presents.

Viewed in this way, I do not think Hume's philosophy of religion yields a satisfactory answer. He does not show that our supposed psychological inability to sustain doubt about common-sense beliefs makes it consistent to decline religious belief. Nor does he show that the indispensability of our secular beliefs is not a feature of religious beliefs as well — unless one means 'secular indispensability' when one says 'indispensability'. His attempt to concede a vague general theistic commitment but to evacuate all real content from it does not so much counter the Parity Argument as show it to point toward a general, rather than a specific, religious commitment.

This strand of Fideist Argument. then, must be conceded more merit than any of the others we have encountered. To assess it more carefully, I shall first describe two contemporary versions of it.

TWO RECENT VERSIONS OF THE PARITY ARGUMENT

The first version I shall examine is that of Alvin Plantinga, in an essay entitled 'Rationality and Religious Belief'.[1] It is a defence of theism against those who accuse theists of irrationality for not having adequate evidence of the existence of God. These critics may well not be epistemological skeptics, of course; but in countering their position Plantinga makes use of arguments which, though original and contemporary, inevitably call to mind Skeptic attacks on the doctrines of infallible representations and Skeptic discussions of the criterion of truth.

The criticism of theism that Plantinga answers is a derivative of what he calls *foundationalism*, which is a widely-held philosophical doctrine about what beliefs are rational. It employs a distinction between those beliefs a person has which depend upon others, and those beliefs he has which do not. The latter he calls basic beliefs. Foundationalism is the doctrine that for a belief that someone has to be a rational one, it must either be basic, or be shown to be justifiable by basic ones; and that basic beliefs are properly only of two kinds — self-evident propositions and incorrigible propositions (roughly, propositions one sees to be true merely by understanding them, and propositions which are shown to be true merely because someone believes them, such as propositions about one's present sensations). Plantinga argues that to commit oneself to the positive view that self-evident propositions and incorrigible propositions are properly basic is to make a commitment which all non-skeptics do make but which is not itself open to justification; and to take the negative view that no other sort of propositions can properly be basic for anyone is self-refuting, since it is neither self-evident nor incorrigible and cannot be held as basic without being its own exception. He concludes from this that belief in God need not be defended in the manner of traditional natural theology. The natural theologian concedes that belief in God needs to be justified by other, basic, beliefs, and then attempts to provide the justification. But Plantinga holds that belief in God can itself be classed as properly basic: that it can be rational to believe in God without basing that belief upon other beliefs or propositions.

He defends this against two objections. First, he rejects the argument that such a view makes belief in God groundless. I think his defence is this: even though a proposition can properly be accepted by someone without this acceptance being based on that of other propositions, it does not follow that there is nothing that justifies it. For it might be occasioned ('called forth') by circumstances that we can point to to justify it. In the case of belief in God, these might be experiences of the wonders of nature, or the sense of divine disapproval or forgiveness. Second, he insists that his view does not open us to accepting any and every belief whatever as properly basic. For, unless one adopts question-begging general criteria like those of the foundationalist, the only tests of the propriety of one's basic beliefs will have to be their results — the judgments they support and exclude.

A similar, though not identical, version, of the same argument is to be found in Norman Malcolm's essay 'The Groundlessness of Belief'.[2] Malcolm begins by stating a position he attributes to Wittgenstein in *On Certainty*.[3] This is the claim that doubts can occur only within a context of a group of beliefs which we acquire without question and without proof. Each of us, therefore, has groundless beliefs which are fundamental to the questions and answers that we frame during our lives. Malcolm gives as an example the belief that things do not vanish without explanation: he suggests that it is quite conceivable that there should be a culture in which this possibility is not excluded, although in our culture we are unable to entertain it, and we frame all our thinking, and ask and answer all our questions, in a manner that excludes it from consideration. He quotes Wittgenstein as offering the principle of the continuity of nature as another example of such a framework-principle.

Each of us, therefore, lives and thinks within a group of framework principles which Wittgenstein calls a 'system'. (The term does not seem to imply that the principles are connected in such a way that one cannot coherently consider subtracting or adding one of them: at least it seems to me that Malcolm's claim that we can conceive another culture which does without the principle that nothing vanishes without explanation would fail if this were implied.) Questions, answers and justifications all occur *within* a given system, and presuppose its principles:

We grow into a framework. We don't question it. We accept it trustingly. But this acceptance is not a consequence of reflection. We do not *decide* to accept framework propositions. We do not decide that we live on the earth, any more than we decide to learn our native tongue. We come to adhere to a framework proposition, in the sense that it shapes the way we think. The framework propositions that we accept, grow into, are not idiosyncrasies but common ways of speaking and thinking that are pressed on us by our human community. For our acceptances to have been withheld would have meant that we had not learned how to count, to measure, to use names, to play games, or even *to talk*. Wittgenstein remarks that 'a language-game is only possible if one trusts something.' Not *can*, but *does* trust something (*On Certainty*, p. 509). I think he means by this trust or acceptance, what he calls belief 'in the sense of religious belief' (*On Certainty*, p. 459). What does he mean by belief 'in the sense of religious belief'? He explicitly distinguishes it from *conjecture* (*Vermutung; ibid*). I think this means that there is nothing tentative about it; it is not adopted as an hypothesis that might later be withdrawn in the light of new evidence. This also makes explicit an important feature of Wittgenstein's understanding of belief, in the sense of 'religious belief', namely, that it does not rise or fall on the basis of evidence or grounds: it is 'groundless'.[4]

This thesis of Wittgenstein's shows obvious similarities to what Plantinga says about basic beliefs, and even more obvious similarities to what Hume says about our natural beliefs.[5] The obvious difference from Plantinga is Malcolm's statement that a framework belief is groundless, although the differences are probably more superficial than real. The obvious difference from Hume is the assimilation of framework beliefs to religious commitments, which is our present reason for discussing this argument.

Malcolm's primary concern, of course, is to defend religious belief as like our framework beliefs, such as the belief in the continuity of nature. He does this by arguing that in both cases philosophical demands for justification as a precondition of acceptance are absurd, and rest on a misunderstanding of the actual language-games we practice. In Western philosophy, he says, we have a deep-rooted 'veneration for evidence', which leads to philosophical absurdities. It causes philosophers to insist, for example, that images and memories must resemble their objects, that intentions must be feelings, or that correct performances must derive from ideas: in each case a theory is invented to supply evidence in support of a recognized item of knowledge or expertise. But such theories are not explanatory, and justification only has place *within* a language-game.

Religion has been a common casualty of the demand for justification, which has historically produced the proofs of natural theology. But it is a misunderstanding to assume that religion has any need of justification:

Religion is a form of life; it is language embedded in action – what Wittgenstein calls a 'language-game'. Science is another. Neither stands in need of justification, the one no more than the other.[6]

Justification may have its place within particular religions, where the status of some particular doctrine may be at issue, and here evidence, such as that of texts, is indeed relevant. But such disputes belong within a context not itself subject to such need for justification. A result of this is that one and the same fact may have religious significance for someone whose thinking goes on within such a religious context, and have none whatever for someone whose thinking does not.

In taking these two essays together I do not suggest that there are no significant differences between them. One obvious point of divergence, already noted, is to be found by contrasting Plantinga's argument that taking belief in God as basic does not entail holding it groundlessly, with Malcolm's explicit insistence that religious belief does not, and could not, have grounds. While I doubt whether their positions are as opposed as their words suggest, I shall not explore this here.[7] I am concerned here with the core argument that is common to both, which I think may be called a *permissive* version of the Parity Argument. The classical versions of the Argument, in Pascal and Kierkegaard, suggest that the unbeliever, since he depends in his daily life upon commitments he does not, and cannot, found on reason and evidence, is in fact acting inconsistently when he refuses to embrace religious faith also, particularly if the reason he gives for his refusal is the fact that it cannot be founded in such a manner. As I understand the matter, the intent of the arguments I have just summarized is to show something rather less than this — that the *religious believer* is not guilty of irrationality; that he is, as Plantinga puts it, "entirely within his intellectual rights in believing as he does".[8] They defend him against the charge that it is irrational to believe in God without adequate evidence; and they do it by arguing that believers and unbelievers alike are necessarily committed to principles such as the reliability of our sensory apparatus or the constancy of nature. (Not necessarily *these* principles, of course, but some such principles as these.) The justification that unbelievers demand for belief in God is not available for these secular commitments, either because (Plantinga) one inevitably finds oneself up against some principles which are ultimate and can only be 'justified' by circular arguments or inconsistent ones, or because (Malcolm) requests for justification and evidence belong within systems of thought and cannot be directed toward whole systems from outside. Even if it is possible to conceive a system in which this or that fundamental secular belief is false, this is not in fact entertained within any system. The status of other beliefs is judged by reference to the fundamental ones, which, in Hume's language, are 'taken for granted in all our reasonings'. Someone whose framework of thought includes belief in God will accord the same status to that commitment that he and the rest of us together accord to the secular natural beliefs. To judge him irrational on that account is to presume that his commitment has to be assessed as though it were a subsidiary or non-basic belief within a framework determined by the secular natural beliefs alone — which is to misjudge the status he accords to it, and, from the standpoint of *his* system of thought, to restrict one's basic intellectual commitments in an arbitrary manner.

Before commenting on this permissive argument and its implications, I must make two provisos. The first relates to the concept of rationality. Plantinga is wholly right to say that it is not a pellucid notion, and I shall try to be circumspect in my use of it. I shall take it in what follows that although Plantinga and Malcolm seem to agree that it is arbitrary to require universally that a belief merits the accolade 'rational' only if it is supported by evidence, and that such a criterion of rationality must be used more restrictedly, they would still agree that the description should be withheld from any commitment that contained, or led to, contradictions; and that a system, or assemblage of beliefs, should be classed as an irrational one if two or more of the fundamental beliefs which constitute it should turn out on examination to contradict one another. Hence, for example, if the Christian faith in God's power and love were to turn out on examination to contradict the Christian insistence on the depth and reality of evil, we would be justified in concluding that Christian faith is irrational. (Plantinga's formidable defence of Christianity against the traditional 'Problem of Evil' is an obvious confirmation of this.[9]) The second proviso is this. I shall assume in what follows that although religious commitment may not be undertaken on the basis of evidence, it still yields interpretations and explanations of facts which, though an unbeliever cannot so interpret them, reinforce the basic commitment the believer has made, and can therefore be offered in support of his commitment, much as success in scientific prediction can be offered in support of, though not perhaps evidence for, a secular commitment to the constancy of nature. We might call this kind of support *internal* support.

With these provisos, it seems to me that the permissive Parity Argument is a successful argument. By this I mean that if it is true that each of us must make some intellectual commitments that cannot be justified without circularity, in order to have standards of justification to use in assessing any beliefs whatever, then someone who holds a religious commitment such as belief in God as one of those fundamental intellectual commitments cannot be convicted of irrationality merely because belief in God could not be justified by evidence to someone who did *not* have it as one of his own fundamental commitments.

I make this judgment without any formal decision on the question of whether Plantinga or Malcolm are right in arguing that we must all make some intellectual commitments without justification, even though the case for such a view seems to me a strong one. It may be, for anything I have said here, that the Pyrrhonian is right in saying that one can somehow manage without any real intellectual commitments at all (at least if we live in a world where others do make them and we can conform belieflessly with their practices). But in that case, it still seems to me that the permissive version of the Parity Argument shows that someone who *does* make such commitments, but does not include religious commitment among them, is in no position to accuse someone who does include religious belief among them of irrationality. For the criteria of rationality he will have to use for this negative judgment can be dismissed by the believer as arbitrarily restrictive. It remains true, however, that if there were some independent and universal criterion of rationality, in addition to that specified in my first proviso, which secular intellectual commitments satisfy but religious commitment does not, the permissive Parity Argument would collapse. While I think that in their different ways Sextus, Hume and Wittgenstein have made this appear an unclear and unlikely possibility, I do not wish to pronounce on such a vast theme here. With these restrictions, we can say that the Evangelical Fideist is right on this matter.

I have said that the permissive Parity Argument, which I have now accepted, differs from the version I attributed to Pascal and Kierkegaard, against which Hume's defences seem inadequate. I must now explore this further. This version accused the secular unbeliever of inconsistency in not espousing faith along with his secular intellectual commitments, since these were equally groundless. I have argued that Hume, who accepts the groundlessness of the secular natural beliefs, is indeed open to this charge if his reason for not espousing religious belief is that the evidence does not justify it. But the permissive version of the Argument suggests a response which he could have made but did not make; a response which would have been a sufficient counter to a charge of inconsistency. I surmise that the reason he did not make it, even though it would have fitted in very well with the rest of his system, is that he never quite came to terms with himself on the matter at issue in Part XII of the *Dialogues* – the matter of whether, in spite of the absence of good arguments to establish it, we do not after all feel the need to ascribe our cosmos to an intelligence.

The response is this. It is true that if one adopts the commitments of secular common sense but not that of religion, one is acting in two opposite ways, and so, apparently, inconsistently. But it is possible to do what we all do when called on to defend apparently inconsistent actions, and point to special reasons for treating the two differently. The reason in this case is the following. If we compare the standpoint of the secular unbeliever with that of the religious believer, we can easily see that the latter differs from the former by *addition*. That is to say, the believer does not reject the unbeliever's commitment to the regularity of nature or the independent reality of objects of perception; they both share these commitments. They differ in that the believer adds on to them another commitment, to the effect that the world they share is the handiwork of a divine intelligence. (Historically, no doubt, the process has been one of subtraction rather than addition, in that all people used to agree that the world in which we live has such a cause, but by Hume's day there were some, including Hume himself, who did not include this among their commitments, and by now there are very many. While this is true, it is not misleading to describe our *present* situation as one in which the believer adds something the unbeliever does not share.) If, in adding it, the believer also wishes to accuse the unbeliever of irrationality in not doing so, it can be retorted that the unbeliever can offer a reason for stopping where he does. It will consist in pointing out that our secular intellectual commitments have borne fruit in the form of a large body of common sense and scientific beliefs, and that in arriving at these beliefs we have not merely supported them with positive evidence, but have refrained from including among them any beliefs which openly *exceed* the evidence: we have established our common fund of beliefs by applying a standard of *simplicity*. Without some such standard, we would not be able to sort out those beliefs which should be part of our common fund of belief from those many alternatives to them which could account for the same data but are more extravagant in the ways they do so. To say that all the phenomena of our world have to be viewed as ordered by a divine mind is to add a dimension which clearly violates the standard of simplicity. The success and importance of this standard is a reason for refraining from adding the religious commitment to our secular ones.

The first thing to say about this response is that it is not a mere repetition of a response I attributed to Hume in our last chapter. There I took him to say that we have to take the secular natural beliefs for granted in all our reasonings, but not belief in God. To this it is enough for the believer to reply that we do need to believe in God to sustain our religious reasonings, if not our secular ones. I now suggest Hume might have said, instead, that in the realms of reasoning the secular natural beliefs make possible we consistently find it indispensable to apply the principle of simplicity, and that theism violates it. It might seem to some of Hume's readers that Hume does say this — namely in those places where he stresses that the supposed evidence for a divine mind falls short of proving it, since we can only infer from an effect to a cause adequate to produce it, not to a cause that is *more* than adequate to produce it.[10] But in these places, it seems to me that Hume is merely showing us (vital though this is to recognize) that the evidence does not justify the theistic interpretation. I am suggesting now that he might have done more than this, and offered a reason for thinking that this is a sufficient ground for not venturing to accept that interpretation, namely the experienced importance and success of the principle of simplicity.

How good would such a response be? It seems to me that it would do for secular unbelief what Plantinga and Malcolm claim (successfully, I have suggested) to do for religious belief — to fend off the charge of irrationality. It would provide a defence against the charge levelled against it, in this case that of gratuitous inconsistency. Its result is essentially *permissive* only: to show that both secular belief and religious belief can be acquitted of the charge of irrationality.

That it would do no more than this perhaps needs argument. In offering an argument, I will have to augment some of the things Plantinga and Malcolm have said. Suppose someone were to claim that the principle of simplicity has more than defensive use: that it is a basis for accusing believers of irrationality in adding to the commitments they and unbelievers share with each other? "After all", such an unbeliever might say, "we can now respond to the critic of unbelief who says we ought by rights to add on theistic commitment by telling him that we do not merely *choose* not to, but can defend our refusal; yet he, in adding such a commitment on, merely defends *him*self by saying we have no intellectual right to stop him". Plantinga's argument particularly might seem open to this comment, if what I have offered as an unbeliever's defence were accepted. But it is easy to see how a believer might augment what he says to deal with this. He could say three things. First, he could point out that the fruitfulness and importance of the principle of simplicity can be matched by the fruitfulness of theism as a source of religious understandings of our world. More importantly, he could insist that we must adapt the standards of human enquiry to the themes into which we enquire, and that although the principle of simplicity is necessary and fruitful in the scientific investigation of nature, it is a hindrance when supernatural themes are introduced, since it prevents our considering them at all. Thirdly, against the austere virtue of simplicity, he could set the appeal of explanatory depth, and say that although belief in God does not undercut the scientific understanding of phenomena, but leaves it as it is, it adds another dimension to it.

To this, in turn, the unbeliever could say that he has no way of being sure that the theist's alleged depth of understanding is not spurious and obfuscatory; and that not only is the believer's religiously-based understanding of natural phenomena, on his own admission, unnecessary, but he can offer naturalistic accounts of why people like his opponent come to believe such unnecessary things. To which the believer can offer a theological account of why the unbeliever refuses to consider anything beyond naturalistic accounts. And so the debates proceed, along familiar and wearying patterns.[11]

Stated generally, the situation the permissive Parity Argument reveals to us would seem to be this. To say that a person's beliefs are irrational is of course to claim that they fail to meet a standard. The accusation of irrationality may be successful if the standard against which these beliefs are measured is one which they indeed fail to satisfy, and is shared by accuser and accused alike. If, on the other hand, the standard they fail to meet is not shared by the accused, or is overridden or modified within the accused's system of beliefs by another standard to which he subscribes, the accusation will fail — though it may be of considerable importance in other ways to understand that the beliefs criticized do indeed fall short of the criteria to which the accuser appeals. The standards themselves cannot be justified in a manner that is neutral between systems of thought, but each side can never-theless support or defend the standards he accepts by making clear the intel-lectual benefits derivable from them within his system; and his being in a position to do this is itself a reason for saying that he, or the system he has, is a rational one. In such a situation neither side is in a position to accuse the other of irrationality, even though each can give reasons (though not neutral reasons) for its difference from the other.

This at least would appear to be the situation which the permissive Parity Argument shows to us when we examine the disagreement between believers and unbelievers in the light of it. Neither can successfully accuse the other of irrationality merely because the other has fundamental beliefs which are not held for reasons he himself would accept as justifications. This defence can, on each side, be supplemented by showing how his own system of thought can respond to those facts of experience which the two systems interpret differently.

A situation such as this, in which each side can deflect the criticisms of the other is ready-made for the classical Skeptic's response: equipoise, sus-pense of judgment and ultimate quietude. So while the Parity Argument, reduced as I have argued it must be to a purely permissive and defensive form, is a successful answer to a familiar attack on faith, it nevertheless seems to me in the end to militate against the Evangelical Fideist's fundamental con-tention that it is non-intellectual factors, and evil ones at that, that must always stand between men and a commitment to God. This is especially clear in our own day, where many thousands have no natural or environ-mentally acquired inclination toward a religious interpretation of their world, even though many thousands of others do have such an inclination. For in the absence of it, we cannot suppose, except as a dogmatic theological assertion, that no one can sincerely align himself on the unbelieving side of a deadlock like the one I have described.

For in a situation of deadlock such as this, our world is *intellectually ambiguous*, much as the Skeptic says it is. I have already argued against the Fideist view that if man is corrupt and God is hidden and man is free, we should *expect* our world to be intellectually ambiguous. I content myself here with saying, once more, that if it is ambiguous in the way I have indi-cated, this would provide an unbeliever with a reasonable excuse for his unbelief — an explanation of it which might well be true even if his intellect were not twisted by corruption. So although the Parity Argument contains important truths about the status of religious commitment, it does not, finally, do anything to show that there is theological advantage in accepting a skeptical evaluation of natural theology. It merely shows that someone who has faith without the benefit of natural theology is not irrational to do so.

A few concluding comments on natural theology and its purposes. Malcolm and Plantinga appear to say that it rests on a mistake – the mistake of agreeing that religious belief needs justification, and then seeking to offer it. I think that the permissive Parity Argument does undermine this supposition, if natural theologians were making it. But I am not at all sure that we can accuse them of this, even though they did, of course, think that they could supply rational grounds for religion. Certainly Aquinas seems to me to have been quite clear that the believer whose belief is solely a matter of faith, which to him means that it is in no way a result of philosophical argument, is not irrational. But he certainly also thought that some of the things such a person believes can be demonstrated, and that by doing this we give a lesser, but still real, degree of support to the other things he believes. The Fideist would reject all this; but unless he merely rejects it because he thinks the natural theologian's arguments are failures, it seems to me he is mistaken to do so. For the success of the natural theologian's arguments would show two things. It would show that the believer's key commitment could be derived from facts and standards which he and the unbeliever shared; and in consequence it would also show that the unbeliever ought to accede to it *by his own criteria of rationality* – for example, without violating the principle of simplicity. Not only would this be shown if someone produced a suitably refurbished version of one of the traditional proofs; it would also come about if we should encounter what I have called a probative revelatory phenomenon.[12] Should either occur, the unbeliever would be shown to be irrational not to believe, or at least to be irrational to *persist* in unbelief, and the Parity Argument would then not shield him. If this were to take place, our intellectual situation would be *dis-ambiguated*. Then, and not until then, would there be a case for saying that unbelief could only be due to some nonintellectual factor such as corruption.

I think the natural theologians were commonly seeking to do something as strong as this. They were not offering arguments in support of religion because they felt that without the presence of such arguments religious belief would stand convicted of irrationality. They were on the attack: they were trying to show that it is irrational not to believe. I incline to think that, contrary to what Evangelical Fideists tell us, the success of their enterprise, or the occurrence of something else that would have this consequence, is a necessary, if not a sufficient, condition for showing that unbelief must be due to sin.

Theologians should therefore welcome, not discourage, attempts to provide intellectual support for belief in God. If they conclude, in the face of the long record of failures, that they have to agree with those philosophers who dismiss such attempts as hopeless, they should judge this result to be what it is — a great pity, and a significant theological *problem*. For what reason could there be for unbelievers always to have reasonable grounds for their hesitations?

CONFORMIST FIDEISM AND CONTEMPORARY PHILOSOPHY

The influence of Pascal and Kierkegaard has been very great, and I have therefore not felt it necessary to demonstrate the contemporary relevance of Evangelical Fideism in detail. (It has not, in consequence, been part of my case to suggest that the recent arguments I have just discussed owe their origin, to any degree, to what Pascal or Kierkegaard said. The arguments are of independent value, and they have shown us a way of assessing specific claims that Pascal and Kierkegaard *did* make.)

It might seem, on the other hand, that Conformist Fideism is a mere historical curiosity. In fact, however, some vigorous elements in present-day philosophy of religion show striking similarities to it, even though their representatives would regard themselves as evading or refuting skepticism, not as embracing it. The similarities are sufficient to show it would be wise to consider whether the defects in Conformist Fideism can be matched in these contemporary views also.

What were these defects? Most clearly, it was absurd to offer Skeptical suspense as the attitudinal core of faith. The problem is not whether this is a viable proposal, since it clearly is not; the problem is why anyone should seriously have attempted it. I suggested that the key lies in the fact that both faith and classical Skepticism are saving ways of life that offer escape from anxiety; and that each has a similar practical outcome — a mode of participation in daily affairs that combines active involvement with inner detachment. This combination has opposed sources: the Skeptic has abandoned all conviction that the practices to which he conforms can be founded on true judgments of fact or of value, whereas the man of faith sees beyond these practices to a transcendent source of conviction and loyalty. This was missed by the Conformists because of their revulsion against religious enthusiasm and intolerance, and their consequent wish to minimize the importance of doctrine in faith.

The common factor which unites the thinkers on whom I shall now comment is the wish to commend religious faith in an age when so many reject it because they are unable to assent to what they take to be its doctrines. The doctrines are rejected because their critics judge them to be superstitious, scientifically false, fantastic, or even incoherent. In the face of this rejection, some defenders of faith have suggested that it does not, or need not, require commitment to these doctrines, so that rejection of faith is due to tragic misunderstandings. I suggest that the faith such thinkers commend would have to have at its core a detachment which is close to that of the Skeptic, and would therefore fail to *be* faith. No doubt the recommendations of the latter-day Conformists might serve to prolong the religiosity of our society, just as the participation of the classical Skeptic must have served to reinforce the practices of the cults of his day, but they preclude anyone who matches their descriptions from having faith himself.

The writers I have in mind differ among themselves, but share a common method: that of offering reinterpretations of the meaning of religious belief and practice. In their reinterpretations they seek to correct misunderstandings of these beliefs and practices that they see as common both to the hostile critics they wish to answer and to traditional defenders of faith who have sought to answer them in the wrong way. These misunderstandings are due to the assumption that faith requires us to assert the reality of a number of supernatural facts — such as the being of a God who is incorporeal, personal, almighty, and loving, who has entered history in the person of Jesus, who died and rose from the dead, and in so doing has redeemed us from a state of sin and enabled us to inherit eternal life: this being not only a quality of life now, but a continuation of it hereafter. To varying degrees and in various ways, they argue that the assertion of such supernatural facts is not central to faith, and that both its attackers (who have rejected it because they do not accept these supposed facts) and its traditional defenders (who have tried to authenticate these facts in order to sustain it) have distorted its true character.

This mode of argument is far from new, since it is in many ways typical of a good deal of Nineteenth and Twentieth Century Liberal theology. But it has gained in subtlety and influence in our own day through the involvement of some of the disciples of Wittgenstein, who have sought to apply his methods to philosophy of religion. Their involvement is in part a response to the fact that the attacks on faith, which have for a long time been based on alleged collisions between supernatural claims and scientific knowledge, have been augmented in our time by linguistic criticisms. The burden of these criticisms, as we find them in the writings of Flew and Nielsen, for example, is well known.[12] They claim that the assertion of the key supernatural facts of Christian faith generates incoherences, since the language we have to use for such assertions, which is the language of action, intention, will, and emotion, has its natural home in discourse about human beings, where it has varied but readily-discernible connections with evidence and experience; but in its religious use it seems to lack such connections. So if faith does not depend on our adhering to outmoded and pre-scientific falsehoods, this is only because in the last resort, its key statements lack a clear meaning. The responses on which I am commenting depend on arguing that, rightly interpreted, faith does not depend on trying to assert such supernatural facts at all. Since it looks to most philosophers as though it does, it becomes necessary to give an alternative account of its nature that can show the irrelevance of the linguistic (and the scientific) criticisms.

This desupernaturalizing, or non-credal, defence, has something vital in common with the argument from Malcolm we examined earlier in the chapter. That, too, is inspired by some of Wittgenstein's key contentions: in this case, contentions about the limits that must be placed upon demands for justification of the ways we think and talk. The non-credal defenders of faith are also insistent that the demand for faith to be justified by evidence is an extraneous and uncomprehending demand. But Malcolm's argument, though he asserts this also, does not suggest that what the believer proclaims has to be desupernaturalized for his defence to apply to it.

I have already made passing mention of important likenesses between Wittgenstein, Hume, and Sextus. Each despairs of philosophical constructions designed to give justification to our common beliefs and intellectual practices; but each seeks also to reconcile us to those practices and enable us to participate in them in company with others without being beholden to the philosophical demand for such underpinnings. Each sees such a demand as one which it is impossible to satisfy and as a source of unnecessary anxiety, and therefore as something from which we should be freed. To Sextus the method of freeing oneself from it is that of sating and exhausting it — by showing that for every theory there is a counter-theory and for every justification a negative critique, until we attain an equilibrium which permits us to return to participation in the everyday without the commitments we have hitherto been trying to sustain by theory. To Hume the method of release is that of treating both dogmatism and skepticism as theoretical pastimes, of confining our philosophical activities as far as we can to issues that arise within the framework of our natural beliefs, and of maintaining a social involvement that will keep needless anxieties at bay and keep intellectual distempers in their place. For Wittgenstein the demand must be undermined by doing philosophy itself in a new way: a way which shows, case by case, how the demand for justification arises from (and worsens) deep misunderstandings of the areas of discourse about which philosophical problems have been raised. The misunderstandings are then seen to be due to chronic intellectual obsessions such as a craving for generality, or a determination to view all uses of language on the model of one, such as naming. The anti-metaphysical aspect of the method comes from the fact that metaphysical constructions are viewed within it as attempts to provide answers to questions that are due to misunderstandings, and are properly dealt with in another way: by assembling reminders of how language is actually used in the areas of discourse about which the confusions have arisen. The result of the process should be a return to that discourse without the theoretical preconceptions that produced the original dissatisfaction with it. Philosophy, therefore, 'leaves everything as it is'. So whereas Sextus' method is the assemblage of the positive and negative arguments of others, and Hume's method is the psychological confinement of philosophical enquiry, Wittgenstein's is the cultivation of such second-order understandings as are necessary to show philosophical dissatisfactions to be confused. This has suggested to many that such second-order understanding can have a positive value in itself, as well as an *ad hoc* utility in combating philosophical perplexity, but this is not our concern here. What is of primary interest is the claim that philosophy leaves everything as it finds it. What are the implications of this when what philosophy is speaking about is religion? We have seen one implication in Malcolm's essay: that religious belief is not something for which external justification can be demanded. I wish to look now at the far more radical view that understanding religious belief as belief in supernatural facts is also a result of this mistaken demand.[13]

I shall borrow a term from Don Cupitt,[14] and refer to the supernatural reading of religious belief as 'theological realism'. Someone committed to it would hold that the supernatural facts which he thinks faith requires must indeed *be* facts for faith to be true, so that if they are not facts, but fantasies (or, even worse, not coherently expressible), then faith is unjustified. Most atheists or agnostics are theological realists, and obviously most defenders and apologists for faith are also. In that sense accepting theological realism looks like a precondition for considering that faith *has* a justification, *and* for thinking it *lacks* it. But this is not enough to demonstrate that a theological realist cannot hold that the key supernatural facts may be rationally asserted *without* justification yet still with rationality (that one can be 'within one's intellectual rights' to include them among one's basic beliefs); or cannot hold that belief in these supernatural facts is a foundational belief of religion that is immune to attack from outside it. Theological realism is not *obviously* incompatible with the belief that philosophy leaves everything as it is. It could only be shown to be incompatible with that understanding of philosophy by a demonstration that when we acquire a better second-order understanding of religious faith we find that its distinctive character is one that theological realism misrepresents. Then, and only then, could it be plausible to suggest that it gets its popularity among attackers and defenders of religion from the fact that each is still confusedly looking for a justification, and misreading the faith in order to supply it.

The philosopher who has argued for this most extensively is D. Z. Phillips.[15] I can make no pretence here to examine his work in depth or detail. My purpose is more limited. It is to see how close the analogy is between the outcome of his analysis and the outcome of the proposals of the Conformist Fideist. In this respect it is important to understand that it is of the essence of Phillips' position that he is giving an account of what faith *is and has been*, not that he is proposing that his readers adopt some other stance toward life in its place, even under the same name.

If a thinker rejects theological realism, but thinks that theological realism is nevertheless an integral part of faith as traditionally practiced (not merely as traditionally described by philosophers), he may recommend that we adopt a position which is free of supernatural beliefs, but still embodies some of the emotional or conative aspects of faith that have so far been bound up with them. He may consider that these have such value that they should be pursued for themselves. If he does not think that these non-realist elements have been *distinctive* of faith as traditionally understood, or exclusive to it, he will then only retain such terms as 'faith' or 'religion' or 'Christianity' because they help to give the weight of tradition to that which he wants us to preserve; though he may not wish at all to insist upon the distinctiveness of it. This, very roughly, is the position of R. B. Braithwaite[16] and R. M. Hare.[17] Both seek to emphasize the core of moral resolution in Christian faith, but wish to abandon theological realism, since, in Hare's words, they do not "believe that the differences between those who accept it and those who reject it have the slightest substance". Such factual commitments as they have are not supernatural ones, and although they consider it proper to call themselves Christians, they clearly concede that the radical nature of the changes they recommend are such as to make the question of whether or not they should do so a controversial one. On the other hand, a proponent of non-realist religion may wish to retain the great bulk of traditional ritual, practice, and spirituality, but to reinterpret it through and through in a non-realist manner. He may wish to do this because he feels that the values he wishes to preserve have a distinct embodiment in the tradition he is reinterpreting, which justifies the continued use of the standard language and ritual to express them. This, I think, is the position of Don Cupitt, who makes statements of which this is typical:

I therefore maintain that by the criterion of religious adequacy (or fitness to bring us to salvation) faith must be understood in a thoroughly voluntarist way and God in a thoroughly internalized and non-objective way. [18]

In offering the reinterpretations he speaks of in this passage, he attempts to transform the continuing tradition of religious life and practice into something that better expresses the most vital religious values.[19] Here again, although the retention of the title of 'faith' for what results can be challenged, it can also be defended. What is clear, however, is that what is offered is offered as re-interpretation. Neither Hare nor Cupitt is claiming that theological realism *has not been* integral to the faith 'as it is', but to dispense with some of what it is in the interest of preserving and revitalizing the rest of it.

What Phillips has sought to do, if I understand him correctly, is to present an understanding of religious thought and practice that shows faith *as it is* to be a non-realist phenomenon. It is therefore fitting that two of his most extensive studies should be concerned with aspects of the traditional Christian faith that lend themselves most naturally to realist interpretations, namely the practice of prayer and the belief in immortality. In each case he attempts to show that the supernaturalist reading of these is the result of a misunderstanding of their real role in faith. To think that in prayer the believer is addressing requests to a supernatural agent is to miss the whole point and value of prayer within the actual practice of faith. The point and value of it is *internal to its practice*. If the point could be understood in supernaturalist terms, then prayer would entail expectations of interruptions in the processes of nature, and would only achieve its point when these were supplied in the interests of the suppliant. The point of prayer is realized, rather, when the believer sees that the world has no obligation to him, that everything is a gift and nothing is his due, when he radically accepts what life gives. The supernaturalist understanding of prayer tends, therefore, to hinder its proper practice, not merely to misrepresent it. He says similar things about the belief in immortality. If this is understood as continuance of life after death, this will tend to make one interpret what the believer says and does as an attempt to order his life now so that he can enjoy the proper rewards hereafter, and this will submit his religious practice to the demands of his ego. The proper understanding of the concept of eternal life is in terms of the *destruction* of the ego:

> The immortality of the soul by contrast refers to a person's relation to the self-efface-
> ment and love of others involved in dying to the self. Death is overcome in that dying
> to the self is the meaning of the believer's life.[20]

The most explicit insistence on the internality of religious concepts to the practices in which they are used comes in a passage a page further on in the same work:

> I am suggesting, then, that eternal life for the believer is participation in the life of God,
> and that this life has to do with dying to the self, seeing that all things are a gift from
> God, that nothing is ours by right or necessity. At this point, however, many philo-
> sophers will say that I have yet to prove the existence of God. . . . To speak of the love
> of God is not to prove the existence of a God of love. To say that everything is a gift
> from God is not to prove the existence of the Giver. I believe these popular philosophical
> objections to be radically misconstrued. In learning by contemplation, attention, renun-
> ciation, what forgiving, thanking, loving, etc. mean in these contexts, the believer is
> participating in the reality of God; *this is what we mean by God's reality*.[21]

I think that the position Phillips takes combines two things that it is important to distinguish. The first is the claim that theological realism is a second-
order distortion of what believers are about, and that when we examine what
they do without preconceptions we can see that what they do has meaning
and purpose in a way that is internal to itself, and is not dependent on reference to supernatural realities (like an incorporeal God) that lie beyond it.
Opposition to this claim would come from a different second-order understanding of what faith is. Both would *leave* faith as it is, but would differ
about *how* it is. But Phillips also seems to suggest that theological realism
interferes with the faith: that someone who is tainted with it will not *pray
properly*, and will respond to death in the wrong way. His thesis here becomes normative as well as descriptive; it supports a particular view of what
faith ought to be, and to contest theological realism as religiously damaging.
Now it is virtually impossible for any account of faith to avoid this, since it
is a mere fantasy to suppose that there is anyone (or at least anyone of moderate sophistication) who participates in the practices and rituals of a religious
tradition without doing so in a way that aligns them with one theological
interpretation of them rather than another. Liturgies and prayers reflect theologies; it is not only the other way around. In itself the normative choice of

one form of religious life as a paradigm for an analysis of the whole of it is not objectionable, if only because it is hard to have practices and beliefs to point to unless one does this. It is a matter not of demonstration, but of judgment, to decide whether a particular characterization of religious faith can pass as a reasonable description of a representative range of religious phenomena, and does not achieve its accuracy by hopelessly biased sampling. Phillips' affinity with such writers as Tolstoy and Simone Weil prompts him to pick on certain forms of spirituality as necessary features of a proper case of true or genuine religious life: forms which stress the centrality of submission, contemplation, denial of egocentricity, and the like. One can certainly sympathize with any bias that the influence of such religious figures may cause, and we may not, while we sympathize, feel that we miss those frequent aspects of faith which they do not stress so much — such as concern for proper ritual, political and social activism, and the rest. The claim, however, is that supernaturalism can be seen to be a misdescription of all the key religious phenomena because it can serve to foster incorrect attitudes towards those chosen as normative: that because a supernaturalist understanding of prayer can make some who pray do so in a way that really asks for things, and that on the preferred version of the faith, asking for things is *praying badly*, a supernaturalist understanding of prayer is thereby shown to be erroneous. This may or may not be leaving things as they are; but it is certainly using a judgment of how they should be as a basis for preferring one account of how they are to another.

Wittgenstein's philosophical prescriptions tend to encourage the assumption of a pre-philosophical innocence to which the enlightened philosopher eventually returns after he has surmounted the puzzlement that philosophers have generated. This assumption is not made by Sextus, or by Hume. Whether or not it fits other realms of discourse, it is clearly a Procrustean assumption with which to approach religious discourse. The vast majority of religious believers, including those closest to Phillips' norms of true practice, have a theologically realist understanding of what they do, and any divisions among them about the right way to pray, or the proper attitude to death, occur within such a framework. Perhaps certain preferred ways of praying, or of facing the fact of death, would have as natural, or even more natural, a home in a desupernaturalized context. If so, there is a tension within the tradition that is being examined, and perhaps this tension should be broken by abandoning theological realism. But if this is our position, we are moving toward the explicitly revisionary stance of Hare or Cupitt, that seeks to preserve what is best, not what there is.

From this I would infer only the following: that a believer who encounters anti-religious criticisms, and then returns to the faith after absorbing Phillips' account of it, will be taking part in the traditional religious life once more, but necessarily in a manner which requires him to withhold assent from a pervasive understanding of what he is about which is as much a part of the tradition he re-enters as the practices he takes part in. He will have to see the practices as having only their own point, not as deriving their point from our relationship to realities beyond them. In this his participation will have exactly the same kind of inner reservation within it that the participation of the classical Skeptics had. He, like them, will suppose that the reservation he attaches to the things he says and does will enable him to get greater spiritual benefit, and suffer less spiritual harm, than other participants. But for him these benefits and avoidances are not the fruits of faith: they have become its essence. So he will not be a defender of the faith to which he has apparently returned, but the advance guard of something else. For he will be continually using a language of relationship and response in a context that, to him, includes neither. Instead of participating in a tradition of response, he will be responding to a tradition. The tradition will have value to him, but it will do so in a manner which requires him to subtract from it the meaning he used to think it possessed. He will stand in a continuing tradition, and perhaps even represent subscribe to a religion, but he will not have remained in a faith.

NOTES

[1] The essay is to be found in *Contemporary Philosophy of Religion*, ed. by Steven M. Cahn and David Shatz, Oxford University Press, New York, 1982. Earlier versions of its arguments are in papers in *Rationality and Religious Belief*, ed. by C. F. Delaney, Notre Dame University Press, 1978, and in *Nous*, Vol. 15, 1981.

[2] The essay is in Norman Malcolm, *Thought and Knowledge*, Cornell University Press, Ithaca, 1977.

[3] Ludwig Wittgenstein, *On Certainty*, ed. by G. E. M. Anscombe and G. H. von Wright, trans. by D. Paul and G. E. M. Anscombe, Blackwell, Oxford, 1969.

[4] 'The Groundlessness of Belief', pp. 203–204.

[5] That there are striking similarities between Hume and Wittgenstein on this matter is not, to my knowledge, recognized so far in studies of Wittgenstein, even though it has more than a slight bearing on the relation of Wittgenstein to skepticism. It has, however, been noted in Hume scholarship. See Peter Jones, 'Strains in Hume and Wittgenstein', in *Hume: a Re-evaluation*, ed. by D. Livingston and J. King, Fordham University Press, New York, 1976.

[6] 'The Groundlessness of Belief', p. 212.

[7] Plantinga's comments on this theme in the essay are very brief. To me they suggest *either* that he thinks justifications of belief in God through other basic beliefs are possible but not necessary for a basic belief in God to be accounted rational, *or* that he thinks the believer can support his belief with reasons, but reasons that the unbeliever would find question-begging – with reasons, that is, that would provide what I have called internal support. With both writers, a decision on how far belief in God has grounds would have to take account of the fact that each has offered a version of the Ontological Proof.

[8] 'Rationality and Religious Belief', p. 270.

[9] See the latest statement of it in his *The Nature of Necessity*, Clarendon Press, Oxford, 1974, Chapter IX.

[10] See, for example, Section XI ('Of a Particular Providence and of a Future State') of the first *Enquiry*.

[11] For a fuller characterization of the stand-off I describe here, see my essay 'Is a Religious Epistemology Possible?' in *Knowledge and Necessity*, Royal Institute of Philosophy Lectures, Volume Three 1968–69, ed. by G. N. A. Vesey, Macmillan, London, 1970; pp. 263–280.

[12] See, most famously, Flew's contributions to *New Essays in Philosophical Theology*, ed. by A. G. N. Flew and Alasdair MacIntyre, SCM Press, London, 1955, and such works as his *God and Philosophy*, Hutchinson, London, 1966. Kai Nielsen's views can be found most conveniently in his books *Contemporary Critiques of Religion*, Macmillan, London, 1971, and *Scepticism*, Macmillan, London, 1973; both contain extensive bibliographies of the controversies to which he contributes. I have offered views on these controversies myself in *Religion and Rationality*, Random House, New York, 1971, and *Problems of Religious Knowledge*, Macmillan, London, 1971.

[13] In addition to the works of D. Z. Phillips listed below, see T. R. Miles, *Religion and the Scientific Outlook*, Allen and Unwin, London, 1959; S. C. Brown, *Do Religious Claims Make Sense?* SCM Press, London, 1969; and D. Z. Phillips (ed.) *Religion and Understanding*, Blackwell, Oxford, 1967.

[14] Don Cupitt, *Taking Leave of God*, SCM Press, London, 1980.

[15] D. Z. Phillips, *The Concept of Prayer*, Routledge and Kegan Paul, London, 1965; *Death and Immortality*, Macmillan, London, 1970; *Faith and Philosophical Enquiry*, Routledge and Kegan Paul, London, 1970; see also his essays, 'Faith, Scepticism and Religious Understanding' in *Religion and Understanding*, and 'Religious Belief and Language-Games' in Basil Mitchell, (ed.) *Philosophy of Religion*, Oxford University Press, 1971. For criticisms of Phillips, see Kai Nielsen, 'Wittgensteinian Fideism', in *Contemporary Philosophy of Religion*, ed. by Steven M. Cahn and David Shatz, Oxford University Press, 1982, and John Hick, 'Religion as Fact-asserting' in his *God and the Universe of Faiths*, Macmillan, London, 1973. Two books I have found of great value here are Carlos G. Prado, *Illusions of Faith: A Critique of Non-Credal Religion*, Kendall-Hunt, Dubuque, Iowa, 1980, and Alan Keightley, *Wittgenstein, Grammar, and God*, Epworth, London, 1976. I have leaned on the latter particularly in what follows.

[16] See his 'An Empiricist's View of the Nature of Religious Belief', the Eddington Memorial Lecture for 1955, published by the Cambridge University Press and reprinted in Ian T. Ramsey (ed.), *Christian Ethics and Contemporary Philosophy*, SCM Press, London, 1966.

[17] R. M. Hare, 'The Simple Believer', in Gene Outka and John P. Reeder, (eds.), *Religion and Morality*, Doubleday, New York, 1973, pp. 393–427.

[18] *Taking Leave of God*, p. 126.
[19] See *Taking Leave of God*, p. 82.
[20] *Death and Immortality*, p. 54.
[21] *Death and Immortality*, p. 54–55.

CHAPTER 8

THE NATURE OF FAITH

In this book I have argued that the fundamental claim of Skeptical Fideism is mistaken. This is the claim that in undermining our confidence in the powers of human reason, the Skeptic is performing a service for faith. This has been presented in two main ways. The Conformist Fideist argues that faith is best understood as one form of the undogmatic participation recommended by the classical Pyrrhonists. This argument misrepresents what faith is, and gains its otherwise strange appeal from its perception of structural likenesses between the Skeptic way and the life with faith as its centre. The Evangelical Fideist does not attempt to absorb faith into the Skeptical tradition, but holds that the destruction of the pretensions of reason is a necessary condition for faith to take root, since these pretensions merely serve the corruption in human nature which is the real obstacle to it. I have rejected this, on the general ground that if the Skeptic is right, it becomes less, not more, likely that unbelief is due to corruption, and that if the claims of faith are sound, the efforts of natural theologians to support them with reasons cannot be dismissed as hindrances. I have, however, accepted a negative, or permissive, version of the Parity Argument. This Argument tells us that we believe many things which it is indispensable for us to believe, but for which we have not discovered rational grounds, and that it is inconsistent for an unbeliever who does this to accuse the faithful of irrationality, merely because they believe in God in the same way. This does not entail, however, that the Skeptic is right in surmising that no rational grounds for our natural beliefs exist. Nor does it entail that those who have faith would be justified in accusing the unbeliever of irrationality for not himself adding belief in God to *his* list of ungrounded beliefs. In these circumstances, furthermore, if there are no successful demonstrations in natural theology, or no probative revelatory events, to remove the religious ambiguity of our situation, this is a theological problem, and not, as the Fideist claims, an apologetic advantage.

I have not committed myself in this argument to a particular view on the soundness of skeptical attacks on reason, or to the existence or absence of justifications for our secular natural beliefs, or of belief in God. I think that the estimate of Skeptical Fideism that I have presented here does not depend on a particular decision on these very difficult questions. I have found it necessary to take a side on some slightly less broad issues, in particular on the form Skepticism has to take to avoid charges of incoherence, and on the degree to which we have voluntary control over our beliefs. There is, however, one fundamental issue on which I have made incidental pronouncements in the course of my argument, and on which the thinkers I have examined have very strong views, which provide the motive for their theories. This is the question of the nature of faith itself. It is quite out of the question, even were I competent for the task, to present more than a fragmentary account of this most fundamental of religious attitudes; but it is necessary to indicate in a schematic way the sort of understanding of faith to which one is led if the arguments of this book are sound.

A brief look, first, at some of the elements that have emerged in our earlier discussion. First, in our short study of the Erasmus–Luther controversy, we encountered the identification of faith with 'piety' (roughly, moral dedication and religious service) opposed by a conception of it which sought to distinguish it sharply from secular morality by emphasizing its commitment and its need for *assertion*. I have suggested that the Conformist view gets its plausibility from the fact that faith, like Pyrrhonism, gives peace instead of anxiety, moderates secular entanglements, and requires regular sustenance, including intellectual sustenance in the face of doubt. Second, such sustenance can be regarded as one example of the way in which our beliefs are under our indirect control, so that the assent involved in them is not itself a voluntary action, but is the result of factors, including the consideration of argument and evidence, which can be controlled by such actions. This indirect control is stressed by Pascal, who attempts to lead his reader toward faith by weakening his emotional resistance to it, and replacing it first by a willingness to consider it seriously, and then by a positive desire to acquire it. Kierkegaard, reverting to the view that assent is wholly voluntary, claims that only God can give us the power to exercise it, and that when we do we are submitting not to a truth, but to a person, and that our state is properly called a passion, not a belief. I shall try to comment on all of these positions, and draw my remarks upon them together into a coherent outline.

I must make three procedural assumptions in order to proceed. The first is that I shall be discussing a phenomenon or state of the human personality which was spoken of by Jesus in the Gospels, by Paul in the Epistles to the Romans and Corinthians, and by the author of the Epistle to the Hebrews. I do not assume that the same understanding of it is to be found in these different parts of the new Testament, but I shall take it for granted that if this is not so, differences are to be regarded as different descriptions of one state, not as descriptions of different states. My second assumption is that it is the same state that Erasmus and Luther and Pascal and Kierkegaard were speaking of when they referred to faith, and that here, too, we have differing understandings of what that state includes. These two assumptions yield the result that the immediate subject of what follows is faith as understood in the Christian tradition. I do not, at this point, assume that it is, or is not, to be found, or even spoken of, in other religious traditions, though the question is an important one which I would like to treat elsewhere.[1]

The third thing I shall assume is that faith, so identified, is something that exists. This may seem a strange remark, but it is a necessary one. The writers of the Gospels and the Epistles, to say nothing of later theological figures, all assume that human beings stand in certain relationships to God which can be righted or transformed if they heed the Gospel message. They made *theological assumptions* when they spoke about human nature. These assumptions would obviously be at work when they spoke of faith, which they thought of as an essential part of a right relationship to God. It might be suggested that only those who make these same assumptions can agree that faith is to be found — just as only those who believe in spirits can believe there is such a thing as possession or exorcism. When I say that I am assuming that faith exists, I mean that it can be known to exist even by someone who does *not* make any of the assumptions about man and his relation to God that the New Testament writers, and their theological successors, make: that faith is an identifiable human phenomenon, and its existence is not only a *theological* truth. Someone who does not believe in God at all can, therefore, quite consistently admit that some people (though not he himself) have faith; and he can even identify some of them, such as Paul and Martin Luther and St. Francis of Assisi. The relationship between this assumption and the previous two is not an easy one.[2] But I think it is necessary to make all three in order to be able to attempt a philosophical analysis of faith as it is found among Christians, yet still be able to consider without absurdity whether the term can be used in describing the attitudes of the adherents of other religions, or to speak of secular unbelievers and their natural beliefs. A consequence of making all three is that a theological claim like the assertion that faith can only come to someone through the operation of divine grace, cannot be a necessary, but only a contingent, truth.

A very common view of what faith is, but one which our previous discussions imply to be an inadequate one, is that faith is the holding of certain beliefs. Indeed, the popular view of faith among those who do not have it is that faith is the obstinate insistence on believing doctrines which do not have adequate grounds — pig-headedly being certain of doctrines that are *un*certain. There have been many motives leading religious thinkers to contest this understanding of faith, particularly in recent years. One has been the desire to avoid a situation where faith seems to require acceptance of pre-scientific cosmologies. Another has been the wish to find examples of faith among adherents of other religious traditions, who do not share the beliefs that Christians have. A third, and more influential one, has been the determination to emphasize that faith is not philosophy: that assenting to propositions merely augments one's understanding, but faith transforms one's life and points toward salvation. This last tradition owes most, of course, to Kierkegaard. Each has provided impetus to attempts to sever connections between the concepts of faith and of belief.

Classically, the major exponent of the view that faith is essentially belief is St. Thomas Aquinas.[3] For him faith is the first of the theological virtues — the others, following St. Paul, being hope and charity. Faith is the cognitive component in the Christian life, which leads on to, and makes possible, serenity and love. Each of the theological virtues comes about in a person through the grace of God. In the case of faith, the central act which manifests its presence is the inner act of assent to the truths that the Church proclaims about God. He considers this assent to be a voluntary action (here he is at one with Descartes and Kierkegaard), but one which I am enabled to perform only with divine help. Only such divine help can give me the necessary willingness and desire to perform it; and, more important for our purposes, since I am assenting to truths which reason cannot demonstrate, yet am doing so with a certainty and assurance that otherwise only belongs when I assent to demonstrations, grace must assist me in the act of accepting them. Faith must be belief in unproven truths, since there is no freedom in assenting to what is proved, and therefore no merit in such an assent. So it is a necessary truth that faith and knowledge are distinct. (So the facts that natural theology *can* prove, such as the existence of God, are not part of faith for those who know the arguments.)

This account leads into some difficulties. One is the fact that it is possible to have the right beliefs in a way that is not meritorious and does not lead to the Christian life. The example that exercises Thomas particularly is that of the devils, who believe that God is but (as St. James says) tremble. Thomas says that they believe only because they are forced to by signs — which, for him, unfortunately confuses the question of faith's voluntariness. He also distinguishes between formed, or completed, faith, which is a virtue, and unformed faith which is not. Formed faith is faith that has blossomed out

into hope and charity, and so is part of the full Christian life, whereas unformed faith has not. This is a somewhat unsatisfactory attempt to account
for the fact that when we say someone's conduct is due to his faith, we do
not only mean that it manifests certain beliefs he has. Such a claim seems to
include his attitudes and emotional stance within his faith also.

It is these, non-cognitive aspects of faith that are central to accounts of it
like those we find in Luther or Kierkegaard. Kierkegaard, indeed, explicitly
says that faith is a passion. Let us follow this suggestion, but recognize
immediately that contemporary philosophy has made it abundantly clear
that there is a logic of the emotions. I think that if this is recognized, a viable
understanding of the nature of faith can emerge.

The characteristic stance of the person with faith is a *trust* which issues in
a freedom from anxiety. If we understand this as falling within the logic of
the emotions, then we must ask whether faith, thus understood, is like those
emotions that have objects, such as love, hate, resentment, or gratitude, or
like those that do not, or need not, have objects, such as depression, joy, or
euphoria. It seems clear that if we say faith consists in trust, trust has an
object (a person, in this case God); but serenity[4] or calm seems to be object-
less. Now someone who has faith is, in the New Testament, supposed to be
serene and free from anxiety, and to be enabled by this to perform acts in
God's service that he or she would not otherwise be able to perform. When
Jesus tells his hearers that they have too little faith, part of his message is
that if they had the faith they should, they would cease to be anxious about
their material needs, and would instead be confident that God would care for
them. The author of the Epistle to the Hebrews lists the many achievements
that the faithful were empowered to do because of the faith they displayed.
The serenity characteristic of the faithful person derives from his trust in
God. But the notion of trust is a complex one. In his recent study, *Faith and
Reason*, Richard Swinburne says

To trust a man is to act on the assumption that he will do for you what he knows that
you want or need, when the evidence gives some reason for supposing he may not and
where there may be bad consequences if the assumption is false.[5]

This gives rise to a problem. Understood this way, trust does not look like an
emotion, but like an action that one chooses to do, or a policy one chooses
to follow. Indeed, as Swinburne goes on to say, one can choose to act on an
assumption that one does not actually believe, like Pascal's would-be believer
who acts on the assumption that God exists even though he does not yet
believe it. One can also act on an assumption that one does believe, but only

weakly. Whenever people trust others from duty, or from familial love, in order to give them a chance to behave better than the evidence suggests they may, they are acting in this way. In such cases it is not at all clear that trust releases one from anxiety; it may well produce greater tension, not less, at least until the person trusted passes their test successfully and the trust is vindicated. I incline, therefore, to think that trust as Swinburne defines it is at most a characteristic of someone struggling to attain, or to maintain, their faith; and that someone whose faith is strong, whose faith can be thought of as a paradigm, is someone whose trust, though still an *achievement*, is not in this straightforward way an action or resolution to act. (A declaration of faith, such as the recitation of a Creed, may express the presence of strong faith, or the resolution of weaker faith.) Unsurprisingly, the model that seems to fit here is that of familial trust − the kind of trust which a parent may have for a child, or a child for a parent, before the cruel facts of life produce disillusionment. This is the kind of trust that we often judge to be pardonable but unreasonable, when we encounter it in others. The mother who is the last to see that her son or daughter is guilty of crime is thought to be overlooking the evidence that convinces everyone else, but to be pardonable, even to an extent commendable, in doing so − at least in being more persevering than the police in constructing exonerating interpretations of it. This is very much the way unbelievers judge the trust shown by those who have faith. Such occasions are occasions when what we call *implicit* trust, a trust which takes good will in its object for granted, seems to collide with counter-evidence. Such a trust is often dismissed as immature, but it is perhaps important to notice that the New Testament does not completely share the criteria of maturity that such a judgment implies.

To call such trust implicit is to suggest two things. First, it is taken to mean that the trust is complete or unreserved. Second, it suggests that it is commonly not explicit, that is, not formulated. When negative circumstances confront the person who trusts, however, they are likely to force an explicit recognition of the stance he or she has been taking. Then it is clear that this kind of trust rests upon *beliefs* about the person who is the object of trust, about that person's character and dispositions particularly; and it also becomes clear that to have this trust necessarily disposes the person who has it to *act* in certain ways and refrain from acting in others − ways that can be summed up roughly by saying that the person trusting has no inclination to protect himself against the one he trusts, and will engage in business or personal transactions with that person unhesitatingly. The emergence of negative evidence may well come as a shock, because it brings the self-knowledge that one does believe these things, and is disposed to act in these ways, but may be mistaken in doing so. (It is quite natural here to compare this shock with that received when one first encounters skeptical queries about secular natural beliefs, which are similarly implicit in this double manner.)

Once the beliefs and the dispositions to action are made explicit, both may of course be abandoned, and the trust disappear. It is quite likely, however, that each will continue in a modified form. One possibility, probably the least likely, is that the trust will continue to be as complete and unreserved as it was before the beliefs it presupposed were formulated, because these beliefs are now seen to be able to accommodate the counter-evidence: either because they explain it satisfactorily, or because they are considered to have such strong independent grounds that the counter-evidence is judged to be ultimately explicable when all the facts are in. In such a case, the dispositions to action that were part of the original complex can continue unaffected. I suggest that this is close to the ideal of faith as this is understood in the New Testament writings and in Thomas' notion of formed faith. Here, of course, the object of trust is God, the beliefs are those typically formulated in the Creeds, and the dispositions to action are those expressed in the New Testament moral prescriptions. In cases where the object of trust is a human being, it is a matter for debate and reflection how far trust can or should continue if the evidence shows the presupposed beliefs to be false. (Christian ethics seem to me to suggest that trust should continue in the face of the knowledge that it is not merited, or at least that this is characteristic of the ideal, or saintly, character.) But in the case which concerns us, that of religious faith, it is not the case that the original beliefs about God can be abandoned. What has to be abandoned is the naive expectation that there will be no counter-evidence.

But a far more likely response to the counter-evidence is a strained or diminished trust, a trust which is real but weak and no longer unreserved. In such a case the original beliefs will be reasserted, but in a somewhat shaken form, in the hope or determination that the counter-evidence can be accommodated within them; and the dispositions to act will be modified so that it becomes more a matter of resolution, more a matter of deliberately acting-as-if the original beliefs were true. This is imperfect faith, faith as it actually is most of the time, faith that has to struggle. The motive of the struggle, both at the reflective level of belief and the practical level of action toward God and one's fellows, is now in part a sense of *obligation* to God, to keep his *commands* in practice and to contend with doubts about him in one's thoughts. Unbelief and failures of love and righteousness are seen as *disloyalty*.

I submit that the ideal of faith is implicit or unreserved trust, which leads to serenity and confidence in conduct. I also submit that actual faith is the miexed or struggling kind, where the trust is only partial, and in consequence the practical dispositions appear in part under the category of obligations, contending with temptation and despair with more mixed success than the mode of life inspired by ideal faith; and the beliefs are not merely explicit, but rendered less firm by counter-evidence. The beliefs also are viewed under the category of obligation − a form of obligation which has to co-exist with the secular obligation to base one's beliefs only on evidence. It is inevitable that the struggles of faith will seem to unbelievers to be no more than elaborate exercises in self-deception; but within faith they will make their own, quite different, sort of sense. It is clear that while ideal faith defeats anxiety, even though it may well not eliminate pain or material disaster, struggling faith will be motivated by a wish to eliminate anxiety, but will only partly succeed in doing so, and indeed will generate stresses of its own in the process.

I think it is quite appropriate to classify implicit trust as an emotion. I would base this in part on the fact that we classify love among the emotions, and implicit trust is at least often a by-product of love. To the extent that actual faith incorporates it, or approaches to its own ideal, it is proper to apply the logic of the emotions to it. To the extent that actual faith departs from this ideal, then it is more appropriate to speak of it in the language of moral resolution. In ideal faith the actions of the faithful are natural expressions of the trust that they have; in actual, or imperfect, faith, they are, when not sheer failures, in part the result of moral resolutions formed in the light of the ideal. In ideal faith the beliefs which we may call the cognitive core of the emotion are held in a manner which Thomas tries to capture when he says that in faith one believes with the certainty or assurance that one has when one knows the outcome of mathematical or other demonstrations, even when one does not have such demonstration. He distinguishes the sort of belief we have in faith (credere) from what we have in other sorts of belief (opinio) by saying that in the latter we affirm, but 'with fear of the opposite' (cum formidine alterius). Unfortunately he thinks that we only have faith at all when this condition is satisfied; I suggest we only have *ideal* faith when this condition of certainty is satisfied. In actual, or imperfect, faith, especially in our day, the intellectual claims of alternatives to the cognitive core of the faith are constantly pressed upon us, either in the form of evidence for beliefs that are incompatible with the core beliefs, or in the form of evidence for beliefs that are intellectually self-sufficient without them. The believer has to face continual suggestions that the object of his trust is not *unworthy* of it, but, worse still, is a figment of his imagination. As he grapples with these, his loyalty and his intellectual integrity may come into conflict, or seem to him to do so, and if this occurs it is likely that his belief, and so his faith, will fade, or, alternatively, that his faith may survive at the cost of real, rather than apparent, self-deception, or of obscurantism. He may, on the other hand (and here it is the task of the apologist to help him), succeed in sustaining his faith in the face of his doubts by intellectually uncorrupt means. But while he is in a state of imperfect faith assailed by doubts, his trust will inevitably be, in large part, a matter of acting-as-if, a matter of resolution, and his freedom from anxiety will be under constant threat.

It is clear, if this picture is at all close to the truth of the matter, that faith, if it is most centrally trust, requires beliefs that are held and sustained, and that in their absence the serenity and reassurance which characterize ideal faith are in jeopardy. But this only shows that the core beliefs are necessary conditions for faith, not that they are sufficient for it. It is possible for someone to believe all the requisite things about God and his relation to himself without having faith, if he does not repose trust in the God in whom he believes. Trust is the natural and appropriate attitude toward a deity who is what Christians say that he is. But we do not always respond to facts in the natural and appropriate way – or the traditional antithesis between reason and emotion would have nothing to feed upon. Even if St. Thomas' devils do not really exist, their psychological state is quite intelligible to us. So is the state of Ivan in Dostoyevsky's *The Brothers Karamazov*, who says he believes all the things the church teaches about God except that he feels the economy of God's world is morally outrageous, and will not worship him. For someone who thinks worship and trust are the proper responses, but does not find it in him, in spite of his beliefs, to make those responses, all that there is, once more, is acting-as-if one trusted: doing those things which would be natural expressions of the trust one does not have, and which appear therefore to one as moral imperatives. This form of activity, especially if carried out within a community of faithful, will induce or sustain the trust that ideal faith requires by making its natural expressions part of one's nature; this will also reduce the anxieties which lack of trust would otherwise occasion.

Since my main concern throughout this work has been the cognitive, rather than the conative or affective, aspects of faith, I will concentrate in the space that remains upon the status of its core beliefs. The first consequence of the brief account I have given is that since it makes the core beliefs necessary conditions of faith, but does not *equate* faith with the core beliefs, it is wholly neutral about the epistemological status of the beliefs themselves. They may be held as basic or framework beliefs, without any thought or suggestion of justification. Or they may, at the other extreme, be held because the believer thinks they have been proved, or revealed to him directly. And they may be held either rationally or irrationally, if this is taken to be a matter of what sort of epistemic status they have for the believer himself. The key point for our purposes is that the Fideists are wrong to suppose that the nature of faith, *per se*, requires that they be held either without justification, or without rationality. If they are right in thinking that it is human sinfulness that keeps men from trusting God as they should, then this sinfulness will be a fruitful source of obstacles both to the trust *and* to the formation of the belief on which it depends; so if there are proofs of God, we will as sinful people be quite able to ensure that we do not end up believing their conclusions. To blame our unbelief on our sin does not require us to say there are no good reasons to believe. In fact, as I have suggested, it makes it more difficult to see why such good reasons should not be ready to hand, for their absence would provide a real excuse for hesitation.

In addition to this, someone who has faith may not unreasonably expect its fruits to include intellectual satisfactions. This is clearly one of the correct insights in Pascal's doctrine of the heart. From the standpoint of faith, once adopted, a dimension of understanding is possible that was not possible before. One can from time to time discern (or consider that one discerns) providential guidance at work in the very phenomena that the unbeliever takes to be evidence against its existence, as well as discerning deeper significance in those phenomena which speak of God to the believer less ambiguously. The less economical understanding may yield greater intellectual rewards. This suggests, though it certainly does not prove, that the Fideist is mistaken in suggesting that the search for such rewards is an obstacle to the acquisition of faith.

How is one to assess the repeated insistence that the beliefs that form the core of faith have to be *certain*? The notion of certainty is notoriously ambiguous between the epistemic status of a belief (which, if the belief is called certain, is said to be the best possible) and the state of mind of the person believing it (who, if he is certain, is said to be free of doubts about it). The view it is most natural to ascribe to the Fideists is that in faith, belief is certain in the second sense, but totally without the credentials of certainty in the first sense. It has been the main burden of this book to insist that faith does not require belief to be devoid of epistemic certainty, but that there is, rather, a problem if it is. It is important to stress here also that

those who have tried to use the arguments of natural theology to support
the core beliefs of Christianity have not always said that they can be given
the highest epistemic credentials (that is, proved); they have often been
content to provide them with a measure of *probability*. Two examples of
this are Joseph Butler, and in our own day Richard Swinburne.[6] When we
turn to psychological certainty, the position is rather different. Certainty
in belief would not necessarily lead to trust and reassurance as we have seen,
though it would *naturally* do so. But it is quite clear, I think, that if one lacks
certainty, even if one considers the beliefs one has to have a good measure
of probability, this lack cannot fail to have the result of making trust less
unreserved, and making the faith to a marked degree a matter of acting-as-if,
that is, a matter of resolution. Now it may be in the highest degree rational
(to adapt Pascal), that if I think it more likely than not that the Christian
God does exist,[7] I should resolve to stake my whole life on this likelihood
and act as if he did. This will only yield an imperfect or striving, faith, that
will deserve the title because it is, self-consciously, adopted in the light of
the ideal of faith, in which the acts flow naturally because of the implicit
trust they reflect. But this means that faith ideally requires certainty, though
in fact it rarely manifests it. This particular form of imperfection in faith
is a form to which the ferment of knowledge and proliferation of theory
in our day, for all its other benefits, inevitably condemns those of us who
aspire to faith at all.

In view of the role I have assigned to certainty here, a comment is necessary
on the counter-evidences to faith and the believer's response to them. Fideism
undoubtedly gains some of its appeal from the fact that trust, and therefore
faith, can only be needed and exercised in a situation where there are experienced facts that give reason to think that the core beliefs may be untrue. One
of the implications of the doctrine that the truths of faith are mysteries is that
since the faithful, in this life at least, only very partially understand them,
they may have little or no inkling of what the explanation of some of the
counter-evidences really is. One of the implications of the doctrine of human
sinfulness is that even if they do think they have such an inkling, they may
have the greatest personal difficulty in acting, or feeling, accordingly. None of
this does anything to show that the core beliefs cannot be epistemologically
certain, or probable. I can know that my friend is innocent of the murder, because he was with me at the time it was commited, without in the least understanding how it is that he has the victim's blood on his jacket. And I can know
that there is less reason to be afraid of flying than of driving on the freeway
while still being terrified in the airplane and complacent in the car.

I conclude with a few comments on possible *extensions* of the concept of faith to include other, related attitudes. I begin with the use of the word 'faith' to cover secular natural beliefs. This is common, and it is harmless, and even healthy, if it serves to draw attention to the fact that these beliefs are held implicitly, and that even if they *have* philosophical justification, this is unknown to almost all who hold them, and is certainly not the cause of their being held. It is a harmless way of drawing attention to this fact, since this is also a fact about the way most people have held religious beliefs too. If, however, it is also taken to imply that there *are* no philosophical justifications for secular natural beliefs, and it is taken to imply this because that is thought in some way to be a necessary condition of faith, then it is worse than tendentious; for faith does not require that the beliefs at the core of it be held in this manner, though indeed they may be.

I have said above that one does not have faith merely by having its core beliefs. In our own day there are many attempts to suggest that one can have faith without them, merely by having the affective and conative elements of traditional faith on their own. I think it is self-evidently absurd to speak of having trust when one has no belief in the existence of an object of it. But there are plenty of attempts to offer us supposed faiths which consist of moral resolutions, or action-as-if there were a God to trust. And there are also plenty of attempts to offer us freedom from anxiety, or liberatedness of personality under this same description. I regard this as an unwise extension. Moral resolution, even accompanied by the use of Biblical stories and liturgical language, differs from faith as I have described it in the key respect that it is not undertaken in the hope that it will restore, or induce, faith in the fuller form, and it is potentially self-deceiving for those who have felt obliged to abandon the core beliefs of traditional faith to use language that suggests they are now engaged in anything other than a *substitute* for it. While faith should issue in serenity and spiritual liberation, it in no way follows from this that serenity and liberation can only come from faith, or that everyone who seeks or achieves those conditions must *have* faith. I do not wish to enquire here what alternative causes might produce some of the affective elements in faith, but possible candidates are alternative sets of beliefs (such as those of Freudianism or Marxism), brainwashing, music, and drugs. To call spiritual liberatedness faith is to identify faith with one of its fruits or manifestations.

In the last chapter I briefly criticized Phillips' view that the assertions of faith are to be understood in a way which eliminates suggestion of supernatural facts. The way he offers is, roughly, that of interpreting them as expressions of certain preferred religious attitudes. These attitudes are in fact the spiritual outcome of the trust that is the central element of faith, especially as it approaches its ideal. It is certainly correct to note that the spiritual attitudes that derive from trust, and therefore from the beliefs on which it depends, may find their expression in the assertion of the beliefs — that one may express the sense of the peace of God, or of gratitude to God, in saying what one believes about him. But this is a long way from justifying an analysis of the beliefs themselves as no more than the expression of the attitudes to which they properly lead. If one were to apply the word 'faith' to someone who felt he had these attitudes, and used religious language to express them without believing that it incorporated the facts on which the attitudes are traditionally based, I would submit, once more, that faith is being identified with its fruits.

These judgments on the wisdom of extending the application of the concept of faith to include widespread contemporary attitudes are of secondary importance. It is of far greater importance, I think, to examine the extensions of it that are found in some reflective examinations of non-Christian religious traditions. But to examine these would require another study. Such a study would have to concentrate on the degree of analogy that exists between the structure of faith and that of the central attitudes of those traditions. It would also have to proceed on the recognition that what the Christian tradition determines to be necessary for faith may not be the only route it can allow to lead to salvation. It is enough for the purposes of this study to conclude by saying that whatever extensions of the idea of faith may be desirable, faith as it is not a state which necessarily excludes the support of philosophical argument.

NOTES

[1] A major discussion of this question is to be found in Wilfred Cantwell Smith, *Faith and Belief*, Princeton University Press, 1979. In spite of the remarkable learning in this work, and the very original and documented study of the development of the notion of belief which is a key part of it, it will be obvious in what follows that I am unable to accept the sharp separation of the two concepts named in its title.

[2] For comments on this issue, see my discussions of faith in *Problems of Religious Knowledge*, Chapter 6, and the essay, 'The Analysis of Faith in St. Thomas Aquinas', *Religious Studies*, Vol. 13, 1977.

[3] I have a detailed discussion of St. Thomas' account of faith in the essay cited in Note 2. For St. Thomas' account itself, see *Summa Theologiae*, 2a2ae, 1–7, and also *De Veritate* 14. The latter is available in English in *Truth*, Regnery, Chicago, 1953, Vol. II, Trans. J. V. McGlynn.

[4] Contemporary analytical discussions of the emotions can be said to have begun with Gilbert Ryle's *The Concept of Mind* (Hutchinson, London, 1949). It is clear from Chapter 4 of that work that it is a mistake to class all emotions as what Ryle calls agitations, and that the opposites of some agitations (such as frenzy or rage) belong in the vocabulary of the emotional life also.

[5] Richard Swinburne, *Faith and Reason*, Oxford, Clarendon Press, 1981, p. 111. Chapter 4 of this book is an important contribution to the topic we are now examining.

[6] See particularly *The Existence of God*, Oxford, Clarendon Press, 1979.

[7] More accurately, that the existence of the Christian God is more likely than any one of the alternative possibilities that are open options for me. See Swinburne, *Faith and Reason*, p. 119 ff.

INDEX

Due